Swimming in a Red Sea

Lawrelynd Bowin with her brother AOB

Swimming in a Red Sea

by
Lawrelynd Bowin

Preface by Fabienne Richard

Afterword by Tobe Levin von Gleichen

UnCUT/VOICES Press
2018

ISBN: 978-3-9818563-0-9

Bibliographic information published by the Deutsche Nationalbibliothek. The Deutsche Nationalbibliothek lists this publication in the Deutsche Nationalbibliografie; detailed bibliographic data are available on the Internet at http://dnb.d-nb.de
Frankfurt am Main: UnCUT/VOICES Press, 2018.

About UnCUT/VOICES Press ...

Founded in Frankfurt am Main, Germany, UnCUT/VOICES Press is the first publisher to focus solely on female genital mutilation. By translating studies of FGM from French, German and other languages, UnCUT/VOICES Press broadens access to these indispensable resources. It also features significant and rare material in English aimed at ending an egregious injury still inflicted on girls worldwide.

The founder Tobe Levin von Gleichen, an affiliate of the International Gender Studies Centre at Lady Margaret Hall, University of Oxford and an Associate of the Hutchins Center for African and African American Research at Harvard University, has been active against FGM since 1977. Co-editor with Augustine H. Asaah of *Empathy and Rage. Female Genital Mutilation in African Literature* (Ayebia, 2009), she served as founding president of FORWARD-Germany and has advised the Austrian Parliament, the Bundestag, Westminster, UNICEF and WHO. See also Levin, Tobe, ed. *Waging Empathy. Alice Walker, Possessing the Secret of Joy and the Global Movement to Ban FGM*. Frankfurt am Main: UnCUT/VOICES Press, 2014.

UnCUT/VOICES PRESS
Martin Luther Str. 35, 60389 Frankfurt am Main, Germany
Tobe.levin@uncutvoices.com   www.uncutvoices.com
Geschäftsnummer HRB 86527, U.G. Haftungsbeschränkt

Also from UnCUT/VOICES Press

Khady with Marie-Thérèse Cuny. *Blood Stains. A Child of Africa Reclaims her Human Rights*. Trans. Tobe Levin. Frankfurt am Main: UnCUT/VOICES Press, 2010.
Prolongeau, Hubert. *Undoing FGM. Pierre Foldes, the Surgeon Who Restores the Clitoris*. Foreword Bernard Kouchner. Trans. and Afterword Tobe Levin. Frankfurt am Main: UnCUT/VOICES Press, 2011.
Hutton, Frankie, ed. *Rose Lore. Essays in Cultural History and Semiotics*. Frankfurt am Main: UnCUT/VOICES Press, 2015. With a chapter on FGM by Tobe Levin.
Kiminta Maria and Tobe Levin. *Kiminta. A Maasai's Fight against Female Genital Mutilation*. UnCUT/VOICES Press, 2015.
Mwaluko, Nick Hadikwa. *WAAFRIKA 123. 1992. Kenya. Two Womyn Fall in Love*. Frankfurt am Main: UnCUT/VOICES Press, 2016.
Kameel Ahmady. *In the Name of Tradition: Female Genital Mutilation in Iran*. UnCUT/VOICES Press, 2016.
Jeanie Kortum. *Stones*. She Writes Press & UnCUT/VOICES Press, 2017.

Table of Contents

Preface by Fabienne Richard   7

Chapter 1. African Childhood   9

Djadja goes to jail – Memories of Clay ... Vancouver, July 9, 2014 ... Galle and her mother after jail – Port Kamsar, August 1988 ... Brussels, May 2, 2016 ... Galle overhears her parents – Port Kamsar, August 7, 1988 ... Lawra Linda alone with her mother during childbirth – Port Kamsar, August 8, 1988 ... Brussels, May 2, 2016 ... ... Vancouver, October 2014 ... Childbirth – Port Kamsar, August 8, 1988 ... After Galle's mother dies – Conakry, August 1989 ... The unknown woman's life within Galle's initiation

Chapter 2 – Moscow, Russia   91

Linda meets Harvey – Moscow, summer 1997 ... Linda tells her father about Harvey – November 1997 ... Linda's helpful Russian roommate ... Moscow, Spring 1998 ... Linda in Amsterdam for the first time – Harvey's house

Chapter 3 – African Marriage   116

Chapter 4 – Unrootedness   126

Back in Amsterdam: No sense of home – December 1999 ... Brussels, October 2015 ... Harvey's first time in Vancouver

Chapter 5 – Children and Motherhood   136

Finding out Linda was pregnant – Vancouver, summer 2004 ... Vancouver, July 2004 ... Linda confirms she's pregnant – Vancouver, Dr. Brian's office ... Expecting the first child – Vancouver, summer 2004 ... Right before birth with Dr. Carter – Vancouver, April 1, 2005 ... Linda is hospitalized before childbirth ... Breastfeeding right after childbirth ... Linda locks herself in her room after Josh's birth ... Harvey's mother intervenes – Vancouver, May 2005 ... Considering a second baby – Hawaii, summer 2006 ... After having two children – Vancouver, 2007 ... Doctor's visit ... Sensitivity to violence and bad dreams – Brussels, November 2015

Chapter 6 – A Premonition   189

News from Father – Vancouver, December 2012 ... Name change – Terrorist-attack anxiety – Brussels, March 28, 2016 ... Lawra Linda fears dying the same age as her mother – Vancouver, December 25, 2013 ... Brussels-attack stress leads to bleeding – Brussels, March 23, 2016 ... Linda in the hospital – Vancouver, spring 2015

Chapter 7 – A Butterfly   210

Sick brother – Sense of responsibility – Vancouver, August 1, 2015 ... The importance of children and life's meaning – Treeing people – Vancouver, fall 2013 ... Motherhood – Family life – Wandering soul in Brussels – April 11, 2016 ... The unexpected visit of a yellow butterfly – Vancouver, August 8, 2015

Afterword by Tobe Levin von Gleichen   221

Acknowledgements   237

Dedication

I dedicate my first novel *Swimming in a Red Sea* to ... The Virgin Mary who's been, over my life time, the greatest Mother to me and The Mother of All Mothers!

My mother Djenab Bah, my little sister Kadiatou Bah (Nenein Bah), my little brother Alpha Oumar Bah (AOB), Theirno Abdul Bah (Goudoussy), Ibrahima Sory Bah (Alhadji).

My husband Harry Van den Ameele and our children Colin James and Brandon Charles Van den Ameele, as well as my mother- and father-in-law Govorina Van den Ameele (Rina) and Jacobus Cornelis van den Ameele (Jaap).

Mathilde d'Udekem d'Acoz whose Mathilde Fund of Belgium supports organizations such as GAMS/CeMavie that serve the most vulnerable in Belgian society, who strongly advocates for women's health, is a guardian angel for youth suffering violence, who welcomes, protects and prevents girls from undergoing FGM and champions the rehabilitation of those who have already been victims of this ungodly deed.

In addition, I would like to dedicate this book to Dr. Fabienne Richard, Executive Director of GAMS Belgium and midwife at the FGM Clinics, CeMAViE, University Hospital St. Pierre, Brussels. Her door was always open wide and her telephone on whenever and wherever I needed her; she fought beside me not only through my own struggles and traumas but also stood by me with countless hugs, encouragement, and hope when trying to save my brother AOB's children. Enhanced by love and integrity in helping humanity, your professionalism, Fabienne, is priceless.

Preface

By Dr. Fabienne Richard

PhD, midwife, FGM Unit CeMAViE, University Hospital St Pierre in Brussels and Director of GAMS Belgium.

Translated from the French by Tobe Levin.

Dear Lawrelynd,

On April 12, 2016, we met for the first time at St. Pierre's Hospital in Brussels, brought together by my engagement in the CeMAVie[1] unit responsible for reconstruction after genital mutilation and offering holistic medical care to excised women. I remember as though it were yesterday. The day before you had stopped by the Travel Clinic to be vaccinated in preparation for a trip to Guinea (Conakry). A colleague at Travel phoned me and said, "Fabienne, I don't have enough time to talk with this lady but she's not well. She burst into tears at the mere thought of a trip to Africa. It's not normal so I suspect something troubling behind it. Can you please see her?" That afternoon my calendar was full but aware that my co-worker wouldn't ring me for nothing, I squeezed you in between appointments. Little did I know that would signal the start of an enduring adventure. … Indeed, you came to my office weeping and explained that, although you had sworn never to return to Africa, you felt compelled to go to Guinea to visit the tomb of your younger brother Alpha Oumar Bah (AOB) who had died under brutal circumstances in Senegal. When I asked why you had wanted to break all ties with your family and nation, you told me about all that you'd gone through, the violence you endured (excision, gang rape in prison where your own father had you locked up at age twelve to break the spirit of the rebellious child in you, and to finish the job, the whipping you suffered on release, as though the preceding brutalities hadn't sufficed). You could have folded, allowing yourself to die, but no, you found the energy and opportunity to flee, far away, to reboot your life, to study, marry, have children and all the while thinking that yes, you'd deleted your past to the point of forgetting the language, the food … you wanted to preserve not a single trace. But your brother's death restored you to family and origins. Your brother AOB, brilliant economist, second in command at the IMF in Guinea (Conakry), was

---

[1] https://www.stpierre-bru.be/fr/videos/cemavie-operation-de-reconstruction-du-clitoris-apres-une-mutilation-genitale Accessed 26 April 2018.

a fervent opponent of excision with a major influence on your family (no one dared touch his children as long as he remained alive). After his death, the family reclaimed its 'rights': they want to marry AOB's wife Mariama to his younger brother and excise their daughters. Simply imagining anyone touching those girls triggers anguish. Your post-traumatic memory is returning full force, you're in hell, you can't stand it. But once again, instead of a tearful meltdown, you invest all your energy in fighting like a lion: you take on the government, visit the Foreign Office, appeal to aid associations for non-citizens' rights, trek anywhere you think you might advance your cause. Your nieces must be protected, they've got to join you in Belgium. Everyone discourages you, this has never been done before, you'll never succeed, no one has ever witnessed an entire Guinean family receive humanitarian visas for Belgium, but you have faith. You don't listen. Some people even advised you to hire a trafficker to get them here illegally, but you refused. You want the legal route, officially. How could you possibly help these criminals make a living? You hang in there. You don't eat. You don't sleep. You spend hours sitting in offices without appointments until the administrator finally decides to talk to you or invite you in. Your determination has impressed me. Regularly, you check in with me, without an appointment (as is your habit) and between two patients I manage simply to give you a warm hug, holding you wordlessly for several minutes. You come to recharge your batteries, as you say. And this will become our ritual, whenever you pass by the clinic.

I'll stop here to let your readers uncover the rest of the story for themselves, but I really wanted to convey how enchanted I am that you crossed my path in April 2016. I've become a better person through your example of courage and determination. You could have died from all you'd been subjected to as a child, but they failed to tame you. The child dissident has become a ground-breaking avant-garde woman!

Chapter 1
African childhood

My younger brother, Alpha Oumar Bah, used to kiss our mother's feet each time she told us stories before bedtime. When we visited her at the hospital, after she'd lost her unborn twins, he'd tickle her while she read until she begged for mercy.

He'd ask our mother to bless him with the most beautiful woman in the world, and she'd tell him that it was always better to have a kind woman than a beautiful one. I'd intervene and ask her to bless him with both and beyond. Little did I know that, one day, I wouldn't see him for such a long time.

Moving away from her toes, I went to kneel on the chair that had been put in front of her. I looked up and wondered what I wanted to tell her, but nothing like what my brother had asked occurred to me. For a moment I wished I were he, because he was charming, quick and witty, knowing exactly what he wanted when he wanted it and expressing it immediately. I could hear him tell me in Fula, our maternal tongue,[1] "Djadja, when you want something, you must say it loud into the sky right then and there, even when no one's in front of you, because you never know who's really listening."

My mother, Djenab, was very attractive; her skin, a colour like ebony, and her hair, long and curly, gave her the timeless beauty that only a Fula woman can have. I remember my father, who was almost never home, giving me a doll after one of his numerous trips; I'd stopped counting his absences because of the heartache they brought my mother, my brothers and me. That doll I never played with but, instead, replaced with a living chicken as a pet. My mother thought that I, even at an early age, would be aware of the danger of diarrhea, yellow fever and malaria that could be spread from nature or the people living with us. She did all she could to keep away the unpredictable diseases or viruses that would come to hunt our community and home. The fact she was a self-trained midwife helped her be medically aware, anticipating a problem rather than

---

[1] Fula is a West African dialect spoken mainly by the Fula people throughout Africa.

waiting for it to happen. When I had my kids, I never missed any of their vaccinations.

Djadja goes to jail – Memories of Clay

My uncle Hussein, my father's only younger brother, had decided that the best way to punish me for falling in love with a young man called Clay was to put me in jail.

Obsessed with our family values, traditions and secrets, he wanted to prove beyond any doubt, at any cost, that I was still a virgin. The relationship between my father and my uncle went beyond the blood that ran in their veins. In many African cultures and particularly among the Fulani, the younger brother is next in line not only for the older brother's material possessions but also to remarry any widow in the family. He'd take care of his own and his older brother's wives and family; this is how, most of the time, polygamy is imposed upon the generation of my time, despite our advanced education and, to some extent, westernization. I prayed often when growing up that my mother would never have to be a widow so that I'd never have to call my uncle "Father." I didn't anticipate, when I prayed, that this is exactly what would happen, and all too soon.

Vancouver, July 9, 2014

Driving back home after acting lessons on Granville Island, eager to join Harvey and our boys watching the Netherlands versus Argentina in the semi-final of the 2014 World Cup, I thought about how I'd ridden Clay's bike to my mother's house on the dawn I escaped my juvenile jail.

The price of my escape had been being sewn together to make sure that when a man got inside me it would be as if for the first time. My clitoris, too, had been removed, and my vulva looked like a flat-iron. Would I ever recover? Would I tell my husband the secrets I was bringing into our relationship, or would it be best to leave the skeletons in my closet for the rest of my life? I kept feeling the wind in my face, as if I were truly living again, and at the same time I wanted to hide what freedom, for a little while, felt like. *Does anybody actually see it?* I looked around and smiled at the passersby as if nothing unusual was happening.

What would have occurred at age twelve if I'd prayed like my son Josh? Would I have said to God that I wanted both my mother and father with me always, or would I have said that I'd rather have them dead because they had not stood up and fought for me when I most needed them to?

For most of my childhood, my father was not around; from the time I was five, he was often making long and strenuous journeys. I had not understood why he travelled so much. I even wondered if it was because he was from a nomadic culture and longed to connect its source and origin to whatever he felt in his body and his sense of identity. He was a missing parent most of the time.

He'd be home at most for a month or two – maybe just long enough to get my mother pregnant – and then vanish in the night like an evening storm that cleared and left a rainbow on the horizon, as if the storm had never occurred. For us the rainbow was the money, food and beautiful shelter he provided. We were extremely blessed, and fortunate in many ways, growing up in Africa, where our basic needs were met without struggle or pain. We might wake up to a kitchen stocked with French baguettes, butter, eggs, cereals, porridge, cocoa, coffee, milk, meat, cheese, chicken and grains – rice, fonio, millet, combo, manioc and corn – plus coconut, ghee and palm oil, and not to forget the shea butter. All this was supplied to our family each morning by the local farmers, the butcher, and the baker. We also had fancy cheeses delivered, such as Camembert and cheddar, whether my father was home or not, by another supermarket worker he had hired. We never lacked for breakfast, lunch or dinner in my house.

My father would feed not only his own family with these groceries but also the neighbours and anybody else who stopped by. Some would arrive in the morning, some in the afternoon, and others in the evening or even, sometimes, in the very late evening.

Since there was so much coming and going in our household in the evenings, I often found a way to sneak out and either play with the neighbouring kids or kick a soccer ball around with some of the boys in my neighbourhood and my younger brother, Alpha Oumar, a soccer fanatic who would do anything for a chance to play soccer.

I played mostly with boys because the girls didn't get me at all. Having only brothers didn't help; I felt more comfortable around guys and their friends than talking with girls about henna, nails, hair and whom I was going to marry.

Most kids in our neighbourhood waited for us to play, because we were the only ones with a proper ball instead of one improvised from condensed plastic, paper and other soft materials, such as old stretchy fabric. Even so, the homemade version would still make each child happy, despite the fact it wouldn't go as far as a real soccer ball.

One night, out of the corner of my eye, I signalled to my younger brother, using his nickname, Alphadjo, to come out with me; I slipped him a ball to hide under his shirt, which he put right in front of his belly. My mother smiled and gave us a nod, so we vanished from the compound into the darkness of the little open area behind the house.

Our big brick home had six bedrooms, two living rooms, two bathrooms, two kitchens and a large compound with walls at least nine feet high. Living in that kind of house, and my father owning that sort of place, put us among the wealthiest people in our tribe, community, society and, even, our country. We'd had a pump installed within the compound, so we did not need to fetch water or use a rope to raise it from the bottom of a deep hole. My father made this water accessible to everyone, whether they were from far or near – all were welcome.

We were treated differently from other kids, even by our extended family, including my uncle, his wife and children, who lived with us. I didn't have to cook, wash my clothes or clean the house. Our maids preferred to stay with us instead of in their villages, where access to anything and everything was a struggle. They did all household chores, including cooking, and ensured that everything was orderly and spotless. I had only to look after my brothers and make sure they did their homework, ate and went to bed on time. In general, our bedtime was very, very early, whether it was a school day or not, because my father believed that early birds succeeded in life; we all had to get up and get going on anything or nothing at all. As long as we were in bed by eight o'clock, he was happy, proud of his family and children for obeying his rules.

We usually awoke at six and recited the Koran for an hour. At seven we got dressed, ate breakfast – a French baguette with rooibos tea, or sometimes Lipton Earl Grey with whole milk, or café au lait, my favourite – and then we were ready to go to school. At 7:30 we hopped into the car and were on our way. Three times a week we had a tutor, who taught us and helped with our homework or anything school related. My father was hardly ever home; he travelled a lot doing import–export between West and North Africa.

Most of the kids we played with were quietly but eagerly waiting for us – so much so that they shouted when Alpha Oumar threw the ball in the air.

"Shhhh! We can't make too much noise," my brother said. We kept playing and passing the ball until everybody felt they had had enough of that and wanted to split into two groups for a real match.

"We're twelve kids," said Alpha Oumar's closest friend, Alhadji.

"Then we go six against six," I suggested with enthusiasm.

"That would leave you out of the game, Djadja," said Alhadji, looking at his teammates.

"Djadja" means "older sister" in Fula, and, out of respect, I was sometimes called that by my younger brothers and their friends.

"Why?" Alpha Oumar asked.

"Because she's a girl and always hanging around. Why can't she go play with girls?"

"Why is she playing with us – she's a girl!" shouted another kid in the group.

"I heard that, and lower your voice," I said.

"There's nothing wrong with her being a girl who wants to play soccer with us. She's my older sister. She'll be on my team, then," Alpha Oumar said, coming to me and taking my hand.

"Alpha Oumar's right. She has legs, and she can use them. What's the problem? I'm fine if you want to play – just don't cry if you get hit with the ball," another kid said.

Once our match got underway, I made most of the goals with Alpha Oumar's help. He was laughing and teasing his friends for refusing to have a girl on their team.

"It's not fair that she's winning," Alhadji said.

"Well, it's your choice. Do you want her on your team to see if she can bring you luck?" Alpha Oumar asked teasingly.

"No. No offense, Djadja," Alhadji apologized.

"What do you want me to do if you don't want me to play in the group?" I asked.

"Go home, where you should be anyway. You're not allowed to be out of the house when it's dark. My sisters never go out without a chaperone, and never at night even with a chaperone," another kid remarked.

"None of your business," I said.

"If she goes, we won't be an even team, you realize," Alpha Oumar said.

"We'll have six against five for the first round, and then, for the second, five against six. How about that?" Alhadji said.

"No. That's not soccer!" another kid shouted.

"Yes, it is!" another shouted back.

I looked at my watch. My mother had given it to me so that if I were outside by myself or with my brother I would know when to go home, and we could agree on a time.

"What time is it, Djadja?" asked Boubakar.

"8:30," I said, without taking my eyes off my wrist.

"I have to go," he announced. "My dad comes home in an hour, and if I'm not there on time and in bed on time, he'll beat my mother." He started to run off without awaiting an answer.

"Beat your mother, Bobo? He should beat you, because you're the one who went out and not her," another boy called after him. "Bobo" means "tiny" in Fula – an expression that could hurt or please, depending on the tone and context.

"None of your business, and stop talking about my mother," he said, a little peeved.

"OK. Then we're even now, since Bouba is no longer playing," said one of the kids.

"Please call me by my full name and not Bobo or Bouba; my name is simply Boubakar."

"You came back just to tell us that, Boubakar? You must like your name," I said, a little surprised, and he nodded with a smile that brought out the dimples in his cheeks, like Alpha Oumar's.

"It's my great-grandfather's name. He was a great leader and a great man, and I hope to be like him one day, because I'm his incarnation, my father tells me all the time. He also says that a person's name holds everything about his destiny and that I should be –"

"But shouldn't they have named you after your birth star and then added your grandfather's as a middle name? In my family, it's bad luck to have only somebody else's name instead of both. Go on and reclaim your own birth name, Bobo," interjected one of Alpha Oumar's friends who was guarding the ball; he threw it at Boubakar's face, and I caught it quickly.

"Go now, before your mother pays for your absence," I said, regaining my balance.

"Are you OK with this, Djadja? It's our ball, after all. If you want to be on the team, we can decide that, you know," Alpha Oumar said as he took the ball from my hands

"I'm fine, and actually I'm going to see Clay while you're playing. Please come get me when you finish so we can go home together, OK?" I said.

"OK, good idea, Djadja, but…"

"But what?" I asked.

"He's a boy, you know, and you're not supposed to see him or be with him," he said.

"Don't worry. Nobody will see us, and you won't tell anybody, right?" I asked, trying to see his eyes under the brightness of the moon.

"I won't, but what if the neighbours see you go into his house?" he said, almost shouting because I was already walking away from the field.

15

"And he's Christian, you know," another boy yelled.

"Don't worry about that. There won't be any problem, but please remember to come get me when you're done," I said, touching my wrist. I realized I didn't have my watch on.

"Alphadjo, do you have the watch?" I had used Alpha Oumar's nickname.

"Yes; you gave it to me to keep an eye on the time for us."

"Please make sure you check it and come get me as soon as you're done playing." I was out of view once I went through the mango trees that marked the way to Clay's house.

"Will do, and be safe!" I heard my brother shout toward me.

I jumped to claim one of the mangoes, but it was too windy. I looked up into the sky. The moon had brightened the beginning of the night, but now it was vanishing into the clouds. It looked like rain, but I shook that out of my mind. In the rainy season, which was June, July and August, it rained almost daily and left behind an emerald-blue sky.

Clay's house was on the main side of the road, about half an hour's walk from our house, which made it easy to get to either by car, on foot or by bike. To avoid being spotted, however, I walked in the field beside the road.

He lived with his aunt and uncle, who had taken care of him since his mother passed away while giving birth to him, and his dad remarried and moved to the village. His aunt was unable to have children, and they treated him like their own son. They made sure he got a proper education, and, after he graduated, they planned to send him to study abroad. He was the pride and joy of his adoptive family. They had even bought him a fancy city bicycle, which he rode to school whenever he wanted.

He was much older than I was, because he was already in Lycee. He was brilliant and always the first in his class. Everyone in our school wanted to be friends with him, and all the girls would practically faint when he said hi to them.

I'd never felt there was anything quite so special about him, but I loved the fact that he knew a lot from books and was the genius kid on the block. He was tall and handsome, and he smelled nice. It seemed to me he always took a shower, brushed his teeth and combed his loose, curly hair nicely. Then one day he came up to me at school as everyone watched curiously ...

"Hi, Kenda."

My full name was Laouratou Dalanda Kenda Bailo Galle Bah. In Fula culture the firstborn usually honours the names of the inlaws on both sides in case he or she is the couple's only child. Since my name was so long, most of my friends called me Kenda or Kinda; some used Laouratou or Bailo, while others preferred Galle. I hated this. It felt like I became somebody else with each name. Even though I tried to get people to stick to one of my favourites, I knew I was wasting my breath and time.

"Hi, Clay."

"You know my name?"

"Yes. And you know mine," I said, a little surprised. "Everybody knows your name."

"Everybody knows yours, as well," he said.

"I think because of my father."

"He's a wealthy man, and he helps everybody."

"Is that the only reason, then?" I asked.

"No. Because you're very competitive in your class, I heard," he said with a tiny smile.

"Competitive but not pretty?" I asked.

"Yes, pretty," he said.

"You make it sound like –"

"Like you're not pretty," he said, cutting me off with another shy smile. "If it makes your ears happy, that as well – but mostly because you're always first in your class."

I didn't comment.

"You're a girl who loves studying and books," he said.

"And?"

"That's nice!" Clay replied with a little more enthusiasm, since he was quite shy.

'*If it will make your ears happy*' – who talks like that? It seemed he'd rather spend time with his books than with anyone in class, hiding out with his volumes when we were all running around the courtyard. He'd be around the corner reading or doing math quizzes with a bunch of boys on the other side of the enclosure.

One of our mutual attractions was a love of reading. He got many books from his church, which was affiliated with a western Catholic denomination that sent over used literature. He scored most of his favourite authors, such as Wole Soyinka and Senghor, and some magazines about Nelson Mandela that we hid between us to read; the regime in Guinea, West Africa, at that time was dictatorial communist, with Sekou Touré as head of the government. Nobody dared to question or challenge him.

We also read a few French books, such as *La dame aux Camélias* and *Le Rouge et le Noir*, which Clay snuck out of his church library for us and some of his closest friends. We had to study in Susu because the new president was from a Susu tribe, and after his coup against Touré he made it mandatory to learn everything in his dialect. Susu became the national language of Guinea but was only one of the local languages.

We parted and went to our own classrooms when the bell rang. I was unable to focus in class. I replayed our conversation over and over in my head.

We kept meeting in the courtyard after that, at times when nobody important was around. He'd let me sit on his bike, and once or twice he had me pedal on my own, catching me before I fell or before we caught anyone else's attention.

Because Clay was ahead of me in school, our classrooms were far apart, so sometimes, to my teacher's annoyance, I'd get to my own class two or three minutes late. She did not like it, but she didn't bother talking to me about it. Instead, she told the principal, who in turn told my uncle Hussein. He came to school a few mornings just to make sure I did not meet Clay, and the whole school was to report it if anybody saw me with him. My mother found my uncle's reaction a bit far fetched and wanted to ask him why he was being so tough on me.

My mother invited him to her room for tea. "I don't think it's fair, the way you're treating my daughter. She's a good girl. She gets good grades, she always comes home on time and does chores even though we have all the helpers. I don't understand your lack of trust in her," she said.

I stood outside the door, as I often did when they were talking. I didn't like my uncle's behaviour toward my mother. I wanted to be there for her in case he turned violent or verbally abusive, which he was most of the time. At least I could be her witness if she ever complained to my father once he returned from his travels.

"Did you invite me for tea or to scold me about the way I'm raising my daughter?" he asked. He stood, setting his cup on the corner table my mother had set up for tea, cookies and coffee, as she usually did when she had guests.

"She's your niece and *not* your daughter. I guarantee you, if she were your daughter you wouldn't treat her the way you're doing right now."

"Where's her father? Pardon me if I want to call her my daughter. She is my daughter, because I'm head of this house, whether you like it or not. You know that she's even learning to ride a bicycle, I was told by one of the neighbours' kids. She bikes, plays soccer and doesn't wear veils or dresses, just to give you a taste of the list of things I believe, and many people in our family and community believe, are bad for her. What kind of girl are you raising, Djenab? If she keeps behaving this way, she'll never marry, and she will bring shame into this house. Is that really what you want for her, for this family?" he said, moving to the door.

"Learning to ride a bike is good. Her father takes her on his Yamaha all the time when he's in town," my mother said.

"That's the problem, Djenab – because he takes her on his motorbike and she sits facing his back instead of sitting side-saddle," my uncle said.

"What's wrong with that?" my mother asked.

"Her breasts would be touching him, or any other man, and if she falls it could be fatal."

My mother held her head in disbelief and did not comment for a while. It looked like she was searching for a better way to talk to my uncle, who just stood there, waiting.

"You're really not seeing her at all; she hasn't yet developed breasts. She will be OK if you trust her, show you respect her integrity as a growing woman. I guarantee she won't bring us shame. I know her, and, trust me: she will be fine, and we will be fine as a family," my mother said, sitting back in her chair.

My uncle had been about to leave but stepped back into the room. "She almost drowned the other day, when only married women go to the river. Can you swear to me that she's still a virgin? Sometimes I even doubt you've cut her like any clean, decent girl should be. Have you? Is she clean? When did you have her cut?"

"Yes. Of course she's clean; why would she be dirty in the first place? Simply because she has a clitoris, a vulva ... for God's sake, a full vagina doesn't make her dirty. And she almost drowned because nobody has taught her how to swim – end of discussion. How could you think otherwise?" my mother asked.

"Is she a virgin or cut clean or both? Which one is it, Djenab?" my uncle raged.

My mother ignored his anger. "I'm not a good swimmer like my sister, and, besides, what's wrong with her taking my daughter to the river to learn about womanhood? It's normal; how else would she know about such things as her first period and –".

"You mean how to seduce men! Your sister is the queen of that. She doesn't even cover herself, and you want your daughter to spend time with her. I'll take care of that, because I'm going to talk to her husband about the shame he's bringing on this family by letting his wife run around half-naked. What she's teaching our daughter is disgraceful, and I guarantee you, once I speak to him, if he's the one who wears the pants, his wife is going to listen to him. And why is Galle around boys all the time? Have you ever seen her play with girls her age? With even my daughter, for instance?" He was bellowing.

"First of all, my sister isn't your daughter; second, she's a married woman; and third, she was acknowledged to be a virgin when she married, so leave her out of it. As far as Galle is concerned, she has only brothers. Maybe she's more comfortable around boys because that's what she knows. Maybe –"

"Maybe what? Do you hear yourself talk?! Do you even hear how you're talking to me?! You sound like the devil! I'm out of here!" He sprang out of the room but returned in a flash before my mother could even reach out to put the thermos away.

"Take her to the hospital to check her virginity. If she's confirmed a virgin, only then, maybe, can I at least give her freedom at school to talk to other kids. Otherwise, the driver will pick her up every day, and that is the end of discussion!"

"Take her to the clinic? Virginity? Why don't you just trust her? Why don't you trust me?" My mother was almost in tears, but she proudly contained them.

"This isn't about you or about her not being my daughter. Yes, she's my niece, but the shame will be our shame, and I won't be part of that. One more word from you and I won't set foot in this house ever again. Since her father is coming back tonight or tomorrow, we'll leave it at that for now, and I'll talk to him then." He stomped out of the room a second time.

"My husband is coming back; that's nice," my mother murmured to herself, touching her big belly.

"Actually, I won't come back in this house again until a doctor confirms that she's a virgin, a clean and honourable girl," he said, coming back into the room and then leaving as quickly as he'd entered. My mother remained calm and dreamy. He passed me and did a double take.

"You've been standing here all this time listening to us?" I nodded, and he left.

* * *

I knocked at Clay's door, looking around to check nobody would notice me going in.

"Did anybody see you?" Clay asked, peering left and right and around me, as if he were at an intersection without traffic lights.

"Not that I know of, but I was cautious," I said with a smile.

"My family also doesn't want me to see you," he whispered.

"I know. What do you want to do?" I asked.

"We can't go outside, for sure, but we can play Scrabble if you want," he suggested.

"I like that. My brother Alphadjo and I play it at home a lot." I followed him to his room.

We walked past the bed and, from his small library, retrieved the Scrabble box. I noticed a big blackboard with a math assignment on it and a map of Europe drawn next to the far-left corner. His city bike was parked by the door. He took it to school whenever the weather was nice. It made him even cooler in the eyes of other students and was additional proof that his adoptive parents loved him and were willing to spoil him. I always felt special whenever he let me secretly ride it, but it wasn't as often as he wanted me to; I feared the reaction of my uncle even more than falling and hurting myself.

"I leave that map there to remind me of my destination," he said.

"Destination?" I asked.

"Yes. I will go to France to study when I graduate," he said as he pointed at the map.

"How? Do they study Susu in France?" I asked.

"No, but I'm homeschooling in French, just like the French kids do, and through my church as well," he explained.

"Yes, that makes sense, then," I replied, walking slowly around his room and peering at each book on his shelves. I even found it admirable that he had a library.

Guinea had been a French colony, even though it became a communist country after independence. The government stopped teaching in French and switched to the local language, Susu, like many neighbouring, independent African nations that had gained their freedom and were opposed to learning Russian. However, many who were able to homeschool their children did so in French, which was kept in strict confidence, secret from the local militia.

Playing and laughing, competing fiercely at Scrabble, we had not seen the time passing.

"I have to go," I exclaimed.

"Sorry!" He glanced at his watch. "I'll walk you home," he added, grabbing his keys and jacket.

"My brother was supposed to come and get me after his soccer game."

A strong wind was making it hard to shut the door, so Clay went back in, quickly closed the window, and then relocked the door.

"You mean AOB?" he asked, adding the initial of our family name to the short form of "Alpha Oumar." AOB was the nickname given to him at school; his friends rarely used his full name.

"Clay, is that you?" his aunt shouted from their side of the compound.

"Yes, *Maman*."

"Who's with you?" she asked. Footsteps approached, and we stealthily ran away.

We heard the growling of the clouds; the wind grew stronger and faster, and then small drops of rain started falling on us. The drops got bigger and bigger. All of a sudden, we were both soaking wet. There was thunder, and lightning flickered around us. We sprinted to shelter under the first coconut tree we saw.

"We can't wait here," I said.

"Why not?" He looked down at me, draping his jacket around my shoulders. I was a skinny girl, so I got cold quickly.

"What if a coconut falls on us?"

"You mean like it did when AOB wanted one of the neighbour's? It won't!"

"Yes, he wanted that to happen, but you know I'm serious. A coconut could kill us!" I said, and he laughed.

"You're right." He stopped laughing and took my hand as we moved away. We held on to each other as if we wanted to make sure the wind would not blow us away. We were both really skinny – not for lack of food but because we were growing tall and slim – so we weren't holding hands to be romantic. Being much older, Clay might have thought like that, but I didn't.

He moved us under another tree. We stood there for a while, glued to each other like two escargots. I felt his strong heartbeat, which was either catching up to his breathing from our dash or simply beating his desire for me, which at the time I didn't understand; I just stood with him and waited. Then, nonchalantly, I took his right hand and put it on my back as if I wanted him to dance with me. I loved dancing and was great at it, but my father had forbidden it to me.

"You're from noble blood, so you can't be a dancer or a singer. You're to be danced for and sung for, and not the other way around. Do you understand? You're not a Djelee – is that clear, once and for all?"

I had nodded yes and walked away when he signalled with his hands that he was done talking.

The Djelee is a tribe, an ethnic group in West Africa, that's gifted at storytelling through music, dance, and voice. They are paid, sometimes a great deal of cash, or offered other forms of reward to entertain in ceremonies; sometimes they perform for the simple pleasure of it. They often do it in a big circle under the baobab tree.

Clay took a few steps back and reached for my right hand. We started dancing.

"There's no music," I said, glancing around.

"There's music in my heart and in yours," he said and gave a small, nervous laugh.

"Music in my heart?" I asked. I pulled a little on his jacket zipper while laughing a little louder.

"Yes, and the music of lightning, wind and rain," he said. I just kept laughing.

My laughter became contagious, and we stopped dancing when we both realized we sucked at it. We turned our attention to jumping in the puddles.

I hesitated at first but then, encouraged by Clay, I leapt into the little pools around us. We even went looking for more, and it felt great; my inner voice had a sense of freedom and self-exaltation. We ran after one another, splashing in all the puddles we could, and then we stopped to hold each other.

I felt a jolt move through my body, and I moved away quickly, but he came closer, keeping my hands in his as I moved my head from his shoulder and faced him. We moved apart and then faced each other again, as if we had entered a tribal circle of fire where each stepped barefoot on the embers without being singed or making the slightest sound of pain. We knew we were not supposed to be here together at that time of night, but we also knew it was too late to undo what we had already done, so why not make the moment special?

I wiggled my toes inside the Adidas my father had brought back from one of his trips. Then I tackled him. He caught me as if he were prepared and awaiting this moment his whole life. I let myself go in his arms. Losing his balance slightly, he leaned back against a tree, still holding me.

We didn't care about rain, wind, thunder, lightning, or puddles soaking our feet. I moved my face close to his, then my lips, and his met mine. He kissed me gently, as if he were sampling an unknown flavour before savouring it. I felt his tongue slide onto mine; together they twisted like dancing snakes. My eyes were still open, watching his expression and its changes during whatever he was feeling at that moment. It seemed weird at first because I could see him, as clearly as possible in the dark night, but then I instinctively closed my eyes, and it felt nice but stranger than I had anticipated from the movies. Then we both swallowed the flood of saliva from our vigorous kiss.

"That was a lot. Are we supposed to swallow each other's saliva when we're kissing?" I asked.

"I don't know, but I suppose so; otherwise it would feel like we drooled," he said. "I'll ask my parents to go ask your parents if I can marry you. Would you like that?"

"Yes ... but you're a Christian, a Mandingo, and I'm a Fula Muslim girl," I replied.

"You're not wearing any veils. There might be an exception in your family, no?" he said.

"I don't know, and I'm not sure what can be accepted other than our usual, but –"

"– our love for each other will cross all the bridges and boundaries in the world!" he said optimistically, cutting me off.

An unusual silence followed, and in the absence of our voices and our rhythmically beating hearts, I could hear the crash of thunder and see the flash of lightning, which made him hold me even tighter against him. It felt foreign, but nice.

"How are we going to get home tonight? My uncle is going to kill me if he finds out I'm not in my bed," I said.

"Does he check every night?" he asked.

"Most nights, yes, and sometimes I put books under the covers with some pillows before I leave for soccer with AOB and his friends."

"Did you do that tonight?" he asked.

"I don't think I did, because we were right behind our house and weren't planning to stay up late, since it was so windy and the moonlight was gone anyway," I said. We closed our eyes and prayed that my uncle did not check my bed.

When light hit us full in the face, we didn't know what it was. Lightning, maybe? Clay reached out to my boyish, undeveloped hips and then moved his hands to my hardly noticeable chest. I touched the fringed seams of his jacket and squirmed a bit, wondering why that part of my body, for some reason, wasn't there yet. Most girls my age at school and in my town, Kamsar, were fully developed, and some from the Susu tribe would leave their breasts exposed at any given time to show they were ready to be wed. In many cases, for better security, they had already been married off to an older man.

"Clay and Kenda, God damn you two for the shame you're bringing to us!" shouted Clay's aunt. She was approaching with a flickering torch. Clay and I looked at each other, realizing that had been the source of light a moment ago. We quietly smiled, as appropriate to the occasion, stood still and waited for his aunt and uncle to reach us.

"How could you do this to us?" the aunt added through tears. "God help me with what you've done now, Clay."

"Let's go home," his uncle said.

"This tree you're leaning on could have even ... oh, Jesus, let me not say the word! Don't you know that in a storm, you don't go near any tree, let alone a palm that's only half standing?" His aunt's hands were up in the air as if she were about to pray. Instead, tears poured down her face like those of a lonely, lost orphan.

"Killed me," Clay said and gently put his aunt's hands down.

"He could have been blown away – both of you – by the storm and the wind. Didn't you notice it?" Clay's uncle asked.

We looked up. The palm was already a wreck, its other half almost entirely gone.

"You must be in love, but, son, this isn't the way to go about it. We'll have to approach Kenda's family properly if you want to have her. I hope they see love instead of your religion or ethnicity," Clay's uncle said with a grimace.

Clay's guardians argued about the timing for his marriage, and love between Clay and me, and then even more about whether to take me home immediately or let me spend the night and accompany me back in the morning.

"You have to take her tonight, because in the morning everyone will see her and laugh at her and us," the aunt said. She continued weeping but was closer to surrender.

"It would help if you'd stop crying. They're just kids and haven't done anything wrong. Let's bring her home in the morning because of the storm. You can't expect us to travel at this time of night," Clay's uncle said.

"You do whatever you want, husband, and then also find a way to let her mother know that she's safely at our house," she replied, drying her face with the back of her long-sleeved dress.

"You can't do that – my uncle will kill me," I pointed out.

"It's beyond killing now, Kenda," the aunt warned.

"Whatever we do will be wrong. What were you thinking?" the uncle grumbled, as if just realizing the hindrance ahead of us. They agreed to take me to their home and return me to mine around 4:30 in the morning, before the first prayer. That way, the storm would have subsided, and it would still be quiet; nobody could possibly be awake so early.

We walked back to Clay's house. His aunt gave me dry clothes, which I put on right away, and plastic slippers, which I put on despite myself. She went into the kitchen and made us some rooibos tea with milk. Clay and I drank it, still trembling like wet chickens and gazing into each other's eyes across the room. His aunt put me into her bed next to her and ordered her husband to sleep in Clay's bed to ensure we wouldn't see each other for the rest of the night.

Two hours later – I could see the bedside clock – we heard a car pull up to the back of the compound. Clay's uncle opened the gate to find my uncle Hussein and my younger brother, Alpha Oumar, in the sedan, and another obscured vehicle right behind. My uncle was so upset that he ordered the driver to park and came in himself to haul me out.

I walked toward our family car as instructed, my uncle in his fury. I was shaking, so scared that I couldn't feel the ground under my feet. The second vehicle belonged to the police. The officers arrested Clay and forced him into it. Already seated in our car, I saw that crying or shouting for him would have done no good, since the tinted-glass windows were up. Silent, I seemingly turned to ice, like droplets on an evergreen in the middle of a northern winter.

I felt cold. It was like I was in a dream in which nothing was going my way, but I was certain I would wake in the morning, laugh at this scenario and resume my daily life. Or maybe not. As much as I wanted to believe my fantasy, I felt the danger in what had just happened. I was humiliated and sad for Clay and his family.

"Nothing happened," Clay's aunt had shouted through her tears as we got into the cars.

"Mr. Bah, this is madness. How can you call the police on my son, on our kids?" Clay's uncle raged.

It was the first and only time I'd seen him so angry since I'd started going to their house. He was a Bible man and never raised his voice to anybody or anything. To observe him like this was scary, and I knew right away he'd never let me see Clay or invite me into their house again. The fact that he was Christian wouldn't help the matter either, so he chose to calm himself down and look after his mixed-up wife.

"It's not only your irresponsible son who's going to jail – she's going as well!" my uncle screamed at the top of his lungs.

"You can't take a girl to jail, Mr. Bah! You won't find any Koran or Bible that says we parents can lock our kids up just because they have not listened to our way of life. They are human and not animals," Clay's aunt said. With her hands on her head, she was tilting slightly on her feet, like an overwhelmed toddler.

"Let him do whatever he wants. Jesus is merciful. I'll go get our son in the morning. I also know people," Clay's uncle said, moving to leave with his wife.

"No! I don't want my only son spending a single night in jail. He doesn't deserve it, and Kenda doesn't, either. This isn't right! It's not fair! It's not even a children's jail, because there is no kids' jail on earth. Please, do something, husband! Please," she pleaded.

"The militia is corrupt as hell – what do you want me to do?" Clay's uncle said, holding her firmly.

He escorted her back to their house, but she ran back to us, begging the police and calling Clay's name like a tigress that had lost her cub to a heartless hunter.

As the vehicles drove away, I turned a couple of times to look at the squad car behind us, where Clay had quietly surrendered to what I saw in his deep, dark-brown eyes would prove to be an eternally shameful situation. His soul's DNA would never be the same again. I felt bad for him beyond words. He could have dated any girl he wanted from our school, and yet he had decided to go with the only one not from his religion or way of life and who wasn't even pretty; she didn't wear dresses or put on a veil like the other girls in her community.

I wore trousers with long, buttoned shirts and sometimes a wrap around my waist to hide my shape, which gave my body a more boyish look yet could easily show my feminine parts. Like my mother did. Draping something over the top of her slacks helped her get out of the house and face the world with less harsh judgement from family and friends.

* * *

The night felt long, and the distance separating us, eternal. The journey to the police station also seemed endless. The rain kept pouring unmercifully. Most of the trees along the road had fallen; some acacias were lying scattered on the street. Debris from cans, bottles and old worn-out shoes was strewn around, and plastic utensils that had escaped their houses and were floating about, making unwanted and irrepressible sounds which nonetheless seemed like love songs to my ears.

I needed something to hang on to. For some reason the police car passed us right as we were about to exit at the next light onto the main road leading to my house. Our car turned toward home, and I wondered why.

When we arrived, my father stepped out with a face I didn't recognize for the anger written on it. This was the only time I'd seen him come back early from his travels, and I was not able to run into his arms and hug him with my usual tears of joy and excitement or note the smell of his cologne, which I would sniff on his bedroom door handle when he was away. He'd wipe away those tears before placing small kisses on my cheeks – although many people had advised him not to kiss me because I was a girl. I thought, now, he'd surely say something, but he didn't.

He kept silent throughout our ride to the police station. It was really late when we arrived; we parked in the back to avoid anyone seeing me enter. The back alley was flooded from the rain, and piles and piles of dirt had flowed in from the road. Electricity was the first thing the storm had knocked out, so it was dark as we walked in. I was going slowly, hopping from one point to another like a frog, when my uncle shouted, "Move your feet, and fast, before it's daylight."

"She is moving," my father said, peering at me from the corner of his eye. "She's not used to slippers and walking in puddles, don't you see?" He didn't wait for an answer.

I was relieved. I had hoped he would stand up to his brother, and stand up for me, and then we would all drive back home.

I looked down at my feet and realized how spoiled I was. Growing up I'd always worn the latest western shoes and clothes. I kept hearing my mother's voice whenever I wanted to jump in the puddles and play like any other kid.

"You can't wade in puddles, Galle." This was my name in my mother's tongue. My parents called me this because both my maternal and paternal grandmothers, as well as their aunt (my parents were cousins), shared the name.

"Why not, *Maman*? It's so much fun, you know," I'd say to her.

"The only time you can, maybe, jump in a puddle is when it rains a lot a couple of days in a row. That way there are no sleeping mosquitoes in the water, which can give you malaria or yellow fever if you stand in it for too long. If puddles are stagnant, they will be there." She had tried to explain this whenever I invited her to hop into puddles with me. That was the end of my desire to jump in the puddles with her, particularly for my brother's sake. As the firstborn, I had to set a good example.

Even so, I promised myself that if ever, or whenever, I had kids, we would swim in the puddles. If those kids were Clay's, we would all leap in whenever it rained. I felt a brief flicker of joy remembering the moment I'd shared with Clay in the puddles tonight.

It was also not too long before this evening began to seem like a slightly happy one, because the wet patch I was striding into with my father right beside me made me think of a streaming river in a desert. My dad had never walked with me this close before. It was pleasant, though at the same time daunting. My father's comment about my slippers gave me hope, so I kept close to him, holding his left pinky with a pull strong enough to make him aware but not enough to draw attention from my wary uncle's eyes. I looked up to my father with all my strength.

"Please, Baba." I used the Fula word. "Don't leave me here. I'm sorry, and I'll do whatever you want from now on. I'll listen. I'll be a good girl, I promise. You know I'm a virgin – I really am a virgin, even if my uncle doesn't think so. I'm a virgin, Papa. I'll never have a male friend again, and I won't ever marry. And I will –".

"You will what? Shut up! You brought shame to this family!" shouted my uncle, his right hand lifted, ready to slap me.

"Please, no hitting; we've gone past that now," my father said, turning to my uncle. "Why are you taking her to jail? You've certainly made it worse for all of us. How are you going to get her back home without anyone seeing? Why did you take Clay with you? What are you doing, Hussein?" He had finally started to talk, and I hoped he'd keep it up.

"He has to confess that he didn't take Kenda's virginity. I'll bring a doctor to confirm if she's still a virgin; otherwise, they'll rot in jail," my uncle said.

"A virginity check in jail? How? Especially if she's a virgin – which I believe she is," my father said, looking at me for confirmation.

"I am, Baba. I'm a virgin; I'm really a virgin," I repeated.

"No family in their right mind would welcome a girl who has been jailed," my father rebuked his brother. "You could have done this at our own discretion."

"Baba, it's not too late. Let's just go home! Please take me home, Baba! Please!" I implored, clutching his hand.

"*Shut up!*" my uncle screamed. Grabbing my arm, he dragged me toward him. I was trembling.

"You see. Just look at her! She talks back! And she does it with her eyes looking right into yours! She has no shame! That's worse than losing her virginity. She talks back like her mother! She talks back!" he exclaimed. My father did not say anything.

"I did propose a virginity check to your beloved wife – another one who doesn't listen to me – but she insists that Kenda is a virgin and there's nothing to worry about," my uncle went on.

"She's her mother, so she must be right. Mothers always know their girls, and she would have known it first, before any one of us, if she had lost her virginity. So she hasn't yet," he said, pointing at me in the middle of the hall.

"I haven't, Papa. I promise that I'm a virgin and will always be a virgin! Please, uncle, believe me," I begged.

"Now she's calling you Papa instead of Baba … she's talking back … she has no respect for her own language and culture and traditions … she's –"

"Please keep quiet," my father said.

"I'll take the words from the doctor's mouth, and until then you'll learn another lesson of life in this place, since you won't listen to me. You'll listen to authority now," my uncle said to me.

My father had stopped listening. He walked out the front of the station without waiting to find out what they would do to me or where they were going to put me.

"Please make sure she's well cared for," I heard him say to the lady dressed in a khaki police uniform at the front.

"Why and how? This is a jail, Mr. Bah. And it's a jail for adult males and not for women, young women, or kids," she said.

"What I mean is, put her in a separate room with a decent bed until my brother comes to his senses."

"You want me to put her in a separate room? In a decent bed? I can't believe what I'm hearing. You bring your daughter to jail and you tell me what to do and where to put her?"

"Here." He handed her something from his pocket that looked like an envelope. "And please do all you can to make sure she's fine until, as I already said, my brother Hussein decides what to do with her." He walked out.

My uncle filled out a form with the help of another khaki-clad guard, then marched out after my father, who was no longer paying attention to what my uncle was saying. I ran to the window and saw them get in the car. My uncle had ordered our driver to wait at the front of the station after we were dropped off at the back.

I still hoped my father would turn around and come back for me. I wondered why, since he was the oldest, he hadn't been able to contradict his brother. What power did my uncle have over him? What was going on? What kind of tradition was this where the younger brother, or any other family member, had such power over another?

The policewoman walked me into the big waiting room, where there were other prisoners. They looked sad and uncomfortable and had leering faces, particularly at the sight of me in jail with them. None wore a uniform like those in the movies Clay and I had watched at his house.

"I'm worried about you, Kenda," the policewoman said as we approached a room that was supposedly better for me to stay in.

"Where am I going to put you?" she mumbled to herself. "How am I going to keep you away from these monsters, who haven't seen a woman in a million ... ?" She fumbled with one of her keys and didn't finish the sentence. The key broke before the door could open.

"This lock has always been a problem, and I've asked my husband a number of times to fix it, but he hasn't," she said.

"Your husband and you work together?" I asked. She stared at me like she had never heard somebody my age ask a question.

"Yes," she said in a tone that made it clear further queries were unwelcome. "I'm putting you in the next room until I can break into this one. I think with all the rain everything is getting stuck together."

I followed her down the corridor. Every now and then, the gas lamp in her right hand flickered.

"I need to add gas," she murmured, still talking to herself. I followed her without a word.

"Can I look after her, Madame Policewoman?" Clay whispered through a door we were about to pass. She paused, lifting the light to peer at Clay.

"I don't think so. How did you end up here with this young girl? The way I see it, all this happened because you two couldn't keep your hands off each other," she said, looking at me, still holding the flame up.

"No. We never touched each other in that sense," I said.

"Which sense?" she asked.

"We're just friends and like hanging out together, but I never touched her, really," Clay said.

"What do you mean 'really'?" the policewoman asked.

"I mean that we only kissed today when we were stuck in the storm, and I wouldn't have gone beyond kissing her," he said through his small cell window.

"Kissing? You kissed a girl who's not your wife or wife-to-be? I'm not surprised you're both in trouble. Is that all?" She seemed a little amused as she opened Clay's cell.

"Yes, I promise," I said, but she didn't seem convinced that leaving us together was the right thing to do. Her wandering eyes, now fixed on us like a snake in the dark, left no doubt about what she was going to do next.

She walked us both to an adjoining room, where she told me to take a seat. But no sooner had she left than she reappeared, as if suddenly remembering something, and snapped her fingers at Clay, who, despite himself, followed her out silently. I lost any sense of security or hope of being with and helped by him. They had left me utterly alone.

I could hear the whizzing wind and see, through the tiny, half-shattered prison window, the unwelcome lengthening light. The senseless heavy rain fell on the station's burned-out roof as though it were in this room – a room I was put into without any remorse. An overwhelming and profound anguish clouded my thoughts. What would life for a young African Muslim girl be like after this curse? What will become of me?

I heard the loud splash of water rushing down the roof into a big bucket – tock, tock, and then whoosh – like a broken clock.

I wished I were one of those drops, even though I could no longer bear the thought of hearing them again. The loud, heavy drips smacking the old tiled floor sounded like water escaping from a tap, over and over again, like torture, as if I were in one of Hitler's cells in Austria; trickling to the floor into screaming holes full of ants and mice, running down the worn wooden door with a broken lock and a key that hardly kept it shut. Each time I glanced at the entrance I dreaded what might come through it.

My relentless uncle and my father had disappeared, leaving my fear to grow overnight. The rain did not cease and I couldn't eat, or maybe I refused to eat until I saw Clay or my mother again.

A young cleaner came in to empty the bucket and replaced it with a bigger one that resembled a small wooden canoe. At first, I just leaned against the wall and peered toward the entrance leading to another hall we had not seen when we had arrived a few days ago. Now we were in the biggest rain of the tropical season, and the policewoman had shown a little mercy to both Clay and me, but it was not for long. She would let us visit each other periodically, but she seemed conflicted about whether this was the right thing to do.

On one of his visits, Clay had looked at me, shaken his head, rubbed it, and taken a few steps toward me.

The policewoman said in Susu, "You're pushing it, young man. You cannot come closer to her. I put you together to watch out for each other, not to pick up where you left off."

She led Clay away into another room down the hall; I knew it wasn't the same cell she had taken him from because I'd counted the steps, and now there were many more.

"I just wanted to tell her I'm sorry I put her in this situation. That was all I was going to do. Nothing else, Madame Policewoman," I heard him say.

The empty room filled with the sound of water dripping into the little canoe. It was taking longer to reach the brim, and the young girl who used to clean it no longer came to empty it. I looked back at the door through which Clay had just vanished, like my father and uncle had. I noticed the hanging clock read 3 a.m. An immense agony of loneliness overtook me. I was not scared, but the disappointment that both my uncle and my father had left me here in the middle of the night kept pounding inside my head. I wondered if my mother knew I was in this cell right now, or was she already having her baby and that was why she couldn't come, or did my Teutonic uncle not let her get away? What had happened to my younger brother, Alpha Oumar – had he been able to get home unnoticed or had my uncle beaten him nearly to death to make him reveal where I was?

I drifted toward the wall behind me and slid down onto the floor, still staring at the clock. I tried to ignore the sound of water dripping into the canoe to focus more intently on the clock's tick-tock. For some reason I had come to like its sound. I leaned my head on my knees and tried to sleep, but discomfort kept me alert and wide awake, and now the clock read 4:30. Then my eyes began defying me; although I fought the drowsiness, they closed.

I felt two arms lifting me onto the bed in the corner of the cell. I kept my eyes shut, thinking with pleasure that it was my mother, who used to pick me up and tuck me into bed, something she often did because I slept anywhere the need hit me. At the same time I thought I was in a dream.

Then I felt strong hands pulling down my pants. I awoke and tried to push them away, but to no avail. It was a man, but in the dark I couldn't tell who it was – the only gas lamp in the room had been removed or was out of fuel. I felt like I was in a prison within a prison, weak and powerless and beaten by my own anticipation of defeat. My uncle's roaring voice kept pounding in my head, like the stubborn rain through the tiny cell window. I tried to scream, but the man's hand covered my mouth and nose. I was out of air, and he kept pressing himself on me. Then footsteps approached my door.

The ping of water into the canoe had stopped because the rain had stopped, leaving behind only the sound of a river rushing into the canals; they were to keep the main road from being flooded. I wished I were a piece of debris the river was flushing away, but, no; I was at this devil's mercy.

"Is everything OK?" the policewoman asked through the half-closed door.

"Answer it," the man whispered.

"Yes, Madam. I –" As he pressed even harder on my mouth, I bit his palm.

"You do that one more time – you move or you bite me again – and I'll kill you! I'll fuck the brains out of you, slut," he said into my ear.

"You were sleeping soundly when I took the lamp. Do you want me to bring it back?" the policewoman asked.

"Say yes, and I'll stand behind the door," he said.

"Yes."

"I'm going to get the lamp and bring it back, OK?" She headed to her desk.

"Please don't hurt me," I told the man, who was now totally outraged and maybe scared as well.

"I won't hurt you. I won't do anything to you that you didn't know before. I'll be gentle and do you very nice – better than the young boy who came in with you. I'm better than him, you know," he said, reaching down to what looked like his robe. Then, sliding my half-opened pants all the way down, he stood me up against the wall and turned on a small torch that had been in his pocket. It made the room slightly brighter, at least where we were standing.

"Don't you want to kiss first?" I asked, not sure whether the policewoman was really coming back.

"You see! You're not a virgin. You know about kissing already, you devilish, cursed *eben*!" (In many Mandingo fairy tales, "eben" refers to a dark, dead tree or a free-spirited black beauty.) Holding his arms over my face, he stared into my eyes a little longer; he could see that I'd bite if his tongue got any closer to my mouth. He slapped my face and yanked my right hand down into his pants under his big robe.

"Feel this and hold it now!" he said, groaning like an animal. It felt like the heaviest thing I had ever held. I felt vomit rising in my throat; I tried to swallow but instead I spat it out into his face. I had hoped that would distract him enough, but his penis kept growing like the world's biggest anaconda. My fear of him grew as his penis did.

He hurled me onto the bed and threw himself on top. I started screaming, and he put his big hand on my mouth before I could move any farther. Despite my punching and kicking, he entered me and my body collapsed.

At that moment, the door opened. The policewoman stood there, holding the lamp, her mouth wide open. Time stopped. Slowly rising, I noticed blood dripping from between my legs onto the bed and, when I stood, down my legs to the prison floor.

"How could you do this to me? Her uncle wants proof that she's a virgin. Do you understand that the doctor is coming to check her virginity, and you, of all people, take it away from her? How could you be so low?" she said.

"You're all the same whores – no good, well-born girls are put in jail. She's here because she's a slut, and she got what she deserves – at least what her family thinks of her. No word to anybody about this," he said and walked out of the cell. The policewoman took me away into yet another room.

"We have to do something with you, my poor girl. What am I going to tell your father – I took a lot of money from him to keep you safe and I failed. I'm sorry. You were right all along. How stupid that you were deflowered in a prison cell by my own husband." She turned her face away from me.

"Your husband," I said, remembering our conversation earlier.

"Yes … my husband. Did he hurt you?" she asked.

I kept quiet.

"Yes, he has, because you're bleeding. Did he go up and down with his penis deep inside you?"

"I don't know. What difference does it make now? Why didn't you let me stay with Clay? He'd never have done this to me. He would have looked after me," I said, tears pouring down my cheeks.

"He likes young virgin girls, and he can smell them a mile away. That's why I put you in that far-corner room, since my own wouldn't open with the broken lock. Once he deflowers the girls, he leaves them to friends until he finds his next virgin. He dislikes women with wide holes; he wants them tight, and the tighter the better. I'm alone in the station tonight. And it's been like this since the rain and storms began." She paused, staring at me as if solving a math problem.

"I wish I'd left Clay with you. How stupid!" She shook her head.

"Do you know how to ride a bike?" she asked. I didn't answer. She took me to another room that looked like a shower and asked me to wash myself. It was too dark, and I felt like I had been broken into pieces.

"Let's go back to your cell. There might be water in the canoe we can use," she said.

We returned to my cell, where she noticed the drops of blood on the floor – my own blood – and the stained sheet. She rushed to strip the sheets as if only then aware of the danger lurking in what had happened. She took the pillow cover, dipped it in the canoe water and started washing me. I was trembling, my legs shaking like an earthquake. Seeing this, she held my feet to the ground for a moment before asking me to sit in the canoe.

"You haven't answered my question. Can you ride a bike?" she asked, inadvertently pressing the cloth even harder on my skin. I said nothing and wondered why she was asking me about riding a bike. There was pain between my legs, whose tremors I could not stop. I felt cold and dispensable, useless, like a lost and wounded beast who has barely escaped an evil hunter in a nowhere land.

In the midst of it all, I worried about what they would do to Clay, who wasn't involved in this. Who would believe me if I told them I'd been raped in a prison cell where I was put by my own uncle under the watchful eyes of my father because I had kissed a boy? Who should I tell this to, or tell it at all, without losing my womanly dignity and honour? Could I tell my mother? *This is a real lost cause.*

A week passed, each night dreadful and gruesome. Nobody came to see me – not even the doctor my uncle had mentioned – except the policewoman, who told me my mother was feeling poorly with her pregnancy and that my father had returned to Senegal but would be back the following week. Each morning she gave me a pill that was hard to swallow. For days now, Clay and I and other prisoners had been clearing the debris the storms had swept into the station yard. In the distance I could see him, and he could see me, each time I leaned to pick anything up or throw trash in the garbage bin set out for us. Students our age passed by every morning on their way to school.

Clay's uncle and aunt had been visiting him daily, bringing his favourite dishes. He tried to pass them on to me, but the policewoman kept them for herself. Was she a kind or an unkind warden? All I can say is that she was pragmatic, and distant in her own pain at times, which I noticed from the way she looked at her husband whenever he came to the station with a different young girl.

"How about my uncle, and where is Clay?" I asked.

"Your uncle's going to send the driver to pick you up after the doctor sees you," she said. "Your mother plans to visit once the result has come in."

"Why not before?" I asked.

"Your uncle thinks she'll get the doctor to alter the virginity-test result," she said.

"My virginity?" I asked.

"Yes, your virginity. You're still a virgin. You might have lost your hymen, or maybe you were having your period for the first time, but you are more than a virgin ..."

She explained that virginity can take many different forms. I felt increasingly lost in it all. Was she trying to cover up for her husband and his friends by making me believe I was still a virgin? She said it so often throughout the week, though, that I started to accept the possibility.

"If I really am a virgin that would be nice, would it not?" I whispered to myself a few times.

"What do you mean by period? Is that the same as the blood you lose when you have sex for the first time?" I asked her.

"Sort of, but it's more complex than that. Did you bleed more in the days that followed?"

"Yes. And it was painful," I said.

"Because I didn't have kids for my husband, that makes me a whore and gives him the right to do as he pleases, but I did insist that he tell me everything about you. After I told him I would gather the whole village and tell everybody who he really is, he confessed that he hadn't gone through with it before I came in. He might merely have broken your hymen."

"What's that?" I asked.

"It's the thread that blocks the entrance to the vagina. It's complex and hard to understand at your age, but the doctor will put it back so you can walk out of here the way you came in."

"The way I came in?"

"Yes. What else do you expect? I'm really beyond shocked, and I feel sorry for your mother, who is almost due and has to go through this shit your uncle came up with." She stood up and stomped out.

The next day, the doctor arrived. Before starting the exam, he asked me to drink something and gave me a pill; both tasted really bad.

"This is to prevent pregnancy in case this man's sperm has gotten into you, and it's also like a painkiller for the procedure I'm going to do on you. The jailor told me to replace your broken hymen with a new one," he said.

"Pregnant?" I asked, lifting my head.

"Please keep your head down. You can get pregnant without intercourse – you know that," he said. He inserted two fingers a little way into my vagina as he kept his eyes there.

I was lying with my legs in the air on the same bed on which a total stranger had forcefully and painfully penetrated me. The doctor's procedure hurt so much that I fainted. When I awoke, I felt stitches between my legs. I checked my vagina in the bathroom and saw that my clitoris was gone and my vulva had been sewn shut, the lips brought closer together than before. It looked ugly with black sutures.

I held my head and howled. Then, to avoid drawing attention to myself, put my fists to my mouth. I calmed myself down and went back to the room that would house me for another week. I was unable to go outside; I refused to eat, growing even skinnier and more withdrawn, like a dog lost in an African flea market.

I had now spent about two weeks in prison without seeing any relative. On the weekend of the second week, the policewoman said I had a visitor. We walked together past Clay's cell; I'd noticed it was empty a few times the past week on my way to clean the yard. I wondered what had happened to him – if he had left while I remained.

I saw my mother on a chair facing the front entrance of the station. She heard my footsteps and turned around. She tried to run to me but stopped, supporting her pronounced belly with her hands. I rushed to her in tears as she sat back down and opened her arms. I was used to seeing my father's open arms when he came home from his voyages, but this time around it was my mother. I stepped back slowly, walked forward again and then sprinted into her embrace, still in tears. She kissed me all over and held me tight as she could.

"I'll see you tonight," she whispered in my ear.

I wondered how, but I was unable to say anything; I was too upset that she was going to leave me here like the others had done.

She left the station right away. I watched as my jailor escorted her out and my mother took something from her bag, like my father had on my first day in prison before he vanished into the stormy night.

I returned to my cell, trying in vain to hide my big tears; I also felt blood running down my thighs, an event I didn't care for in the least. The warden, having followed the drops on the hallway floor, gave me some cotton cloths.

"Use these each month when you bleed, clean them and keep them ready for the next moon cycle," she said. She left before I could ask anything more. I had not stopped bleeding since I'd first seen the red dripping from me.

Staring through the window, I saw the young girl again, cleaning my blood from the hall. I felt sorry she had to do that because of me.

I didn't leave my cell to eat dinner and didn't bother stopping by the policewoman's office with my questions, and she didn't come to see me. But somewhere around 4 a.m., a hand brushed my shoulder. I jumped and screamed.

"Shush," the warden said, her right hand covering my mouth. "Keep quiet and come with me."

I walked with her to the back of the station. There was a bike right at the entrance, hidden well enough to go unnoticed from the inside. I recognized the bike. It was Clay's.

"Ride it to your mother. She'll be waiting for you behind your house. Don't take the main road, and be safe," she said.

I stared at her, wondering how in hell I would ride it home. She showed me how to sit on it and balance my body. She pushed me out of the gate, holding the bike frame long enough for me to do some pedalling before she let go.

I managed. In fact, it felt like I'd ridden a bike my whole life. Concentrating on that took my mind off the pain between my legs and the heavy cloth now filled with blood. I was starting to speed up when I heard the chain come off. I got it back on, but now I was all muddy and dirty.

Looking at the sky, I noticed the clouds were clearing. The dawn was about to pronounce itself, the sun just below the horizon. As I continued to pedal, the breeze on my face gave me a feeling of liberation. I couldn't wait to see my mother, but I wondered what would happen when my uncle saw me. Had my father returned from his trip? Was he upset with my uncle? What had happened to Clay, and why was I riding his bike? Who had brought it to the station?

When I arrived, my mother and Clay's uncle were waiting. They took the bike right away and vanished through the mango trees behind our house. I followed my mother without speaking. She was taking me to my aunt's house – my father's and uncle's only younger sister lived a two- or three-hour drive from us. My mother's usual taxi driver was waiting at the roundabout. We arrived at my aunt's around six, the time when most men in her village were setting out for their morning prayers. The taxi left with my mother in it.

"Your aunt will bring you home next week. Stay low, my sweet daughter," she said through the window.

My aunt's house sat about a fifteen-minute walk from the main road. She was the only person my uncle listened to and was afraid of disappointing. She was very irate that nobody had told her about her brother's behaviour.

I didn't stay past the second day with her, because there was news that my father had returned and that my mother was due any moment now. We returned to my home – the home I hadn't seen for almost a month. It looked distant and unfamiliar because of changes that had been made to prepare for the wedding of my cousin – my uncle's daughter.

I realized then why he had forgotten me in jail. He had been busy with his real daughter's engagement and the wedding to follow right after. A Fula wedding celebration of partying, eating and dancing could last more than four weeks. Women would spend days putting henna on their hands, lining their eyes and trimming their brows, colouring their hair or braiding it to perfection. It was a grandiose festivity that went on, in total, for months.

When I entered our courtyard, all eyes were on me; everyone was wondering where I'd been all this time. My uncle and my dad pretended I'd been visiting their sister.

The night before the wedding, my mother and Aunt Halle called me to my mother's room. I was wearing a dress my father had given to my mother for me when he came back from his trip. At first I thought they wanted to make sure I had it on frontwards, not backwards, my usual way. Mostly white, it had a sprinkling of black, red, yellow and green dots all over it. Then my mother invited me to sit on her bed while my aunt locked the door. They asked me to remove my panties, lift my skirt and spread my legs as they shone a flashlight at the space between my thighs.

"What do you think?" my mother asked my aunt, her face turned away.

"I really don't see anything wrong with her vagina, other than that the vulva seems to be tightened like any other girl in our tribe. They didn't close the big lips, though, and that worries me a bit, because there should be only a small hole for peeing and it should be … clean," she said, keeping her eyes on my vagina.

"What do you mean, closed vulva? How did this happen?" My mother wouldn't look; she expected my aunt to do it for her.

"Yes, it's tight in the far back. But what do you mean, 'How did this happen?' Isn't this how a woman's vagina is supposed to look?" my aunt asked.

"Can you please double-check?" my mother pleaded.

"I can't check; inserting my fingers might not be safe and could ruin her virginity. A doctor would be better at this, you know, if you want my opinion. She's fine because she's cut and sewn. You don't have anything to worry about, my dearest. She's untouched and clean. She'll be re-opened with a warm flame on her wedding night with her lucky man. And I can't wait for that day to come, my dearest Galle," my aunt said. She lowered my dress and sat next to me.

"You're fine," she said to me. I said nothing, but my mother wasn't satisfied. I could see it in her face. My aunt excused herself to go wash her hands. My mother came closer and looked into my eyes.

"Did anybody touch you, Galle? I thought you had run away from the cutters, that you escaped."

"I did, and I hit one on the head with the rock like you advised me, but …"

"But what, Galle?" She paced a bit and looked behind the door to see if anybody was eavesdropping. "Now I'm hearing from your aunt what I've feared my whole life. How did this happen, and when?" she asked. I didn't answer.

She started coughing, and as she walked away a drop of saliva fell on my dress. It looked red, like blood. I leaned down to see more clearly, thinking it might be one of the pattern's red dots. Surely I was being paranoid, but I couldn't stop myself from speaking up.

"You're coughing blood, Maman," I said.

"No, not really. Go outside, and never tell anyone what happened."

As I stepped toward the living room, she said, "Stay with your cousin, and don't go sitting with your brothers, not even your brother Alphadjo, or any other boys in the room. Do you hear me?" she said.

"Yes, Maman."

"And stop saying 'Maman.' Say 'Nene.' You're Fula, from noble blood. From now on, you must always speak your language."

I didn't reply right away, other than to nod as if I were starting to dance to music I liked.

"Must I really, Maman?"

"Be careful, Galle. I'm worried about you. Please try, at least, to pretend to obey, even if just for this week. All I'm asking is that you be what everybody around you wants you to be, seven days at a time – or know, at least, how to fake your way around your uncle's and his wife's eyes and ears. The house is full of relatives this month. If you don't want to be dead before your time, please do what I recommend, just this once," she said, clasping her hands.

On my way to rejoin the festivities, I glanced through a window along our corridor. The day was bright with a clear blue sky; outside were benches, plastic chairs, some tables and mats strewn around. A beautiful crowd in colourful ceremonial clothes with embroidery around the seams and necks had gathered, relatives among them – some I knew, some I'd never met or even heard of – and neighbours who had come in to help prepare for the wedding. Because they were doing most of the work, they had fussed very little with their looks.

I saw my father walking into my mother's room as if he were sneaking away from the crowd. I returned to eavesdrop at the side of the door. I wasn't able to hear much, until my mother practically screamed with joy.

"We're moving to Conakry! Away from Kamsar! The timing couldn't have been better, husband, and that's nice! Thank you!" she said.

Kamsar is a port city in Guinea, in the region of Boke on the mouth of the Rio Nunez in West Africa. We were moving to Conakry, the capital of Guinea. I wondered if this was due to all that had happened between my uncle and my father or simply because my father wanted to make sure nobody found out what I'd been through. We would live in a place where girls are untouched and protected, I dreamed.

I wondered what it would be like, and how big it would be; if people spoke Fula or French, since the city housed the central government. I felt relief and nostalgia at the same time, since my two brothers and sister had all been born in Kamsar. Nenein Bah, my only sister, was three and half years old; she might remember Kamsar, I thought.

Their voices lowered, but I remained curious: would my father mention my imprisonment? Cracking the door open and keeping my ears wide open, I heard nothing about me or the jail.

My cousin's wedding-engagement festivity went on through the night, and guests stayed at our house; some slept in the courtyard under the stars. The next day they all left, and my aunt was taken back home to her village by our driver.

Neither my father nor my uncle had mentioned anything about my virginity, jail, or Clay. The entire family simply assumed that I'd been with my aunt, and I was relieved to escape being a source of gossip and cause for laughter, both for my sake and my mother's. I felt grateful to my aunt, my mother and also Clay's uncle, who had helped organize my escape.

Later, in town, I caught a glimpse of the policewoman. Nothing came of it but coldness; I wanted to bury the memory of her face in the back of my mind as quickly as it had come.

At school, my ears perked up whenever anybody mentioned Clay.

Galle and her mother after jail –
Port Kamsar, August 1988

We were still living in Kamsar while my parents secretly prepared to move to the capital of Guinea. My mother even visited at the end of 1986 to scout out a place and help my father open a new construction shop right in Conakry's big Madina market.[2]

"Why are you leaving us?" I recall nagging my mother as she hugged us goodbye on the day she left Port Kamsar.

"Finding a big house around the Madina isn't going to be easy, so I have to take care of that. Once everything is in place, we'll all go. You just get busy with school and homework; I'll be back before you know it," she tried to convince me.

"Are you going to get us a house or are you sick with the baby? I heard you cough a lot at night." I talked against her shoulder, which I wasn't ready to release. She said nothing but, assisted by my aunt Halle, my mother's younger sister, got into the car without turning around. She would be gone for two weeks, which felt like an eternity to my brothers and me.

My mother seemed transformed into a happier version of herself when she returned to Port Kamsar; she had so much hope and energy. She couldn't wait to go back as soon as she gave birth so we could start school on time in the same neighbourhood, since we wouldn't have a car right away. It seemed to me my parents, too, would have to begin their lives over again in Conakry, leaving whatever they had built over the years to my uncle and his family. For the sake of peace, my mother didn't mind as long as she had her freedom.

On the morning of August 8th, my mother began having cramps; my father had left, despite her plea the night before that he stay. I could see the sadness that she always tried to mask with a tiny smile like the Mona Lisa's, almost impossible to read. Now she was cold, distant and impatient, in an even worse mood than she was when she had left a few weeks ago for Conakry.

---

[2] One of the largest markets in West Africa, Madina Market witnessed in 1977 the Market Women's Revolt.

She asked me to go look outside for her usual friendly taxi driver and ask him to take us to the hospital.

"Maman, why don't you invite my uncle's wife to come with you?" I asked.

"I don't want her to come. Your uncle put you in jail because of her," she said.

"Are you sure about that?"

"I hear her talk badly about you to him all the time."

"Did you ask her to stop or find out why she gossips about me?"

"Yes, you know me; I don't have time for that kind of life. I tried several times. Now let's get going," she said, rising from her bed. I didn't move.

"I want you to come with me. You've been here for me at every birth, and this is how I trained to be a midwife, you know," she said with yet another forced smile.

"Yes, I remember that jail, and I think I'll always remember it," I said as if speaking to myself.

"Look me in the eyes, Galle. Are you talking to yourself? Are you OK? Look at me. Did anything happen in that jail?" she asked between contractions.

"No," I said. "Are you in pain?"

"Don't lie to your mother, Galle. Tell me now, right now, what happened in that damned jail of theirs. I'll never forgive your father for always being away and not standing up to his brother about putting you in that place, which I'd rather leave unnamed."

She said this firmly, without raising her voice, which always scared the hell out of me. One way or the other I'd have to tell her what happened – especially in response to that soft but controlled tone.

"I'm not sure this is the right time to tell you, Mother." I tried to persuade her to relinquish her quest. She looked at me, biting her upper lip.

"Tell me before I tear it out of you." She looked different, so changed that I wondered whether she was still my mother and not a devil.

"There were men in the jail!" I screamed.

"Of course, I know there were men in the jail –"

"Those men –"

We kept cutting each other off; we weren't hearing each other's words, and then the unthinkable words escaped.

"I was raped in that jail, Mother! Are you happy now that I told you the truth on your way to the hospital to have another baby?" I screamed. It felt like a bullet had shot out of me, hitting the last target I would have wanted: my mother, when she needed peace and strength to bring her infant into the world.

God, what have I done? I waited for her reaction. I was surprised to have judged her for having another baby while her husband was away again. I felt worse for that than for letting the fact of rape slip out. I swore to myself I'd be kinder to her.

For a second my mother looked as if she wanted to scream or kill somebody, but she remained calm. What was going on in her mind now that she knew what had happened to me? Would I ever find out? It was not her way to be confrontational.

She coughed a little and turned around to spit in a small red vase next to her bed. It had been there for the longest time, but I'd never noticed it before.

"Are you spitting because you're outraged?" I kept thinking I could see why my mother wouldn't want my aunt to come with her.

"Yes, I am. Do you want to come with me?" she asked again, ignoring her cough.

"Yes, of course, Nene," I said in Fulani.

"I'll deal with your aunt and uncle when we come back. For now, let's go have a baby," she said with confidence, as if nothing painful was happening. How could she shift like that? I envied her strength.

I fetched the taxi while she grabbed her packed bags from under the bed. She joined me without waiting for me to come back for her. I wanted to tell her what I'd heard my father say at the door, but I hesitated; maybe I was dreading the consequences of my eavesdropping. I felt sorry for her without knowing why. The taxi driver, more of a friend to her than any other chauffeur, didn't ask, as we got in, where we were going.

"Oh, I forgot the bag on the chair, next to the window, right beside the tea table," she said.

"I'll go get it for you, Nene." Running back, I approached her room – the one at the farthest reach of the house. I opened the door with the key she had given me, quickly grabbed the bag and bolted for the door.

I heard a crash next to the leg of the bed. It was her little red vase, and from it oozed a mist of blood and saliva as well as the scent of eucalyptus. I wondered if I should clean it up before dashing back to her, but I chose to leave without doing so since she was in pain and needed to get to the hospital right away.

I glanced at the key still in my left hand. My parents and my grandmother had tried all kinds of tricks, and had slapped that hand, to get me to give up using it.

Once I had locked the door, nobody other than my father would be able to enter, and he was all the way over in Senegal so why trouble myself with the mess and the blood? Once I was in the taxi, the driver sped straight to the clinic. He must have guessed our destination since my mother was a midwife. I kept wondering about the broken vase.

In the taxi my mother didn't appear to be in pain. How could she exercise so much control? She seemed strong and determined, keeping her excellent posture. The day had just begun, the sun promising another beautiful African breeze.

Through the window, I felt the wind on my face. Pedestrians crossed here and there without waiting for us to stop, and some, bare-footed, ran past with a wave to either the driver or my mother. It was dusty outside and fast becoming crowded with shoppers filling up the open market. I'd always loved the breeze on my cheeks in a car and watching people start their days with so much energy and laughter. I even wondered what they'd had for breakfast to be so jovial. I knew the driver always wanted his windows closed, but because I accompanied my mother, I took advantage of the opportunity.

I wondered whether, at that very moment, my mother still wanted my father to herself. Did she really need him, or did a neighbour's gossip occupy her mind? Was she trying to discreetly suppress her pain, like a sea turtle until she arrived on shore and dug a hole to lay her eggs? I don't believe she was thinking about me having been in jail; she had weightier things to worry about just then.

I wish I had asked what was going on in her mind then. Did she want her life to end to avoid confronting her husband about his affair, if there was one? She was not the type to have self-doubt. As I'd heard my father say, she was a strong woman with her own mind.

What was that blood in her red vase?

Brussels, May 2, 2016

I left my children's room after tucking them in. I did not sit in a rocking chair as I used to. Josh had just turned eleven that spring, and Owen was now nine years old. I had lingered a little longer over Josh, rubbing his beautiful, curly hair and giving him little kisses. Then he had whispered in my ear, "I still have to have a proper birthday, you know."

"Yes. I know I owe you, big time, and I'll make it up to you," I said, cheek to cheek with him.

"It was not your fault you had to travel." He kept whispering.

"I'm glad you understand and have patience with my lack of focus as a mother lately. I love you, sweet angel," I said as I rose.

"I love you too, Maman. You're the best maman in the whole world – don't you ever forget that," he replied, clutching my wrist.

Returning to the kitchen felt exactly like it had one time when I was coming from my children's room in Vancouver. I recalled that night as if it had just happened.

It was spring 2015. Josh and Owen were having their birthday parties together, and we had invited their friends to join them for bowling. Josh was turning ten and Owen was eight. It was a great celebration; Josh and Owen were born in April and March, and they had always been fine with a combined event. This year, however, things had been totally different.

I saw myself walking into my old kitchen the same way I went into my new one, not sure why I was heading there. I opened the fridge, searching for something I couldn't find. Had I lived in this apartment before we moved in? And why did I feel this now? Why was the past coming back to me?

I did a big cat stretch and lay on the kitchen floor for a while, feeling an ache in my body I couldn't put a finger on. I straightened up like an old lady missing her cane and shuffled into the living room. I wasn't sure what I really wanted. The night seemed much longer than usual.

My mother's face kept coming again and again to me, as if she were attacking me. "What do you want, Mother?" I asked.

I tried to meditate my way out of the night I had last seen her alive, but it was in vain. That night kept growing in my mind, relentlessly; I tried to get a reading of my mother's presence but couldn't, not even in my deepest meditation. Why did some nights feel infinite?

For some reason I heard the voice of my meditation leader. "Lawra Linda," she said.

Lawra Linda is the name I chose to use in my passport when I left Guinea. Lawra could serve as a short form of "Laouratou," and Linda would be a western form of "Dalanda." These honoured both my paternal and my maternal grandmothers but, most important, they simplified my name without killing its roots.

"You've been coming to this meditation, to each workshop I've provided, over the past eight years, but I have the feeling you're not facing the truth of what is really bothering you. Whatever it is, you have to find a way through it and forgive yourself so you can move on. With patience and persistence in your self-discovery, the realization will come. I hope you are able to see it and surrender to whatever it is and wherever it finally takes you."

I embraced my knees and curled myself up small, as if I were giving myself a big hug. "I surrender, God. I'm surrendering; yes, I am, and I have. Please help me with what I don't know about myself," I murmured. I wanted to cry but no tears came.

At that moment I realized decades had passed since I'd seen my father and at least five years since I'd been with my young brothers, except for Alpha Oumar, whom I had met several times in Europe, and in Washington when Obama was running for re-election.

Maybe, I thought, it was time to travel with my siblings, to go to anywhere in the world except Africa, and this idea made me feel better. I felt relieved knowing the globe was big enough to avoid visiting my birthplace; all I needed was a big bank account. How long it had been since I'd even spoken to any of them – more than a year.

As for my father, I couldn't recall exactly when he'd last phoned to wish me a happy birthday, but it had been the first time in a long time. He usually forgot. But how could I not miss him? I even remembered the last call he finally managed.

What was happening to me? I'd practically forgotten that world, so why, now, did it all rush in like a storm on a sunny day? Had I moved to Belgium for all this to unfold overnight? Why had I said yes to coming here in the first place?

Galle overhears her parents – Port Kamsar, August 7, 1988

I recalled the conversation I overheard between my parents during my cousin's festivities. Having gone to my mother's room to thank her for helping me escape from jail, I heard her ask, "Why are you leaving for Senegal tomorrow?"

"I have a meeting about the last fruit truck before the rainy season starts. You know how the road gets," my father said defensively as he changed into pajamas – something resembling a long robe and short, loose pants with a drawstring waist. Seating himself on the bed next to my mother, he put on his slippers. Neither saw me at the door. I turned around, pulled between my desire to walk away and to enter, but I was curious to know how my mother would go about convincing my father to stay with her.

She caressed his face, rubbed his shoulder and gave him a small kiss on the cheek. I kind of knew why she wanted him to stay, but I was not sure if my father got it. I thought my mother should make him understand one way or the other.

"The thing is, even though the doctor said I'll give birth in two weeks, I feel this baby is ready to come anytime now. I would want –"

"You're worrying over nothing," my father said, gently cutting her off and taking her hand. "You have nothing to worry about. Besides, you're a midwife and have always had your – let me correct that – our children by yourself." Rubbing her belly, he put his ear to it.

"This baby is different; he's bigger, and I'm feeling weaker as well, after all that has happened between Kenda and your brother, which you chose to ignore and never talk about. Has it ever occurred to you at least to ask? She's different since returning from that hell you put her in," she said, stroking his hair.

"Kenda got what she deserved, so please leave it at that. For the moment, let's focus all your energy on you, and stop thinking you're a weak woman. If anything, you know you're strong not only for you but also for your daughter – you managed to steal her away from jail without involving me, and nobody noticed. Maybe you're tired, but you're never weak! You're a strong woman and a proud African Fula." He looked her straight in the eye. My mother smiled and leaned into his shoulder, like I would when I wanted a long cuddle with him.

"Please don't go," she pleaded when they faced each other. "Like you've just said, I've always had our children alone, but I feel that I need you this time."

He gave her a quick kiss on the forehead. Taking her face in his hands, he gazed at her intently, as if he wanted to read her soul, but he abruptly released his hold.

"Since when does a woman need a man beside her while she's giving birth? Where does your insecurity come from? You'll be fine; besides, my brother is here, and his wife, if you need anything. Now let's go to sleep. My driver is going to be here first thing in the morning."

"I always thought I was married to you and not your brother. How could you expect me to trust them after what happened to Galle? Shouldn't I be worried?"

"About what? The experience will only make Galle tougher, teach her to stay away from boys and keep her legs closed until she meets the right man and hopefully gets married after graduation," my father said as he walked to the window.

I kept myself between the doorframe and the entrance where they wouldn't see me, hidden from sight even if my father approached. I could be seen by anyone coming up the corridor from the living room, however.

"What woman gets married after she finishes university? I don't understand where all this comes from, Abraham. Should I be concerned about another woman in your life who is feeding your ears with this nonsense?" my mother said in a restless voice.

"A woman? Me, with another woman?" he asked without looking at her. He approached the entrance and closed the door without peering behind it.

"Where did you get that from?" he said, sitting next her.

"In your eyes, and the neighbour's wife told me to watch for constant travelling. You seem –"

"You're listening to the neighbour's wife?!"

"She's not just a neighbour; Mamadou Gando is also my best friend, and I'm not 'listening' to her. That's why I'm asking you directly. You used to let your driver deliver to your stores and you travelled only twice a year, but now you're on the road all the time. I'm due any minute and of course you're leaving tomorrow. This is the second time I'm giving birth while you're not around. I won't do this anymore without you," my mother declared.

I heard footsteps in the corridor. It was my uncle Hussein's wife. I had to either step into my parent's room or run, which my parents would hear and then realize I'd been listening in. I knocked and went in without waiting to be asked. My uncle's wife passed with her daughter and entered their bedroom. I was relieved.

Lawra Linda alone with her mother during childbirth – Port Kamsar, August 8, 1988

"Push! Keep pushing and keep on pushing. You're almost there, Djenab! You're a very, very, strong woman … you can do this … please don't give up – push!"

"Mrs. Hellen, please calm down. I'm not dilated enough to be pushing," my mother told the head nurse. "We both know you can't ask a pregnant woman not fully dilated to push," she said mockingly. I could feel the confidence in those words even though she was in pain.

"I think the baby is too big for my hips," she continued. "How about we do an emergency C-section?" My mother bit her beautiful, full, rounded lips.

"Oh no, no, and no, my darling Jena. No C-sections for African women! Not necessary for a Fula mother. We are born strong with hips to bear children and give birth naturally!" exclaimed the head nurse proudly. "Please have faith that you can do this the natural way."

"Yes, I believe you and have faith as well, but don't you think five kids entitles me to a C-section, when I can actually have it in this hospital?" my mother challenged her.

"No, my dear Jena. A C-section in a clinic like ours increases the danger of hemorrhage, infection, and scarring. There's also the risk of never being able to have a baby again."

"This is my last one, so I see no reason why," my mother sighed, almost defeated.

"We women, we always say that. 'This is our last one,' but we keep on having them, regardless, for fear of not being accepted by our husband and our society. You're lucky you have so many boys and –"

"And two girls." My mother was including Nenein as she pointed at me and bit her lips again in pain. I wondered why this woman was refusing to heed her needs.

If this nurse had permitted a caesarian, would my mother have lived?

Vancouver, October 2014

I returned to my bedroom, took off my bathrobe and lay down next to my husband, Harvey, who was half asleep and still waiting for me. I had on only a silk undergarment. He reached out to my belly as my head hit the pillow next to his.

"Your scars healed well, Linda," he murmured. I didn't say a word but nodded, looking at him. I let go of his shoulder and reached down to touch my scars for myself. He was trying to make me believe those welts had healed. Had they really?

Childbirth – Port Kamsar, August 8, 1988

"Djenab, are you listening to me?" the nurse asked. My mother's eyes were half closed. She wasn't answering anymore but kept taking breaths so deep that my lungs pained me watching her. I stepped slightly out of her line of sight.

"Great start, Jena! You were born strong with hips to bear children. You've done it successfully every time. You're made for this, for a natural birth." The nurse kept repeating herself as if she were marching Russian troops in the Second World War.

My mother, feeling helpless, rationed her ebbing energy and breath so she could have sufficient strength to give birth naturally.

I wasn't really sure why we were in the hospital in the first place. But I hadn't asked any questions; I'd just followed her and accepted the fact that she didn't want my uncle's wife to accompany us. And Mamadou Gando, her best friend, was out of town.

My mother had had each of us by herself at home. Only once she had already cut the umbilical cord would she tell her best friend, our next-door neighbour, to come in. I was always the one there to help her get whatever she needed or had forgotten to put in her birthing kit.

She was known to be courageous for doing it alone, and that was not because she was proud. It was simply because she understood this independence as a gift to herself and a gesture made to other women in our city. Therefore, she was listened to, and I was her proudest accomplice in these multiple successful birthings. I didn't enjoy that position at first, but I came to love being her assistant and witnessing the first breath of each infant she brought into the world, right before my eyes, drawing air into their tiny, fragile lungs.

"I ..." Between deep breaths, my mother tried to articulate her needs again. Would anyone listen?

"I think you're going to kill me if you keep pushing me the way you're doing," she told Mrs. Adama, one of the midwives.

I could see on my mother's face that Mrs. Adama's presence made her happy; the nurse was also Muslim. She even wore her veil and kept a small Koran in her pocket that she took out and read to my mother every now and then. She looked determined, no matter the odds, that my mother have a natural birth.

For some reason, the rhymes of the Arabic verse were soothing not only to my mother but also to me – to all of us, actually. Mrs. Adama had a beautiful voice as well as big, lovely brown eyes and well-manicured hands layered with henna drawings – this was all you could see of her body.

My mother's breathing kept growing stronger, deeper and faster. Mrs. Adama had stopped reading and focused on my mother's belly. She burned some incense and a white candle to create a more relaxed atmosphere and added the calming scent of lavender with some Moroccan oregano oil.

I stepped a short distance outside the door to take a breath for myself. Through the window I had seen cars speeding by in the rain with no windshield and, often, with no window glass, either; most passengers were soaked. The day that had started with the birth of a beautiful sun had turned into a small tropical storm. Those outside looked tranquil as they went about their everyday activities. The skies were starting to clear, giving hope to merchants in the bazaar that they would sell something before closing shop and to customers that they would have something to buy for their families.

I watched pedestrians on the far end of a side road trudging happily along with buckets of rice, cabbages, yams, plantain and green beans as well as bags of carefully packed palm, the beautiful colours of orange and yellow seeds on their heads or backs. The world around them felt chaotic and hectic like an endless muddy road. It seemed at times like they were heading to an amazing party, the celebration of their lives.

Observing the world outside the hospital offered me some relief from witnessing my mother's agony. So I walked down the long hall and kept going until a little veranda with a small fountain and vibrant tropical flowers came into view.

The rain had stopped, leaving behind a fresh floral scent and an oozing red-earth smell that was almost impossible to miss, no matter how inept your nose. It rains a lot in Guinea in August.

I sat there for a moment, looking avidly at the yellow flowers. When I rose to go back, I realized that my skirt was damp. I pulled it a little, turning around to check that it was only water and not mud on my beautiful red-and-white dress. To my pleasant surprise, I was wet, but no dirt was on my dress. I smiled at myself and walked back into the hospital, passing a few patients who waved at me with kind expressions. I lingered when I saw one of the women weeping, silently, in her bed alone. *Why is nobody with her?* Then I remembered my mother's own tears as she tried to give birth, so I hurried my steps to her room. She was asking for me as I came through the door.

"Please stay with me, Galle, my beautiful Kenda. Don't go anywhere ever again and leave me alone."

"I won't, Maman." I placed myself again at the door as though I had never left. I did not like being in her room for some reason. My body was half in and half out, as though I were waiting for her to stand up and lead me home again – like she used to do after giving birth – and then ask me to help her shower after yet another victory, giving me her big wide smile.

She smiled at me, in her pain, so kindly that I felt sorry for her, but this time around, her smile was not wide or happy. She was in agony. Of all the times I'd seen my siblings born, she had never been this weak and frail. I was overcome with the sense that she was not there anymore. There was somebody else in her eyes, or maybe the pain of the birth was taking over her soul.

Mrs. Adama sat astride my mother and, with her solid-looking hands, her knees on each side of my mother's legs, was massaging her from the top of her ribs to the bottom of her abdomen, first gently and then strongly. I heard Mrs. Adama say, "Your belly is still too high. It should drop a little more for this baby to come out. This is a strong boy, all right ..."

I wondered, watching from the door, how she knew my mother was having a boy. There was no ultrasound machine anywhere, but she knew somehow.

"Is there a doctor around who can operate on me?" My mother called again for head nurse Hellen. She kept insisting she needed surgical intervention, even though no one listened to her.

"There's no surgeon on site. Mrs. Hellen's been checking on you every hour. It's a lot for her to be coming to you so often, since she's the hospital's only head nurse. Let me give her a message."

"Kenda," Mrs. Adama called. "Where are you?"

"Right here, Mrs. Adama," I said, approaching quickly and looking down at my mother's face. The room was so small that it made little difference whether I was inside or outside at the door. I could feel and see the white walls covered in the kind of paint that would pull off after too much rain, and it rained a lot in a tropical country like Guinea.

Taking laboured breaths here and there, my mother, bathed in sweat, looked tired and hopeless. I could see the absence of my dad in her eyes; a couple of times I heard her murmur his name through dry, longing lips: "Abraham, Abraham, Abraham..."

What is she thinking? I wished to give her supernatural powers to rescue both of us, or the three of us, in fact. I've always wondered if, when I meet her again, the first thing I'll ask will be what was going through her mind while she called my father's name and struggled on her deathbed.

I extracted the shea butter from the bright deep-blue bag she had prepared. Mrs. Adama took it quickly and put it next to the candle;

she helped my mother turn onto her left side so she could massage her back and hips. I put some of the butter on her lips and gave her a sip of water.

"You're a fine daughter, Galle! Everything is going to be all right." My mother tried to console me. I looked at her as though I could force her to promise me that; I wanted to lock my eyes on hers while Mrs. Adama massaged and lubricated my mother's vagina with the shea butter.

She looked more relaxed and hopeful, but I could see how much pain she was still in. At that moment I vowed never to have children of my own. No man would come close enough to my vagina to begin with.

"Galle, I'd like you to go wait outside, because your mother is ready for her last push." Nurse Hellen was back for the final checkup; she gave my mother another shot of painkiller.

"Jena, we'll have to try a bit harder for a natural birth, since that's how we've always done it – and there's no surgeon here. We're also lacking morphine to perform a C-section," she added in a worrisomely hurried manner.

I retreated as though I were leaving the room, but I stood at the same spot as before, right beside the entrance. Curtains separated us now, but I could still see my mother's head and long curly black hair.

"How about taking me back home?" my mother asked nonchalantly.

I felt that anywhere would have been better for her than this hospital room. Where would that be, though? I refused to believe I might be leaving without her and her newborn. I felt a rage of selfish heat rising in the deepest, darkest veins of my heart. I wished for my mother to live, if worse came to worst, instead of my brother. After all, I didn't know him, and I'd rather not, because I wanted my mother. I couldn't imagine my world without her in it. Nothing and nobody mattered but her. I kept my eyes on her as if they, locked into hers, could keep her strong and increase her desire to fight for me, my brothers and, to a certain extent, her unborn baby.

"Oh, my dearest. That would be a waste of time, Jena. Please focus all your energy on this moment! This moment is all you have, and all we have, so give it your full attention. Let's open these hips, shall we?" nurse Hellen said encouragingly.

"OK. Then here we go!" My mother pushed so hard and screamed so loud that I'd still hear her some nights later – the echo of her voice while she pushed out my brother. Through the drapes, I saw two women pressing the top part of her belly and, before I could blink, my brother appeared in Mrs. Adama's hands, wailing as if to test out his lungs. They wrapped him quickly and placed him in my mother's arms, all smiles.

"Galle, my brave baby girl, come see your brand-new little brother. He's big, like an elephant. He almost killed your valiant mother," she said with a sweaty smile, tears rolling down her face. This was one of the very rare occasions I saw her cry. A sense of relief was in the air; both nurse Hellen and Mrs. Adama were happy – spent but elated. They left the three of us alone to go back to their other duties.

I approached for a glance at my mother and brother. For a moment, it seemed as though no pain or struggle had visited her. Her eyes were big, wide and happy, and her smile so intense that the fiercest tornado could not blow it away. She was back, and I was assured of going home with her. Yes, she looked finished, overused and exhausted, but she was joyful at the same time. She was in the midst of a serene moment, firmly anchored in the now, a present surrounding her with so much light that I wondered if anyone else in the room saw it.

She glanced at the window, then asked me to take my newest sibling, whom I was afraid, at first, to hold, just in case I dropped him. I understood the meaning of her now-gentle smile. She was a mother of encouragement, so I took him in my arms, but I held on so tightly that she said, "Relax your grip a bit, my beautiful daughter. You are definitely the lucky one! I was hoping to give you a little sister, but here you are with another brother."

She paused for a moment, looked down at her cover, and lifted her right leg a bit. I backed away to give her more room in case she wanted to stand up, but instead she sat up a bit straighter. Her back was against the pillow Mrs. Adama had given her after cleaning her up from the swamp of blood and tightening her belly with a strong, wide leather belt. *Wow, that looks more painful than the birth – why does she have to wear it? I won't be needing that, for sure!*

The belt was to flatten her stomach, and the discomfort seemed not to faze her. After all, she'd gone through childbirth so many times before. My newborn brother was her sixth.

"You'll take care of your brothers for me?" she asked as she started to pull herself down right after she'd pulled herself up.

"But you're here, Maman. I won't have to," I said, gazing into my brother's eyes. He was captivating. "He looks like a little angel, Maman."

"He isn't that little, my daughter. He's a big angel, then, let's say." She corrected me with a laugh. "Please put him back in his crib. ... No, wait – let me look at him again."

She pulled my arm toward her a bit and gave him a kiss on his forehead. She was very tender for an African woman. She loved showing us affection, assuring us how much she loved us and how we fulfilled her life. She was truly an awesome mother.

"Your big sister here will take great care of you," she continued. I kept quiet at first, then I wondered.

"Why are you saying that, Maman?" I started to worry. Blood was dripping through the mattress onto the floor. I put my brother down fast so I could run to call the nurse. She stopped me and asked me to make a vow.

"Promise me that you'll be there for your brothers? I'm bleeding too much…" She showed me red fingers withdrawn from under the covers. I looked down and saw she was indeed bleeding heavily. A small pool had already formed. *How could this be?* Everything had seemed to be going so well after the birth.

What should I tell her? To hang onto life for me, for us? Should I say anything at all? I could no longer stare into her eyes, because she had closed them so fast; every now and then she forced them open to search for mine. *God, what should I do?*

I felt an urge to tell her something, but, for some reason, I also didn't want to tell her anything. She had to fight for her life and for her children's lives, and I hoped she could hear my heart's desire.

Will she, God? Please don't let her take the easy road. It wouldn't be fair to her to take the easy road.

Underneath it all I could feel my own agitation, so I tried to calm down, knowing I needed to think and act right. I wanted to burst out of that hospital room, race down the long white hallway and run as far away as I could get. I saw myself taking long steps, fast, through the forest to an unknown lake; there was a great sense of peace, serenity and quiet, as I had felt when I had taken my short walk to the hospital fountain and the tropical yellow blossoms. I had started taking baby steps away from my mother.

My feet, though, ignored me, as though they were detached. Feeling them shaking, I put them together, squeezing them against each other. Then I looked down at my mother, remembering I was really still with her. I was not in the forest or the little clinic garden.

She was losing blood very, very rapidly. Although I wanted to be clear and focused in mind and being, I was still confused about what to do. Should I stay or go? I wished I could run. Despite the effort to hold my legs together, my feet continued trembling, like a tiny earthquake was about to crest under them. I was sprinting in my head and fixed in the room with my mother. God, I felt lost, confused and helpless in that moment!

My brother started crying. *Was he hungry?* I hadn't seen them feed him since they put him on my mother's nipple, which he had sucked delightedly as if he had been doing it for years. For a moment, I saw my mother's lips move but I didn't hear her, because I was wondering where my daddy was and why he was still not here with us. She looked at me and kept talking faintly but seriously, as if determined to engrave her last words on my soul.

"Yes, Maman. You want me to take care of your children – my brothers ... but how?" I finally asked. I started to feel logic and presence in the moment my mother made her request.

"How do you expect me to care for your children while I'm still a child myself?"

"No ... No, don't think like that!" She pressed out each word, something that was not her style; she had never raised her voice in her life. It felt like she was losing patience and wanted me to just listen and say yes to anything and everything she wanted.

"You are capable of taking care of them. It's in your mind; you can do it, you know. You can do it, you know…" she kept saying pleadingly. "Please promise me."

I felt trapped. I stood there like a deer in the headlights, wondering what to say, glancing from her to my baby brother, just born, in his bassinet crying and soothing himself with his thumb. I looked back at my mother, fled the room and called at the top of my lungs.

"HELP! HELP! PLEASE HELP ME, HELP MY MOTHER! PLEASE HELP!"

The whole hospital could hear me. Nurse Hellen, Mrs. Adama and a doctor in a white coat with some mysterious medical gadgets around his neck raced toward me. The doctor looked like the surgeon who had been missing when my mother had asked for a C-section. Had he really been absent, I wondered. How long had we been in the hospital?

I glanced up at the main entrance. The clock hanging there read 1 p.m., and below it a big calendar announced the date: August 8, 1988. I ran hopelessly back to my mother. The doctor was checking her with the thing around his neck.

"She needs a blood transfusion," the doctor declared, looking at me as if he were asking me to give her blood. *But I'm just a kid!* I stared into his worried black-chalk pupils, illuminated by the rays of sun tearing through the only window in the room. I'd thought we understood each other. *Then again,* I wondered, *why not? Do children give blood? In which circumstance and at what age would kids give blood?*

"Is anybody with you now? Any of your mother's relatives?" he asked, since I had not replied.

"She needs blood urgently!" he shouted over my mother's worn-out body. He looked down as if he wanted to take the blood from under the bed and infuse that into her.

"Yes … No …" I mumbled, half out the door.

"But I can get my papa … oh, sorry," I said, re-entering the room.

"Where is he?" he asked crisply.

"He isn't in town, I just realized. I'm sorry. Is she going to be OK?" Why not my blood?

"She really needs blood, and it doesn't matter who gives it, as long as it's the same type as hers," he insisted.

"What do you mean by the same as hers?" I moved closer as if to understand him better that way. He looked at me as if he didn't have time to teach me anything just then. He had a much bigger challenge than being my instructor.

"Oh, I see." I backed away from him but kept sight of my mother.

"Any aunt?" he persisted.

"No one accompanied us, but I can go get an aunt ... I can go get ... I can go ... I can run there ... I'm a good runner. I'm the best at my school when it comes to running. I can get my aunt."

"No. What's your name?"

"My mother calls me Galle."

"The hospital is far from where you live. Did you take a taxi here?"

"Yes, we did, and I can get another one and bring the whole family. There's a taxi driver who always takes us wherever we want. He's like a family chauffeur, and whenever my father comes back from his travels he pays him. I can go get him. I'll run to him right now," I suggested enthusiastically, jumping to my feet like a toddler ready for its warmed-up bottle; I wanted the best way, the quickest way, to help.

I realized that every second spent in this room was a waste of time, one moment less in my mother's life. Why was he just standing there? Why wouldn't he say Yes, go and get your aunt? And even if he didn't? Whose permission was I waiting for? I certainly wasn't waiting for it from God, since I already sensed – no, knew – of his existence and place in this moment in my life. I felt urgency in that space and time between my mother, the doctor, my newborn brother – it was precious to us all, but I still believed my mom and brother would be coming home with me. So why not believe, hope and fight for them? I wanted so much to remain that little girl who had a mother and no worries in the world except for school, easy chores and tons of homework. I dared, or chose, to believe with all my heart that my mother would come home. Yes, she will!

"I think I can give her my blood if we're the same type?" Nurse Hellen, who had just rejoined us, offered kindly, her eyes worried.

"Why would you think you can give her your blood?" the doctor asked.

"Because I've done it before. Without hesitation and without wasted time!"

"Thank you, Mrs. Hellen, but I'm afraid I've lost too much blood. It's too late." My mother spoke up.

"Stop that nonsense, Jena. It's never too late. Please hang in there. And fight! Mrs. Adama is coming to stay with you while the doctor and I verify my blood type," the nurse said with a force that could halt a herd of elephants. The doctor took her away, and there was no fuss as to whether they'd chosen the right thing to do.

Once more I found myself alone with my mother and her newborn; he was eagerly sucking on a bottle. I glanced around again. It was very bright, yet there was a sense of calm in me and inside the room, despite the turmoil inside and around it. It gave me hope and faith that everything would be all right. I felt a gentle smile playing at the corners of my mouth.

They had changed my mother's mattress, bed sheet and clothes, and added blankets. They had drawn them up even over her head because she was growing increasingly cold. I touched her feet, which were showing a bit. Her toes were losing their colour – nails painted pink, skin beautifully moisturized with pure, organic shea butter – and the iciness of those feet shot all the way up my arm. I covered them by pulling her covers down a bit and massaged them with my small, skinny hands, continuing kneading from her toes to her belly to her ribs.

"Please don't touch my ribs. They hurt a lot. I think one of them cracked …" My mother could hardly muster the strength to speak.

"Your rib broke?! How?"

"While they were pushing your brother out. I felt a knee on my ribs, but I couldn't tell if the pain was from giving birth or from a broken bone," she said, managing a small smile.

"I arranged with your uncle Soleman, when he came to your cousin's wedding, to take you to Europe the next time he visits Guinea. You'll do better with him, because his world understands and respects women."

I was lost in the things she wanted me to understand, because we hardly ever spoke of my father's other younger brother, a diplomat in Moscow. Helplessly I listened, staring like a hawk. She was beautiful and fragile-looking with an air of grace I don't think I've witnessed since. A little energy seemed to be reanimating her. She talked for a while about her sister Halle, about my brothers and my only sister, Nenein. For a moment, she had the vitality that she had lacked over the last hours.

"Take care of your brothers. Please promise me."

I kept quiet, focusing on her as she kept trying to make me swear to care for her children. I thought that not giving her an answer would make her stay with me and fight harder. I didn't feel in limbo anymore. I just stood my ground, listening and looking at her like a lioness eyeing prey that will feed her babies in the depths of the Sahel.

Despite my hope, I felt her fingers getting even colder. I put my hands under the covers to check if she was chilled anywhere else. Except for around her chest and neck, she was frozen.

"I'm really cold, my daughter. My darling, dearest daughter … you know that I love you and that I'm sorry?" Her right hand pressed mine against her left breast as if she wanted me to feel the last tiny beats of her heart. She was calm yet convinced that she would not survive this birth. I tried to distract her by changing the subject.

I spoke compellingly: "You know they're bringing you new blood, so everything is going to be fine. We'll all go home, and you'll raise all of us. See us, and see me, marrying and having grandchildren, whom you'll help bring into this world. You're the best midwife in town. You can't die from giving birth. That would be cheating the women whose children you delivered. They won't forgive you."

I pronounced this with charm, laughter on my face and the silent fear of losing her in my eyes. At that moment it felt indeed like she was not going to die – I actually knew it. So, happy she was finally attentive to me during this precious time together, I said with a big smile, "Of course, I promise to take care of my brothers! I always watch out for them, even when you're around. You're going nowhere but home with us."

Thus, I had promised! I felt a moment's pause, as though I'd just done something terrible I would regret for the rest of my life. The energy I'd felt prior to making this vow had drained. Had I just abandoned my own ground and power with this pledge?

It almost felt like I had deceived myself, and I hated myself right there and then. I needed to throw up and yet I didn't; I couldn't remember the last time I had eaten. My tummy rumbled. It felt like something in my soul had escaped the moment I said those words. I needed to eat something, anything, to return the warmth and rebuild the shield I'd had all along.

How selfish she's being! I looked at her and felt half disdainful, deceptive yet hopeful. The earth under my feet gave me support to take her home; we would go home together and again eat, laugh and swap stories, and I'd brag to family and friends about her survival skills. Her strengths and beauty inside and out and desires for herself and her family ... She would see me marry and give her grandchildren ... Yes, I believed.

Then her hand left mine as her body grew frigid and heavy. I put my ear to her chest, hoping for even the tiniest of heartbeats, but detected only silence. I surveyed the room, as if I were hoping to discover a presence besides me and my newborn brother. I looked up at the ceiling as if to spot the angel of death who had just snatched my mother from me, but no blue sky could be seen – just ceramic-looking tiles overlapping each other like the scales of a dead fish. I looked down and saw the stillness of my mother's fresh blood, which was thickening into a long snake on the floor.

I dragged myself toward my brother's crib, lifted him and held him gently yet firmly against my chest, as if I wanted him to hear my heart sing my love for him. The journey with my brother began right then and there, in spite of everything.

I had to ensure that nobody saw us leave. Walking out the death-room door, I bumped into Mrs. Adama on her way to my mother. She called me several times as I kept walking, not looking back, without tears – not a single drop. I felt heavy, light, angry and overwhelmed, a burst of fire in my veins.

I felt a desire, too: the urge to escape with my brother in my long lanky arms. And at some point I really was running, because I heard Mrs. Adama race after me down the street yelling my name, waving her arms and pleading, "Slow down! Stop! Come back to the hospital!" I didn't stop.

I hailed a taxi – it was not hard to find one – and got in with my new brother still firmly in my arms. I said nothing to the driver who, it seemed, just drove and drove and drove before he slowed down and stopped.

"I forgot to ask where you are going." He smiled as if he were laughing at himself. "You're Mrs. Jena's daughter," he continued enthusiastically. "I'll take you home. By the way, how's your mother?" I kept silent.

"She was going to have a baby very soon." He kept his eyes on the road. "Actually, wasn't it the day before yesterday that I dropped you both off at the hospital? Don't you remember me?" He turned his head and waited for an answer.

"You're the lucky one! She's a great woman, an angel! Your father must be proud and happy to have a woman like her. We all say that about your father. She brought my very first daughter into this world," he went on dreamily.

It was noisy outside. The driver was taking the market route home. I wondered why. Did he think I'd want to pass by my father's big shop? I didn't enjoy this detour; I wanted to go home, or anywhere where I didn't have to be an adult with a baby.

The taxi ride lasted an eternity, but somehow I didn't mind. Maybe I thought I would have more time to myself; my brother and I didn't have to worry yet about telling my mother's death story.

Glancing at the newborn, I felt a sense of complicity. I found myself innocently smiling at him, like when I had my doll in my bedroom, away from my younger brothers. It felt good; memories of a happy time and my beautiful blonde toy crossed my mind. I played with my brother's teeny-weeny fingers. They looked very white and were extremely soft; it felt great to touch and lightly massage them.

In that moment I fell in love with him. I didn't miss my mother anymore or see my brother as an obstacle to my childhood. A sense of responsibility arose in my gut and an awareness assuring me that we – he and I and my other brothers – would be fine.

I knew at some point my new sibling would have to be fed, cleaned, changed and put to bed. But for now, I didn't need to worry about that. He was asleep, nestled quietly in my arms, his bottle of milk tucked in next to me. I wanted to go home at the speed of light. Hadn't the driver noticed that I had a newborn in my arms? Couldn't he sense that my mother's body was being removed from her hospital bed? I kept looking at my tiny charge, filled with desire to tell him what was going on. I felt, in fact, that I had been telling him, and the driver, too, my mother's story, the story of both my mother and my brother, with me selfishly in the middle of everything.

The driver started talking again about my childhood and the greatness of my mother's deeds. I wanted to escape his words; he sounded like a broken radio that would not shut off. I had no time for his stories, because they would make me weak and I didn't need weakness just then; I had no time for it. I felt the right degree of aloofness, charged with a willpower I'd never felt before.

Outside the window I saw a world with people wearing happy faces. The sky was clear, promising days without rain. I lifted my hand from my brother to roll down the window.

"Oh, my princess Kenda, please leave it up. We'll have dust and splashes in the car," the taxi driver said briskly but kindly.

"How do you know that name?" I asked.

"That's what your mother and the rest of the family call you, isn't it?"

"Yes. But there's no dust, Mr. Mohamed. It just stopped raining." I seemed to reply from afar.

I left the window down and assumed he was fine with it, or he would have said so. He was used to getting what he wanted when he wanted it. A direct and honest man, he spoke his mind kindly with either a sense of humour or simple forthrightness, depending on the situation.

I noticed that his old Mercedes was clean inside and smelled nice. Every now and then, he burned some incense, imported from Dakar and Morocco, that he'd bought from my father's shop. The noises of rusty, broken-down Peugeots and trucks entered the cab, but having refused Mr. Mohamed's advice to close the window, I had no right to complain.

I wondered how people could use these vehicles for transportation when half the parts were broken, and passengers' feet so often showed through the bottom. You could see from the different colours that the cars had been painted several times to upgrade their appearance and attract desperate passengers. Yet they ran, and customers had faith in them, always anticipating a safe arrival home, wherever that was. At times riders would have to get out and push the car to release it from mud or the deep and dirty pools the rainy season had left behind, yet they continued to hail the wrecks and advance toward their destinations patiently; they would even smile and joke while pushing them and tramping their feet in the muck. Was insurance offered for these types of cars? I guarantee that the only insurance the cars, their owners and their passengers knew was faith; that was all that mattered to them. My curiosity lingered, however, as to whether the driver had car insurance.

"Mr. Mohamed?"

He turned his head slightly, his eyes fixed on the road.

"What do you want, my princess?"

"Do you have insurance for your car?"

"What is that?"

"I mean if somebody gets hurt in an accident with your car. Would you have financial help?"

"What financial? Why does a young girl with a good upbringing talk like this? I don't understand what you are asking me. I did not go to school like you. You will have trouble getting a husband because you talk serious most of the time you open your mouth."

We both laughed.

"Go again?"

"Insurance for your car?"

"If I understand what you're asking, when my car breaks I fix it myself, and when I'm driving I am careful, and I have faith that I will get everybody home safe in my car, and the people around me do, too."

"So your insurance is your faith?"

"Yes! Faith and God."

"Faith and God," I repeated, as if trying to convince myself.

He went on. "You have faith, and you believe it's so strong that everything will be fine and you'll make it through."

"Faith and God," I said.

"God: you just call him when you need him – he'll be there."

"But I shouldn't need to call him," I objected. "He or She should just be there; if there really is God –"

"No, no, no, Kenda. It's a 'He' – there's no 'She' in God," he said, firmly cutting me off.

"He's omnipresent, so there's no need to call him." I finished my own sentence. *Your God just killed my mother and left me with a newborn. How can you explain that?* Anger was rising in my chest.

"OK ..." Mr. Mohamed, slowing a little, turned to look at me. "Your father taught you the Koran as well? How are you going to marry? You seem to know everything," he said seriously. He waited for an answer I did not give, so he kept at it.

"Are you OK, my princess? You sound like you're angry at God, who loves you dearly. You're the lucky one; you have rich parents who give you all you want. You have your mom and dad, your whole family with you, and I know for sure that you'll marry very well!"

"I just want to get home now." I blurted out the words like a spurt of hot tea.

"We're almost there. Once we pass the market it won't take long. You know that, don't you?" Mr. Mohamed said reassuringly, implying we had been down this road many times so I must know it well. He was, indeed, spot on.

I tried to calm myself by saying, "Yes, and thank you!" He was, after all, the great man whom my mother respected a lot and who knew my mother well, too.

I felt tears welling, but I took a deep breath and looked outside again. My eyes drifted from my mother's newborn, my youngest brother, who made it five brothers I had the duty to look after, to see if the world around us had changed since my mother and I had taken the same route in the opposite direction, with the same driver, Mr. Mohamed, two days ago.

Mr. Mohamed was a very short Turkish man with muscular arms and a big heart. He was eager to work and provide for two wives. For a few years before he bought his taxi, the Turkish embassy had employed him, so he knew a lot about many subjects. That was why my mother liked him. She felt that by taking his taxi she could learn from him. Since she had helped bring Mr. Mohamed's third son into the world, he had promised he'd drive her anywhere she wished; he saw this as the only fair way to repay my mother for her service to his family and kindness toward her community.

The rain that had stopped a few hours before had left big puddles here and there on the road. Some of the oldest Peugeots simply drove right through them, soaking passengers' feet and splashing pedestrians. I saw a woman, a bucket of groceries and rice balanced on her head, smiling even as she was drenched by passing cars. I wondered what was going through her mind. It was not difficult to guess – she had food for her family for a day or two, or even for a week, so why worry? I looked at the dark faces of the passers-by; they didn't expect to arrive at their destination with clean, dry feet. Once home, they would rinse them off and get on with their daily routines without a worry in the world.

My little brother squirmed in my hands as if he wanted to stretch. Instinctively, I loosened my grip and he unconsciously reached for my thumb. I wondered what the gesture meant. What did he want? I didn't pay too much attention to him. I felt the need to look away, since the promise I'd given our mother on her deathbed would compel me to deal with him for the rest of my life.

In the receding market crowd, I saw some unexpectedly wide, beautiful smiles that seemed habitual. They looked squeezed, like opened sardine cans, with kola-coloured teeth that said they had no care in the world. The women were distinct from one another in shape and height, and their skin tones varied so much they resembled a makeup palette. I noted a spectrum from lightest to darkest, with the fairest exquisitely dressed, composed, graceful and more relaxed. I'd have bet that, in general, the lightest-skinned women would have a driver waiting to take them home with groceries, items from the beauty section, and expensive new fabric for their next outfits. Their chauffeur or one of their young helpers would often tag along behind them.

I could guess that most of these women were Fulani. They would marry extremely well, their spouses being the richest or most elite men in their village or city. Often, the women were educated in madrasas, had been homeschooled using the Koran, or had attended public institutions merely to learn to read, write and pray with their husbands. By the time they were fourteen they would be wed to affluent leaders or merchants, *commerçants*, like my father. God forbid that these women should study past knowing how to perform their five daily prayers or master subjects beyond elementary school. If they did, they wouldn't marry, being considered too smart and therefore likely to disobey their husbands. Parents deliberately took girls out of school to ensure they could find a good spouse.

My father, to the contrary, didn't believe a woman should be less educated than a man. In fact, he thought the opposite and often got in trouble with his brother for hiring a tutor to help me with my homework so I could be the best of the best at school. Being one of the most educated women in my family didn't come without a price, paid both by my father and me.

After Galle's mother dies – Conakry, August 1989

Before the school year started, we moved – in the middle of the night – to Conakry, as my father had wanted. The only ones who knew we were going were my uncle and his wife, who seemed very pleased, since our big house would finally be theirs while my father had to start over on his own.

I wondered why he always allowed my uncle to get what he wanted even though my father was the oldest and worked the hardest.

My aunt Halle was now staying with us. She'd have been the one my father wed if she had not already had a husband, according to Fula tradition. My father chose to postpone marriage, however, even though he had promised to marry the next available sister, Marie, who was about thirteen. The same age as me, my aunt Marie was eager to marry him. For some odd reason I never liked the idea and loathed having her around. Maybe that's why our father waited.

It had been a year since my mother died. She had been buried right away and we had stopped visiting her grave. My father never got to see her after the night she had tried to persuade him to stay. He now spent most of his time and energy finding us a new life in the capital. He had rented a four-bedroom house with one living room, a shower and toilets in the big city of Medina in the municipality of Matam in Conakry. This house was tiny compared to what we were used to.

He kept saying the same thing, which none of us listened to any longer: "Your mother would have loved this house, even though it's small."

We children – Alphadjo, Nenein and Leonis, who was now one year old – learned right away to accept and love our new place as our own. Thierno Abdul Goudoussy, whom we all called Goudoussy, stayed in Kamsar because he was very close to our uncle's son. They were inseparable, and, considering his sensitivity to our mother's death, my father had told my uncle that Goudoussy could stay for one year more before we would all reunite in Conakry. I knew my mother would not have agreed to this, but I didn't challenge it, because I had told Goudoussy our father would fetch him if at any time he wanted to join us.

* * *

I love taking my time in the shower and always massage myself with a moisturizing cream. My mother used shea butter on my skin and on all of her kids when they were little, and after she died I kept this up, massaging my younger brothers with shea butter whenever I gave them a bath before they went to bed or when they were sick.

As I grew older I kept using it, because my aunt Halle had said to me one day, when I was about thirteen, a few months after my mother died, "A woman must, at all times, ensure that she's beautiful – no excuses. Otherwise you'll never marry, or, when you do, you won't be the favourite, because the man always favours the woman who is womanly. Your mother never spoke to you about being a woman?"

"No."

"Do you bleed?"

"What, bleed?"

"Every woman bleeds once a month."

"What kind of bleeding are you talking about? I cut my finger once, so I'm careful with a razor." I tried to show my aunt the scar on the upper left side of my thumb.

"No, that's not what I'm talking about."

I didn't understand what she was trying to say; I'd never spoken with my mother about blood, even though she was a midwife. She had been an extremely quiet person who talked only if she had to. She had a beautiful oval face with kind, dark eyes and a gentle smile that revealed pearly white teeth. Her long, dark-brown hair curled in a way any woman would envy, and she knew that. She loved brushing it while looking in the mirror before bedtime. I would stare at her and wish to grow up to be just like her. She was very tall – six feet one – svelte, smart, funny, kind, gentle, generous and, overcoming her natural reticence, sociable. I was mesmerized by her; she knew so many people and did a lot for our community yet said little about what she had achieved.

I was hoping my aunt had moved on. A story about blood was a bit too much for me since my mother had passed. I still couldn't believe she had died and left me with a newborn. Then something clicked in me, and that something didn't want to come out easily. I began to weep.

"Oh, no. I didn't mean to make you cry. Why are you crying?"

I looked at her, a question mark on my face.

"Are you referring to the blood that came out of my mother when she was giving birth to my brother? Is that the –"

"Oh, no! That's not it, sweet love! Oh, what have I done? Do you still think of your mother that way? I'm not talking about *her* blood."

She turned away, realizing she had gone too far. The conversation had taken a tone and direction she hadn't anticipated. Yet, secretly curious, I was keen to hear what she had to teach me.

"I'm talking about menstrual blood." She sat down and placed her hand on my shoulder as if trying to be comforting, or simply friendlier, as she explained. I always knew there was something more to it when my parents or relatives like my aunt discussed women's menstrual cycles in their matter-of-fact way.

Even though I would listen politely to an informative lecture from anyone, I'd dwell on it or search for more about the subject until I found my own way to understand or interpret it, or see if there were anything hidden in the process of delivery from the adult's point of view.

After my mother died, every woman older than I in my family turned herself into an audio textbook about how a woman is supposed to be or look, whether I listened or not. They felt I needed to know and it was their duty to teach me now that my mother had passed and I was living with just my dad.

Was it to avoid hurting us kids that my father did not remarry right away? Or maybe he was not ready to rekindle the kind of love he had had for my mother, even though many candidates were lined up. A wealthy man from the great Fulani tribe, he was introduced to a girl or two at least once a week. His brothers soon gave up the idea of getting him remarried. Only once his children agreed, when the time came, did he tie the knot again.

"My mother, your grandmother, taught me how to prepare for my first menstrual cycle and become a woman. It comes once in every lunar month," she said, walking to the window as if to show me the moon, or search for it, anyway. Following her, I noticed a small crescent in the distance and some women balancing jugs of water on their heads walking by and nonchalantly chanting some Fulani song. The sunset turned a deeper pink and orange before gently fading, perhaps wishing to go unnoticed, as it had done for many years before.

For some reason my perception was heightened. I started hearing all the sounds around me as though I would turn deaf in the next hour. I got lost in the sunset, which I might not otherwise have noticed and now was attending to or was forced to see, hear, feel and smell. I felt all my senses on that day.

My impatient curiosity was growing, ready for anything that came my way. I was thinking that nothing could be worse than my mother's death, whatever my aunt had to say or teach me.

"Can you take off your clothes?" she asked kindly without turning around.

"OK. Why?" I was a little shy about removing them in front of her.

"Actually, no. Don't." She took my arm. "Let's go swimming in the river. It's still not that dark. We'll enjoy more of the sunset. Has your mother ever taken you there just to watch the sun disappear as you swim?"

"No," I said, remembering the last time I'd gone swimming with my mother. I'd wanted to sit and wait for her, but she said swimming came naturally to all girls who are clean and virgin; there was no need for me to worry about leaping into the current and having fun. I was reluctant, but I had to jump in because the eyes of the other girls and women were on me, and for sure I'd be the talk of everybody if I didn't at least give it a shot.

But as soon as I plunged in, the river carried me away. At first they all thought I was joking around. I screamed until I swallowed too much water. Unable to see anything but the river, I found myself being pulled deeper and deeper into the current.

I awoke with my mother crying on top of me, thanking God for my life, while everyone else stared at me, murmuring that I was neither clean nor a virgin. My mother asked them to stop and took me away; her face told me she had a million questions, which I chose to ignore as if I didn't know what she was going to ask. She in turn reserved her concerns and queries for another time.

"I'll teach you to learn to love the water again," Aunt Halle said now.

"Yeah?" I was curious but still scared of that river.

"Let's go!" Her enthusiasm was infectious, and usually I'd be happy following her to the ends of the earth, but this time we were heading to the stream I'd almost drowned in.

Once we had arrived at the bank my aunt asked me again to undress, which I did. I was willing to try swimming again. The only thing I left on was a small drape of cotton around my waist, worn to hide my private parts though it revealed my breasts. Many a young girl would flaunt her bare torso to show off her readiness to wed; in fact, sometimes hiding behind too many clothes made people suspect she was no longer a virgin.

Among the Fulani, starting at around age thirteen, the already well-developed girls were required to conceal their bodies when leaving the house or compound or when in the presence of guests. In the river, however, most women would be naked; men knew to stay away to ensure the bathers' privacy. Only the older women covered themselves, while the young ones strolled around and swam either with just a cloth around them or in their underwear without a bra.

Now unclothed, I felt happy and free, as though suddenly my aunt had become a girlfriend. I could relax with her and listen without inhibition. My mother and I had not had such a relationship, not because she had been unwilling; she was simply not a talker. By offering me her genuine smile when I looked at her, I felt encouraged and valued, and I expected nothing more. I'm not sure I expected anything, really. I was happy she was with me whenever I wanted and needed her, and so was she.

While I was taking off my clothes, I glanced around as if to reassure myself we were alone. I took in the fading sunset, dispersing behind the mountain slowly and tranquilly. With the approach of darkness, the crickets and frogs made their presence known, as they did every night around the river. A gentle breeze rustled the leaves and the grass in the woods, rippling the water gently before my mentor broke the calm by diving in with exuberance. My aunt Halle was about twenty years old and happily married to a cousin whom she had picked herself; her eyes always sparkled because she saw herself as the lucky one, choosing her own mate, which is exceedingly rare in our culture. Very fair skinned, with big brown eyes and long, beautiful hair, she stood five foot eleven. Without doubt, she was one of the most gorgeous creatures I'd ever laid eyes on.

She jumped into the stream completely naked. I noticed the pronounced nipples on her D-cup breasts and that the rest of her body was slim. Her twenty-four-inch waist and thirty-two-inch hips gave her a curvy silhouette, like an "S." Since her wedding she had had to conceal more of her body under a long robe and cover her hair with a veil. I think she felt liberated in the river, enabled to show off her lovely form.

"When are you coming in?" she asked, swimming away. I stood there, looking and listening. Longing to join her, before I knew it I had stepped into the water.

"Why are you wearing all those clothes?" she asked. "Take them off; you won't need them in here. Besides, we're alone; nobody comes to the river at this time of night."

I was shy about showing my body because it was unlike most girls' my age: at twelve they would be almost fully grown, with pronounced breasts and a beautiful bottom that seemed to have a small brick on each side, which many African men admired.

"Are you sure?" I asked again.

"Certain. Come on ..."

I hesitated. The water was up to my knees, and then she paddled toward me.

"I'll teach you how to love the water again," she announced. "I'm sorry you almost drowned. Don't let fear stop you from enjoying the gift of freedom." She was laughing loudly as if she were trying to attract attention. I could hear the echo of her mirth in the distance; it seemed to come from the deep end of the trees, and the mountains, too, farther away.

Now dusk had deepened. The sun had departed behind the hills, leaving room for the crescent moon to shine on us. My aunt and I started swimming together – or, to be more accurate, she began to swim. I was on her back, gently holding her neck, but feeling as though I were also swimming, and gave some feeble kicks with my feet. Freedom and peace had nested in my heart, so I trusted her moves and even forgot that I was clinging to her.

She turned around and, asking me to trust her even more, rolled me onto my back, facing the dark sky. Moonlight glowed off her cheeks and big firm breasts and onto my warm brown skin. I felt so light I thought I was floating. I thought about the sense of freedom my aunt Halle had mentioned, the kind of liberty she meant – or was there another kind? It really didn't matter what type; I just felt pure joy from deep down, from drifting in this beautiful river and quietly accepting our own presence.

I also thought about my mother, who had loved swimming with me the same way my aunt was doing tonight. My mother adored the water more than anything; she swam almost every day or found another reason to be near it. I had expected them to bury her next to her beloved river, but they didn't. She always said that human beings were made mostly of water, so returning to it was like going home to meet ourselves halfway to our true destination.

As the night darkened, the moon grew brighter. The sense of joy, the security I felt in my aunt's hands, and my mother's memory, made me realize why I hadn't yet learned to swim – I love to be swum with rather than swim on my own, kicking and performing all the physical work it required. The near-drowning had given me a perfect excuse to take advantage of my aunt's support in the water.

Crossing to the other shore, we leaped out of the river with enough laughter to wake up a village, but we didn't need to worry, being miles away from any living human. I realized I was naked, like she was, but I also saw how our bodies differed. Why did she have such big breasts while I had none? The only thing you might notice on my chest were two dark spots on each side.

"Laouratou?" my aunt said. "I see you still don't have breasts."

"Of course, I have breasts … they just don't show like yours," I said, covering up a little.

"Mine." She pressed hers against each other and looked at them with big wide eyes and a laughing mouth. "My breasts are the best a woman could dream of and that men would die for," she said proudly, her hands dancing in the air.

Why would men die for your breasts – aren't they for breast-feeding babies?

"Stand up," she requested matter-of-factly.

Here we go again; the adult is about to teach another lesson. Then it dawned on me, the real reason this river swim had begun.

"Auntie, are we here so you can tell me about 'the blood'?"

"Yes, that too, and much more. Can you spread your legs and let me see if you're circumcised?"

"Why are you doing this to me?"

"I hope you're circumcised."

"What are you talking about?" I inched away from her.

"I mean you have a clitoris right below your pubic bone. It looks like this." She spread her legs to show me hers, but it was not prominent; in fact, I couldn't spot it even though her inner labia weren't fully sealed.

"Mine is done beautifully. It's not as harsh as some, because a doctor in a hospital operated while I was sleeping. You know, I'm lucky. Many girls get this without anesthesia. They take everything off including the labia and leave them fully sewn until they marry," she said, proud at having escaped that cruel fate. "Now, don't touch me, but watch while I do it. Imagine being in a classroom with a doll while your instructor instructs you about a woman's parts."

"OK. Only this time it's you and not a doll," I replied, my mouth half open. I was intrigued and confused at the same time. How come her vagina and mine were different? I looked around, fearful that somebody might be watching. But, as commanded, I peered as she spread her long slender legs even wider. She had dark-brown curly pubic hair, but because she was so fair I thought I could now make out her clitoris.

"Is that your clitoris?" I asked, approaching for a closer look.

"Yes, but it's not a real one, because the real one is gone. This one is what came out of what was taken off," she said.

"Wow, for real? Do you feel pain?" I asked.

"I don't know why you pretend you don't understand anything about this." She seemed a little peeved that I still didn't get what she was talking about.

"My sister, your mother, was a midwife, and she didn't teach you anything?" She turned her back, plunged back in the river and started swimming away as if I were not there.

"No," I said, even though she was no longer listening.

As to what had changed, I had no clue. Her needs or fears were incomprehensible to me. All I recall of that evening is her desire to know if I was circumcised like her and her annoyance that my mother had failed to teach me these aspects of becoming or being a woman. I thought I now understood my late development, my being skinny like a stick with no breasts.

After she returned for me, we swam back quietly and walked home without talking. She was singing to herself while I wondered what else my mother hadn't taught me. *I can't ask my father, but I can ask his mother.* So, as soon as we reached the house, I went directly to my father's room, where my grandmother was visiting, and gave him a hug.

"You stayed very late at the river with your aunt, but you don't look happy, my dearest daughter. Is everything OK with you?" my grandmother asked under my father's watchful eye.

"Are all women circumcised?" I blurted out.

"Oh, I see…" my father said and turned away slightly.

"That Halle!" my grandmother exclaimed and looked at my father indignantly.

"Well, in some cultures, yes," my father answered neutrally.

"Why?"

"So their sexuality is tameable."

"Why?" I asked again, looking back and forth from one to the other.

"So they don't have sex before the wedding," my grandmother responded with a gentle smile.

"Oh, I see." I paused to think. They waited. "Is that good or bad?" I asked.

"Sometimes yes and sometimes no, depending on who you are and where you came from," my father replied.

"It's bad to lose your virginity to any man but your husband," my grandmother said in a serious voice.

"Was my mother circumcised?" I asked.

"Yes," Grandmother said proudly. "All Fulani women are circumcised."

My father kept his face turned away but said, "You know that your aunt and grandmother are with us if you want answers to that kind of question. You can always ask them. You are growing older now, I am your father, and we can't talk about your private life in such detail."

Now, my father was direct and would talk pretty much about anything, although my mother had recommended he leave it to her to inform me fully about such things. Nonetheless, I grew up knowing that my father was always there for me if I couldn't answer the difficult questions by myself.

"Don't you want go to bed now? It's almost bedtime." He kissed my forehead and wished me a good night's sleep as Grandmother escorted me out.

I entered my own room sadly, joining my aunt with whom I shared it along with my tiny newborn brother. She had already nodded off. How could she have gone straight to sleep after what she had started with me? I wished I'd never spoken to her about becoming a woman, and I wished she weren't here anymore.

I hated that moment with her because I was starting to question if I was circumcised. I found myself wishing I had been if it meant having big breasts like hers. *Should I ask her or my father about my vagina?* He had told me such topics were now out of bounds. I felt forlorn, since he was really the only one I could imagine talking to about anything without feeling judged. He would be direct, telling me what he thought with no fuss.

Dissatisfied, I rose from bed, entered the bathroom and locked the door securely before gazing at myself, fully dressed, and then staring straight into my beautiful big brown eyes. In those I saw fear as well as tears for no reason other than realizing my mother really wasn't here on my journey to become a woman.

Did she have me circumcised like all Fulani women? I strongly doubted it, because I'd no breasts to speak of. I was not sure I ever would have any, or if I'd ever have a man to marry me, because I didn't look like a woman. How could a man want such a skinny girl?

I examined my scrawny legs, slim not for lack of food or poor eating; my father was a rich man who fed not only his family but also the whole community – there was no way I was starving. I felt such a rage of sadness that before I knew it I was on the floor sobbing like the victim of a whipping. Then I felt the presence of a woman who wanted to reach out to me. I didn't lift my head nor was I curious about who she was, but for some reason all my tears dried up. I rose, wiped my eyes, opened the door and returned to the bedroom, glancing around as if willing my aunt to wake up and tell me what she had been upset about. I fell into bed and let the dark night deepen and take over my heavy lids, carrying me to distant Neverland until dawn came.

The unknown woman's life within Galle's initiation

A year passed, and I still hadn't gotten any answers to my endless queries about womanhood, not even after that night at the river with my aunt. My breasts were still small and I had no hips or a bottom anything like hers.

Growing up, however, my leanness didn't trouble me. I recalled an evening shortly after my mother died, in Conakry, when aunt Halle and my grandmother called me into their room.

"Are you OK, daughter?" Grandmother asked.

"Yes, I am, if you're referring to the loss of my mother," I answered politely.

"I want to let you know that your aunt Halle has told me you're not cut. Is that right?"

I froze. *What now?*

"Yes, I am," I said.

"When? As far as I know, nobody was invited to your ceremony. Did Djenab keep it a secret? She never wanted to talk to me about it and got angry or changed the subject whenever we mentioned it."

"That's right," Aunt Halle said. "My sister never told me about your being cut. She hated it, but because of it you almost drowned. Why didn't you tell me you're not clean?"

"In jail I was cut," I said.

"You were cut in jail?" my incredulous matriarch exclaimed. She stood and paced around the room. "You were in jail?" they asked in unison.

"Yes," I said.

"Who puts a child in jail? Why?" my grandmother asked.

"My uncle," I replied.

"Your uncle? Did you read this story in some of your white people's books, or have you gone totally mad?" my now-angry grandmother asked.

"Maman, stop scaring her; she's telling the truth. Well, she looks like she's telling the truth. Are you, Galle?" my aunt asked.

"Uncle who?" Grandmother asked.

"She has only one uncle, Mother: Hussein, of course," Aunt Halle said.

"Come close to me," Grandmother ordered, and I did. "Remove your pants and underwear." I was shaking as I did so.

"No need to shake, sweetheart," she said, but I couldn't stop.

"Nene, I don't think it's the right time to check her. She's trembling too much," my aunt intervened.

"Put your pants back on and come sit on my lap," my grandmother said.

They both helped me into my clothes. But before I could cuddle on Grandmother's lap, the baby wailed. Aunt Halle helped me change him before he took the bottle I'd prepared earlier.

She whispered, "I still need to teach you to swim and much more about yourself and being a woman, my sweet girl. And don't fret about your mother's passing. I won't replace her, but I will be your guide going forward." I listened to her as if once again it was story time before I fell asleep.

* * *

My aunt Halle took me again to the river, where she always felt like a beauty queen and where she had tried in vain to teach me to swim. She loved the water most under a full moon. I wasn't sure if she did that because there was more light for us, since we would go at night, or if it was simply a coincidence.

This time around, I couldn't wait to remove my dress. A blood stain on the back was driving me crazy. I didn't know if it meant my first period or not, because I'd been bleeding a lot, which I kept to myself because of the rape. I often thought the rape had caused the bleeding, that the rapist's penis had torn me inside. This blood would come randomly because the cut had not healed; it would never heal and there was nothing to be done about it.

Descending to the shoreline, I dipped my feet in first, then sauntered in up to my knees, then to my hips, and only stopped when the water encircled my waist.

"Take a deep breath, hold it, and go all the way in," my aunt said. She did exactly what she was asking me to do.

"You mean like this?" I readied myself to dive in but stopped short on seeing the water change into the red that was coming out between my legs. I turned around and fled.

"Kenda, where are you going? Come back here," she shouted after me. I was running as fast as I could.

"God, you have quick feet! Where did you get them from?" She was following me. "You're naked. Do you know you're naked, Kenda?" she said. She stopped chasing me.

I looked down. She was right. I dashed back and she wrapped me in a big towel. After washing me in silence, she showed me how to put on a pad – not a pad exactly, but a soft white cloth she had prepared.

"I know your father will give you the white women's tampon when he finds out you're a woman now. Until then, this is what we all use: a simple cloth that you can rinse yourself and keep until the next full moon. You have to come here and wash it discreetly, so no men see it. Understand?"

"Can't I just throw it out and use the other ones?" I asked.

"No," she said.

"Why not?"

"Kenda, you have to learn to take things as you're told. This must be why your uncle had you locked up. Women must be only beautiful and quiet at all times. There's no need to be proud of our intelligence because we're already intelligent, even though we make men believe otherwise," she said, smiling up at the moonlight.

I kept quiet but wondered how to make sure I wouldn't need to clean my cloth. I decided to talk to my father about it.

"Don't tell me you're going to talk to your father about it?" she said.

"You read my mind," I answered.

"Yes. Tell me, now, why don't you want to touch your own blood?" She seemed really interested.

"In jail ... My mother's ..." I stammered.

"When are you going to stop thinking about that nonsense and your mother's blood in the hospital?"

She stood up and I followed her footsteps home. Instead of going directly to the room where the two of us and my baby brother spent the night, she decided to take me to my grandmother's house after we checked on him. He was sound asleep like a bear in winter.

Chapter 2
Moscow, Russia

Linda meets Harvey – Moscow, summer of 1997

On the day my mother died, she told me about her arrangement with Uncle Soleman, who had attended my cousin's wedding. When he next visited Guinea, he'd take me away with him. When my father finally decided to marry a girl his older brother had chosen for him, Uncle Soleman came to the wedding and invited me to Moscow without telling my father, knowing full well what would have happened had he asked his permission. With the complicity of my aunt Halle and my grandmother, everything came together.

I vividly recall Uncle Soleman asking me before we left, "With the hundreds of names that you're called, which one should we put in your passport?"

I paused, wondering how to handle his question. Nobody had talked to me about my name like this. I listed all the different names people used for me, and he asked again, "What would you want to be called?"

"Laouratou Dalanda Kenda Bailo Bah," I said with a smile.

"How about Laouratou Linda Bah?" he suggested

"'Linda' isn't African."

"You're right, but Dalanda and Kenda are the same as Linda, and where we're going it's a good thing to consider. You'll understand when we get there. Now we have a passport to make with an African name and a Western name."

This is how I ended up in Russia being called Linda.

I was a contestant in the Miss Africa competition in Moscow when I first saw Harvey Van den Ameele in the crowd. I was pulled toward him by a scent. It was not a strong cologne or anything that would draw too much attention, but for some reason I drifted toward it. I wondered where or who that scent was coming from.

"Hey, where are you wandering off to, Linda? You don't expect me to deal with these journalists on my own, do you?" my friend Tessa shouted. She was the daughter of the Zimbabwean ambassador. "You're scaring me, Linda. Why are you sniffing around like a dog?" she asked. She stopped a few steps away from Harvey and smiled like she had won the jackpot.

I turned toward her. "This man right here is the one, and he's the father of my children, if I ever have any," I whispered into her ear, keeping my eyes locked on Harvey's. He was waiting patiently and smiling back at us.

"Something is definitely wrong with you, Linda, and you have gone officially mad. Aren't you the one who just told me to take the Miss crown from you because your father was going to kill you if he finds out you were even in this competition, and now you're the same person telling me a white man is going to father your children?"

She expected a reply but I was busy eyeing Harvey, who just stood there watching us. Every now and then when passersby would block my view of him, he'd move a little to the left or right to keep our eyes and smiles connected.

"This man will just sleep with you to get some black pussy and won't go beyond that. You know that?" she said, standing in front of me. I moved past her to get a better look at him.

"Have you seen all these girls with blue Mediterranean eyes and hair like harvest corn fields on a Zimbabwean farm? He doesn't want an African girl for a wife; he wants a long-legged Russian or Ukrainian."

"And this would be the time to say hello, before you officially choose a wife for me," Harvey interrupted.

"Sorry! Did you hear what I was saying?" Tessa put her hand in front of her mouth and took two steps back.

Harvey introduced himself like a proper gentleman, and Tessa turned around to talk to some of the Russian press, offering her take on the first Miss Africa competition ever held in Moscow.

* * *

Harvey had learned I was in the midst of a move to Canada when we met at the competition, which his company, Adidas, was sponsoring.

I was tired of hearing him talk about the sacrifice he'd make by immigrating to Canada with me, defending myself each time we argued about his joining me in Vancouver. Yet I knew deep down that I needed him and couldn't live without him, even if the door was really open wide for us both. When I was around him I felt secure. He got me.

Vancouver, 2015

Harvey did not smell exactly the same anymore, but it was pretty close. Some mornings, when I couldn't find that scent, I was thrown off course. Had something gone wrong with my nostrils? Had they forgotten his true smell for having lived with him all these years, or was I simply distracted by my love of looking out the window, when I woke in the morning, to welcome the world I felt so blessed to live in: peaceful, warless, worriless. I couldn't wait to jump out of bed to thank my feet and my whole self for being here. To greet with open arms another fabulous day and run to my two beautiful sons, Josh and Owen, whom this handsome man had given me, to tell them how much I loved them.

I touched my neck and glanced at him again to reassure myself he was actually sleeping right beside me – a little needlessly, since he was snoring. I wanted to tell him how much his sons made my life worth living every second, minute, hour, day, week, month and year, but I kept the thought to myself.

I ran my fingers through his hair, sandy brown in winter and blond in summer, either to feel something familiar that had been mine for seventeen years or because his locks were simply too cute to pass up. I think they were too cute to pass up. Westerners' hair can be really nice to touch, and there was something about his lovely soft silky mess in the morning. Would this be why most African Canadians or Africans in general use all kinds of chemicals to straighten, texturize or, more expensively, wave their hair, or get it custom-made into wigs if they are really, really wealthy?

In those days I had my mother's tresses: lush, long and curly, and I needed no extensions. As I stroked his hair, I noticed how unruly it was. He'd never leave it like this, not in a million years, for any other person to see. He always left our house with his hair gelled, well groomed for going out into the world. I often felt that each early morning we shared something special, something that was unique from having seen and heard each other for years. It's a privilege to see someone in all the different moments of life and still love them for the person they are each morning. Is that why I'm still with my husband? Or is it because somewhere, deep in my subconscious, I find a way to hide myself in him and his world? Would that have kept me with him for all these years?

Why not mess with his hair now rather than get him all worked up by touching it after he's ready to leave for work? I found this the perfect time to tousle his head, and sometimes I did. Well, on those days, no need to wonder how he reacted.

* * *

In my husband's family everyone is blond and blue-eyed except for my husband, who has his great-grandmother's eyes. She was an Italian Romani with olive skin, just like Harvey's; it tans very quickly. When I met him he looked like an Italian *Vogue* model, or perhaps this was how I wanted to see him. He loved life beyond life itself – he was a free spirit, like a wild white horse you see only in the old Marlboro ads. I was crazy about that wildness and the anticipation of continuous adventure with him. Above all, I loved his scent, maybe more than I loved him; there was something about it that could turn me on anytime and anywhere. It was not just the smell of his aftershave; it was the aftershave combined with his sweat.

He left for work and I went to drop off our kids at camp as usual. I left the house wearing a multicoloured dress I had had a long time, a floral print with a lot of saffron in it and tiger stripes around the bottom and edges. It made me feel cavalier; Harvey had bought it when we were in Moscow after his company's spring fashion show. When I wore that dress on the catwalk, the audience would scream, and I would stifle my excitement at looking so great in it. Harvey loved it on me and could hardly wait to buy it for me.

Linda tells her father about Harvey – November 1997

Moscow was windy, dry and cold but also beautiful and refreshing. My gorgeous long coat made me look rich and invited envy from many of the Russian girls at my university. I'd wear it with Wolford pantyhose and a short skirt, just above my knees, and high black boots. With my family and my Russian girlfriends insisting I stop being a tomboy, I had to make an effort at least every now and then. And I admit, in that coat and footwear, showcasing my long, slender legs, I felt truly womanly.

I didn't know at the time what it meant to be a woman other than dressing in nice clothes and having to marry one day. I knew I'd have to look the part and that moderate-sized breasts were not enough. Being dressed like a woman for once made me proud; my slim legs made me look girly and elegant. I also soon learned that western men loved them. They couldn't stop staring and often complimented me on them. How many times did our driver say, in Russian, "Beautiful long legs you've got there, Mademoiselle."

"Are you telling me this because you like me or because it's the truth?" I asked.

"Both, but not like a boyfriend – like an uncle who knows you're an attractive girl and that you're going to marry well," Sergei said.

Sergei, my family's personal chauffeur, drove me everywhere. Sometimes I'd sneak out on him to take the metro, but he always found me and said, "I need this job, Mademoiselle, so please let me give you a lift." He had kind, deep-blue eyes and thick hair, dirty-blond in winter and pure gold in summer.

"You're not here only to drive me. You're here to spy on me, too, for my uncle," I said.

"That, too, but either way I want you to be safe. Russia is changing, and I'd rather you didn't meet up with any hooligans."

"Yeah, right … OK. OK, I got it. You'll drive me and I'll always tell you where I'm going," I said, lifting my hands slightly so he could hold my arm like a child's. Then he teased me; with those legs of mine, I'd soon be married to a new Russian. The new Russians were the ones who had acquired great wealth after the communist era.

We laughed about it, although I always wondered if any man of any race could love my legs, scarred from climbing mango trees as I grew up in Africa. I didn't care at the time, because I was attracted to none of the men our embassy or the Kremlin sent my way. Therefore, why dwell on marriage? My whole life, people around me had talked incessantly about weddings or about whom I'd marry. I've always wondered why it has to be like that.

Why can't a girl grow up without being told she has to marry and have children? We're into the twenty-first century, where women in our society thrive and have assets and accomplishments beyond being mothers and wives, yet it feels at times like we're going backward. Aren't we good enough for anything other than saying 'I do' and producing babies? Is it a man's world for them and another one for us, a separate woman's world? Would I have married if I'd not been ordered to, as I was growing up, by every single person no matter their sex, language or culture? Or would I have been just me, and much more?

* * *

I was returning home after my exam, delighted at how it had gone. I felt confident and couldn't wait to tell my father about it, but, for some odd reason, I kept practicing the words I planned to say.

"My political science exam went really well, Papa."

I imagined him laughing, his broad white-toothed smile and proud face on the other end of the line. I thought to call him and share not only the good news about my results but also, for the first time, to tell him about Harvey. He wouldn't mind then; he wanted me to marry by the time I finished university, since we both knew that landing a husband after graduation would be a whole new ballgame.

It will be a win-win for both of us: I give him a major in Political Science and he lets me marry the love of my life, Harvey Van den Ameele... I'm not sure I'll take his last name, though.

I finally got to the phone and excitedly dialed his number.

"Hello? Papa?" I spoke in French.

"Yes, how are you?" he answered.

"Great!"

"How did it go?"

"Extremely well!" I said.

"Wonderful, *ma fille*. I told you that you'd end up loving Social and Political Sciences. I want you to be a diplomat like your uncle."

"As long as that pleases you, it's fine with me," I answered.

"You make me very happy, and your mother in heaven is happy with you right now, too."

"Oui, Papa." I paused. He seemed somehow not happy enough to learn about Harvey. *Maybe another time.*

"Is everything OK with you? I sense some sadness in your voice," he continued.

"Really?"

"Oui. I'm your father; I know you."

"Oh … *Vraiment?*" I said.

My father always had a sixth sense. Even before I knew something about myself, he'd tell it to me. Even so, I often wondered how much he really knew. As a child, I'd always told him the truth, even if I was scared to the point of peeing my pants, because he'd find out anyway. Why had he not trusted me the same way when I was twelve years old and under my uncle's thumb? He had played the role of mother and father with me and my younger brothers for years, often making me too lazy to think for myself. That was why I'd been very happy on my own, away from him, to figure things out – to get better acquainted with myself, perhaps, even though at the time I didn't know what it would really be like to discover myself as a woman.

"Are you still a virgin?"

The loss of my virginity was his ultimate fear. Every time we spoke on the phone, he asked. I always answered without thinking about it, but this time I felt a bit exposed, embarrassed to talk to him about it. I felt defensive and kept trying to change the subject. He had always told me there was no need to rush into sex, because, once I started it, I could never become a virgin again.

His take on having sex for the first time was that it was supposed to be special, with a special person, for whom you wait as long as it takes. But what did he really know to even claim the right to talk to me as he had all these years about sex?

"Do you remember your cousin?"

"Which one of the hundreds of them?" I asked. His eldest brother had four wives and at least eighteen children, some of whom I knew and some I didn't, because I'd left Africa at a young age. Some of those I'd never met had died in the Liberian civil war.

"The one who was almost twenty-five before she lost her virginity," he said in Fula.

"Yes, your older brother gave her to the richest man in the village for money," I said in French.

I did remember this cousin, because she was an example of cursed beauty; people in the village were afraid of her because she was very, very fair skinned and extremely pretty, with long lustrous hair that grew naturally down to her lower back. She was curvy with all the right elements in all the right places, which made both women and men scared of her. She looked too perfect and was therefore said to be a *djinn* – a devil.

"It was not for money. The chief of the village did us a favour, protecting her dignity and ours. To lose her virginity the right way, she was given to this man, since no one else had proposed and she was getting too old. She wasn't made for marriage but couldn't remain single, either. That was her curse, and the family couldn't accept it," he said. "She died a year later, in childbirth, because she broke her vows with her husband from a former life. Do you remember now?"

"Yes, I kind of knew, but what does it have to do with me?" I wondered how he could possibly believe the tale he'd just told. My cousin had died in labour, like many other African women who had suffered, and consequently paid the price for, genital mutilation.

"It has to do with the fact that not only are you too educated, you're also on the small side of the spectrum when it comes to the kind of woman African men like," he said.

"Are you really saying I'm too skinny and accomplished, and you stood there and let your younger brother ruin my reputation? What do you really expect of me?" I said.

I was angry that my father, of all people, would tell me I needed to marry my own and yet give all the reasons it was almost impossible for me to land an African man. To make it even worse, I shouldn't marry a white man, either. *What does he really want from me?* I wondered as his lecture went on.

"Oui?" I said without thinking about why I was even answering, since I had not been listening, had lost interest in listening, to him.

"Your 'Oui' should not be a question!" he said, raising his voice and speaking more firmly.

Here we go again about my virginity – something I never felt like telling him the truth about, the truth that I always wanted to bury in the deepest and darkest place of my being for as long as possible.

"Papa?"

"Oui, ma fille?"

"I'm turning twenty soon and you're still asking me if I'm a virgin every time we talk on the phone."

"You'll never be too old for me to ask this kind of question. When you're married I won't, but maybe something else will come up. As for now, just relax and answer me."

I really wanted to tell him about Harvey, but this conversation wasn't going well at all. It had gotten worse before it had begun.

"Papa. I want you to listen to me carefully without being angry or questioning me before I finish what I'm about to say," I said with all the courage I could muster.

"OK. Go ahead then."

"I met somebody." I paused.

"Yes, I'm listening."

"I love him for real," I said and held the phone tightly.

"Really?" he said, still respecting the fact that I'd asked him not to cut me off until I was done talking.

"Yes, and he's white," I finally admitted.

"A white man?!"

He said this so loudly that I moved my ear from the phone and hung up abruptly. I sat there with my hands over my mouth and stared at the receiver. After I had confessed my love for a Westerner, I didn't want to hear what he'd tell me next. He had sounded outraged.

When he called back he was a bit calmer and willing to try to understand.

"OK, he's white … white from where? Russia?" he said now in Fula.

"No. He's from the Netherlands," I said in French.

"A Dutchman?!" he screamed.

"Yes, Papa."

"How did you meet this man?!" He was livid again, and I wondered if I should hang up and never call him back, but something in me kept me going.

"I don't know how," I answered in a small voice in Fula.

"You don't know how?!" he howled.

"I don't understand what you want me to tell you," I said in my high-pitched little voice.

I was really scared and wanted to hang up again, but this was my father. I couldn't do that a second time.

My hands were shaking, as were my feet. I looked around the room and remembered the couch beside the phone. I plopped down on it immediately and looked out the window. Not a soul was to be seen, but there was snow falling. I imagined myself twirling and dancing in it, my hands open in the air as if waiting to be rescued by Harvey; the two of us would salsa and shimmy until dawn to the song of the drifting flakes, immune to the cold simply because of our untameable love, the fire between us – a fire no one could stop.

"Hello? Are you still there?" I heard my father ask. I returned to our conversation.

"I'm here."

"Is he one of the diplomatic kids?" he asked, a little calmer for some reason, as if he sensed my anguish or the distance between us.

"No … and he isn't a kid," I said. There was a pause.

"*Allahakoubar!!!*" he proclaimed in Arabic – "God is mighty and glorious" – as if he were talking to himself. He was losing his patience with me.

I felt even smaller on the couch and was starting to get cold, maybe because I'd opened the window to see more snow fall on its frame. I needed a hug – something – some kind of magic blanket that would take me away and help me forget this conversation, like the floating carpet in the fairy tale *Aladdin* my mother used to tell me and my brothers before bedtime.

I was starting to shut down on him as I wondered how to tell him the whole story. An uncontrollable anxiety rose in me. I didn't know exactly what to call it, but my heart was pumping so hard it felt like I was running a marathon.

"Have you hung up on me again, young woman?" my father shouted. I could hear his angry voice from the distance of my carpet. Then I realized I'd been away on that carpet for a while now, somewhere in the endlessly beaming stars amid the snowy sky.

"You never did this before? Is this something I should be worried about?" he said.

"Maybe." I finally responded, still with a high-pitched voice as if I were ascending from my dream world into reality, where I'd finally have to face my truth. I realized I had to, in fact, fight for Harvey if I wanted him for myself.

"OK. I think I was too intense with you," he said gently and paused. We both waited as if for a whistle to signal the start of a competition.

"You can't be with that man. It doesn't matter how you met him or when, or that you love him or whether he's the wealthiest man on the planet. He's simply not your kind or your type. He's never going to understand who you are, where you come from and what you're made of," he said after what felt like an eternity.

"He wants to meet you," I said encouragingly.

"He wants to meet me? How about the hundreds of other family members we have; does he know about them?" he said.

"Yes," I said.

"And he's fine with that?"

"He's more than fine, Papa!"

"He knows that you will have sex with him only when you marry?"

"Yes, Papa." I continued using the French word instead of calling him "Baba."

"He's fine with that, too?"

"Yes," I said, a little more hopeful.

"He didn't ask you for sex? Sorry, please let me rephrase that. You didn't give yourself to him?" he continued.

"Tempted, but he never let me," I said.

"He's a good man," he said with a sigh. It felt like there was more breathing space between each of our contributions to the conversation.

"And?" I asked excitedly. He paused.

"But that doesn't mean he's the one," he said in his worst voice ever, the quiet yet firm one. His tone made me think this was not a done deal, not in a million years. *Why is he taking away my hope?* I'd rather have him scream than use the voice that goes through me like a ripple on a quiet lake after a child has thrown a pebble in it. I froze. I felt deceived.

"Who is the one, Papa?" I said in tears; they were streaming as if I were cutting an onion. My tears were disobedient; I couldn't stop them.

My body began falling into my twelfth-year memories. I tilted my head and looked into the ceiling, decorated with fine Russian artistry and painted yellow – my mother's favourite colour – to bring myself back into the present. This was no time for self-pity, particularly with a man who had stood by and let another man put his own daughter in jail.

"A black man … a black Muslim man," he said.

"A what?!" I shouted.

"A black Muslim man!" he repeated.

"Do you really want me to marry a black Muslim man?!"

"Yes! Your own kind is always the best pick!"

"Has anybody asked for me in our city?" I said, remembering how I'd left Conakry, Guinea.

"No," he said.

"Why?" I asked again determinedly.

"You're too educated for them. We have to marry you to one of your cousins or one of the ambassadors' sons."

"Too educated ... too this and too that ... and now an arranged marriage?!" I said.

"What's wrong with that? Your mother and I got together that way, and it worked out well."

Really? I bet it did!

He changed the subject. "Have you met anyone at university from another African country?"

"Yes. But you wouldn't let me get close to men of any other ethnicity in Guinea, and now you're asking about another African man from the African continent. I don't understand –"

"And?" he interrupted. I wondered if he were listening at all.

"They treat me like their sister," I said.

"Why?" he asked. "Are you behaving like a lady?"

"What do you mean, behaving like a lady?" I asked, surprised.

"One of the arts of being a lady is staying put with your girlfriends and waiting for the man to invite you for a drink rather than taking the initiative." I wondered if I were really speaking to my father, whom I used to know, so I went with the flow.

"Oh, really ... why can't I ask them to go for a drink? It's different here, Papa."

"The protocol of love is never different, no matter the land or the culture you're in. It's all the same: a man likes to feel like the man. You can wear pants out there all you want, but you have to remain a woman, a young woman, a lady. Guard your boundaries and keep your expectations close to your heart; stand by your principles at all times until the one who deserves you comes around. I truly believe he won't be a white man," he said.

"That's racist, Papa. For a man who has travelled the world like you, that's an insane thing to be coming from your mouth."

"Believe it or not, part of my job is to preserve our roots, our African culture, even though I'm a traveller. Sleep on it, and don't meet him again until I call you back. If you're still thinking about him, then we'll talk more. By then he'll be hanging out with one of his kind." He said this with a short mocking laugh.

"I can't believe you're going to end the love of my life just because he's white."

"You should know better. He's white, and that's the end of it!" he growled.

"He's white, but when you cut him there's the same blood as yours! You haven't been the father I've known since my mother died. Your new wife has certainly gotten into your head and your way of thinking, but I really love this man. Why are you making this difficult for me, for both of us, when I've been your daughter and done exactly as you always wished? Why?" I ranted.

I was ready and willing to fight him on this, because I couldn't stand the idea of not seeing Harvey anymore.

"My new wife has nothing to do with this. Besides, you and your brothers told me it was time for me to remarry, since you were all grown up. Only then did I do it."

I felt defeated, like a falling leaf in autumn, because he was right. The guilt of not being there for our mother when she needed him most had kept him waiting for our approval to remarry, even though his brother was onto him about remarrying every single day. He had all kinds of women lined up for him, great alliances with well-born Fulani girls who would do anything to marry into our family.

"I'm very firm on what I've just requested you to do, and you will do it whether you like it or not. I won't let you ruin your life for a … for a …"

"A white man. I get it, and goodbye!" I hung up. I didn't care. Although I was shocked at myself for doing this, it was the first time such a thing felt right to me.

My father didn't call back; months passed. He wouldn't talk about Harvey and neither would I. He sent my uncle and aunt to see how I was doing. I hadn't seen Harvey for weeks, or months – it felt like forever. I'd cry on my pillow every night before I fell asleep. I refused to go to the embassy and stayed at my dormitory with Elena Ivanovna.

Linda's helpful Russian roommate

One of my Russian roommates, Elena, helped me get news of Harvey by calling him every now then on my behalf. Harvey couldn't understand why Elena was calling him and I wasn't. I felt ashamed about the whole situation, embarrassed as though I were naked in the middle of a river that fails to cover your privates unless you sit in it.

Is she going to sit in the water or come out and stand up to her father? I heard Harvey ask a few times when I was listening in. "Is everything OK with her? Why can't she call me directly?" I told Elena to let me tell him myself when the time was right, but she didn't. She told him my father had forbidden me from seeing him because he was white.

"Now he'll go see his blondes and forget about me," I whispered.

Tessa would shout from her room, "I was right about interracial relationships between blacks and whites," even though, most of the time, she didn't know what we were talking about. In her mind, no white man would want a black woman except out of sexual curiosity; for him, it would be a casual adventure and for the African woman, a chance to acquire a western passport.

"I heard that," Harvey would say. "Why can't we see each other? I miss her a lot, you know, and I want to be with her. Can you tell her that, Elena?"

Elena was kind and understanding; she refused to take sides, but she did her best to reassure us both: if it was meant for us to be together my father would accept him, and I wouldn't be replaced by a blonde blue-eyed Russian or Ukrainian girl on campus, as Tessa was predicting.

I'd met Elena Ivanovna in my first year at Patrice Lumumba Friendship University. We had bumped into each other when I was coming from the library, my arms overloaded with books. It was the beginning of fall and very windy. Most of the volumes tumbled out of my hands not only because I couldn't keep my balance but because I was still too skinny for the Russian weather and afraid that debris from the endless colourful leaves would blow into my eyes. Before I knew it, Tessa and Elena had come to my rescue.

"This must be your first year of school?" Tessa asked in English. I smiled, holding the remaining stack of books.

"What language do you speak?" Elena asked, one of my volumes in each of her hands.

"French," I said.

"You must love reading, or you're determined to get this language barrier out of the way." Tessa still spoke English, which I understood a little. "You know, you can always go back and take more classes later on. Russian is a hard-core language, but once you get the hang of it, it'll be yours for life."

"I love French," said Elena who, with Tessa, was following me. "It used to be very popular in the Russian aristocracy, and Tolstoy used it a lot in his books." I'd continued walking since I also wore a cumbersome backpack.

She likes books, and I hope she's my roommate. As it turned out, she was, and Tessa took the other room in the apartment. It was a three-bedroom flat with a common living room, bathroom and toilets. The small corridor led directly into the living room, where Tessa and I spent hardly any time because we both lived at our embassies – we stayed on campus around exam time and sometimes found excuses to use the apartment for dancing when we didn't have exams, or to cook in the main kitchen.

We were in the middle of a Russian winter in all its glory. I was sitting in our living room, right beside the window I'd opened for fresh air. Tessa hated having it ajar, but Elena and I did it anyway. Sipping a strong chai with lots of honey, I watched Elena from the corner of my eye as she applied red nail polish as though it were summer.

I gazed through the window and opened it even wider because of the smell of her polish. Nobody was on the streets. Naked trees in what would become a beautiful green forest during the summer caught my eye. I stared into the endless snow, so white it felt like the sky and the earth were one, with very little light seeping through.

Everything looked dark and distant; it was winter all around, and all I could hear and see were the whistling wind and a moving dune of snow, like a sand storm in a faraway summer in North Africa.

I turned around, folded myself back into the chair and took another sip of the hot chai, savouring its warmth in my hands. Elena was now humming her favourite American song, "Billy Jean."

I kept looking at her as if for the first time. Fragile and pale, she gave an impression of being ill, particularly at this time of year; her deep gaze lent a gleam of profound meditation and self-control to every gesture. The blue light in her eyes reflected every movement of her hands.

Although she was fully grown, when she sang her small, thin, rounded lips would expand and grow like an infant's. She was also a virgin and orthodox to the core. It was nice to have her with me, not only because of my need to learn her language quickly, but because we had many things in common even though she was a westerner.

She was waiting for the right man to come along. We talked about the kind of man who would be our kind. To my surprise and hers, mine, for now, turned out to be a *toubab* (the West African word for a white person). She was adamant that her husband would come from her church.

My Russian had gotten much better since I'd met Elena in the fall; I had needed the Russian winter to really get it.

There was not much going on that morning other than the increasing snow. The road looked deserted, and students had left for the winter holidays. Even Tessa had gone; she was in Paris with her family to celebrate Christmas and the New Year.

Elena decided we would go shopping. The night I had spent sitting by the window, my chai keeping me awake, didn't seem like a good time to her. She was getting ready to see her parents in Saint Petersburg, so she needed to run some last-minute errands. I was glad to join in. We always spoke Russian when Tessa wasn't around.

"Has your father called back yet?" Elena asked as we left the residence.

"No," I said.

"He still hasn't given you his blessings about Harvey?" she asked.

"No ... and I miss them both," I replied.

"I understand." She turned her head to me and then resumed walking to her car, like a mother checking on her kid.

"Yes, I'm warmly dressed. What do you think I should do?" I asked. I held her hand; we were like two babushkas that needed each other for balance and warmth in such weather.

"Do as he said: get great grades, and he'll come around," she offered, walking quickly.

"I see, but I'm doing that already," I said, matching her speed. "You know, Elena; all I've been is a good girl to him and everybody else."

"Beside my mediating between the two of you, have you had contact with Harvey since the summer?"

"No. Last time I saw him I was on the dance floor with him," I said.

"You went dancing with him?" she almost shouted, which made us both look around. We held back our silly laughter.

"Yes!" I replied, my eyes taking in the people near us.

"I know," Elena started. I interrupted her, since I'd heard what was coming a million times.

"I won't meet my husband on the dance floor!" we said together.

"I won't at the mosque or at the church, either," I added.

"Maybe that's what your papa wants for you, to find a man at the mosque," she said.

"Finding a man at the mosque without wearing a veil? Besides, they don't find me attractive," I said.

"Who?"

"The black men," I said.

"You're too skinny for them, my dearest monkey," she replied.

"Really?"

"Yes ... did you get that before? Maybe wearing a veil and big robe might work to your advantage if you want to find a husband among your kind. Yes, you *can* find a black Muslim man, you know." She paused, then blurted, "That is, of course, if that's what's going to make you and your father happy."

I kept listening.

"Look; at university, all their girls are more substantial: tall with big lips, big breasts, big bottoms, big hair; very solid looking. They are bigger in ... *everything*. I think the black man likes the very curvy woman much more than the model type," she said.

"Are you insinuating that black women have bigger clitorises than western women?" I said through pursed lips. By the look on her face, I read she had really meant that.

"Yes, of course!"

"I can't believe you're orthodox and go to church every Sunday. You're a dirty pig –" Before I finished talking she had thrown her snowy hat into my face.

"Well," I went on, "I'm not sure about that. After all, most African girls are cut by the time they're twelve years old."

"Oh, Linda – I'm sorry I got carried away. Yes, your sister. I'm sorry – really sorry. The girls I'm talking about are the ones I see in our common showers. Well, of course you can't assume all African women share the same lifestyle and culture. Majoring in international studies, I should know better. I'm sorry, and you know I mean it." She was in tears, so embarrassed that she resembled an overripe strawberry. She gave me a hug, which I welcomed.

"And anyway, how come you know about their clitorises and I don't? No; forget I just asked that. You've already answered me, and don't you dare ask me if I have mine intact," I said, my tone defeated and demure. She gave me a soldier's salute.

"As an insider, you won't see what I see. My mom and I talk about it when you're not around, for instance, particularly when she wants to lecture me about my body. She says that to attract men I need big breasts and more meat on my bones. Something like an 'S'." Elena drew the letter in the air. "You kind of have an S-shaped body, even though you're skinny. You're so slim a fall wind could blow you away."

"Yes, of course you had to remind me how you rescued me with my books that day. Do you really mean I have an hourglass shape? I thought I looked more like a boy," I said, touching my hips.

"Yes, that too." She examined my body from head to toe in her new, amusing way.

"You're a tomboy, which is another thing, but you don't have a boyish body. Besides, you always wear nice lingerie."

"You're worse than the KGB. You know I grew up with boys and played soccer instead of doing ballet like you. I dress like a woman, though, don't I?" I asked a little defensively.

"Sometimes," she giggled with a mocking face. "You do dress nicely in Parisian clothes – like I said, your fancy lingerie and all that – but in general you're more of a tomboy than a lady."

She kept laughing, and I loved it. So often she was very serious; this was the most I'd ever seen her laugh.

"That's what my father said: that I need to be a lady in order to attract a black man."

"Wow, your dad is something," she said.

"You can say that again," I replied.

"Wow, your dad is something." That brought us another laugh.

"It doesn't matter what the colour of a man's skin is. Men like their women pretty and chic! Your dad is really something," she repeated wistfully. "You actually talk about that … I wish my father wasn't such an alcoholic. He could have been a great daddy."

"He's still coming along," I said.

"Yes, you're right. I shouldn't judge him. The thing is, most Russian men who didn't die in the Second World War are alcoholics, and the ones who lived and are advancing, if they don't have their own wealth, are lost between the new Russia and the old Communist regime," she said.

"The women, on the other hand, are growing strong," I said.

"You have your mother, and I don't have mine. We're kind of even, don't you think?" I added to console her.

"Yes, I do have my mom, but she has some complex about my body. She thinks I don't have breasts and my lips still look like a baby's," she replied.

The way she said it made us laugh again without minding the people around us. She always talked in demonstration mode, which made her simultaneously eloquent and funny. It was one of those moments when she knew how to use her best asset: her eyes.

"Most Russian mothers compare their daughters to themselves – perhaps all mothers, universally, do this," I said.

"Where else or who else, though?" We chuckled.

"Just watch what happens when you have kids. You'll have the biggest ass with giant cow-milk breasts," I declared, laughing until I was breathless.

"That, my dearest, is the trade-off for every woman who has given birth. Wait until you have yours; then we'll see how your boobs stay the same," she said, gesturing at her own.

Moscow, Spring 1998

Harvey and I finally managed to convince my father of our love for each other. That I passed my exam with excellent grades helped, and Harvey's staying away proved to my father he was not in just for a one-night stand with an innocent black girl from Africa. Harvey had also agreed to accompany me to Conakry and marry according to our customs. He'd wear the traditional groom's attire and take a Muslim name.

I was not sure whether going through these steps would have any effect on Harvey, or the point of it. All we wanted was to finally be able to sleep together in the same bed and make love like any other couple who desired each other, and we were ready to do anything to make that happen. The collapse of communism in Russia had driven many expats to leave the country. Harvey was one of the first to go, because Adidas had decided to keep only their German controller and hire locals to carry on at a lower cost. Recruiters he used to work with found Harvey a job back in Amsterdam.

Linda in Amsterdam for the first time – Harvey's house

After the great news about summer exams, which had gone well for both Elena and me, my father and his whole family had decided to meet Harvey.

We flew to Amsterdam. I'd been through the Schiphol airport many times, but I'd never actually gone into the city. It was easy to get a cab from the designated taxi stand. Sitting inside with our luggage securely in the trunk, I could see and feel how speedily this city moved. The sound of trams, buses, cars and cyclists was everywhere. The number of bikes on the road and parked on the side streets surprised me.

"All these bikes stay outside?" I asked, holding and playing with Harvey's left hand.

"Yes. Why?" he asked.

"Nobody steals them?"

"No," the taxi driver answered. His slightly British intonation was mixed with some other accent.

"This is the Netherlands, my dear. These bikes stay outside no matter the weather, and nobody steals them. Also, most cars are parked on the road side, no matter how expensive they are. Sometimes owners cover them, but really, they are all simply what you use to get from A to B," the driver continued. I saw his smile in the rearview mirror. "And look to your right before crossing or turning, because you'll always spot a pedestrian or another form of transport passing by."

"I'm not sure I like having to leave everything outside," I said.

"Here we are," the driver announced, stopping in front of a slightly slanted old red-brick building.

"What a beautiful home. It looks like it's tilting to the front," I exclaimed.

"Most Amsterdam houses are like this nowadays. They're getting old, dear. Will you be staying for a long time?" he asked. He looked at Harvey as he opened the door.

"We're going to get married in Africa," Harvey said eagerly.

"That must be interesting! What love can do, young birds," the driver said as he set our luggage on the sidewalk. He was keen to help.

To get to Harvey's door we climbed three steps and then, once inside, another four. It was a very big house, with high Victorian ceilings and some tall, open windows on each side. We put our bags down in the middle of the floor.

"Can we go to the van Gogh Museum?" I squealed. "Can we go there? Please don't say no, Harvey."

"Not this time around. We'll have plenty of time when we come back. What if your daddy knows we've been there? We don't want to take any chances. Do we?" he said, kissing my forehead and giving me a warm hug.

We were waiting for his best friend, Wouter, with whom I'd be staying for a few days before Harvey and I flew to Guinea; in the meantime, Harvey showed me around. He had a remarkable telescope in the middle of the living room looking out the largest window. It was amazing to zero in on the passersby and the neighbouring cafes, bars and restaurants as well as the neighbour's garden. We heard the doorbell. Wouter had come to fetch me.

Natasha, Wouter's girlfriend, found it strange that I would be staying away until we married. She herself was due any moment with their first baby, and they weren't married.

"If you don't tell, nobody would know you're spending the night together," Natasha said. Her tone and face suggested both Harvey and I were sick and needed help.

"I think it's best to do it the right way. I promised her father that I'd respect his wishes and culture, and I think, to some extent, this is important to Linda," Harvey said, and I wondered.

During our stay in Amsterdam, Harvey's parents visited us and offered their blessing, but his mother was not too fond of the situation. I asked him about it before our trip.

"Do you think your mother likes me?"

"Yes, she does, but no woman is good enough. Just keep that in mind when you start having doubts. I wouldn't worry about it, my soon-to-be wife," he said and kissed my forehead.

"Is this really, really what you want?" I asked.

"Yes, it is. If that's what it takes for your family's acceptance and permission to sleep with you in the same bed, I'm all in!" he said excitedly, lifting me slightly off my feet.

"Oh, and a small detail … there's one condition," he added as he put me down.

"Is an unexpected condition at the last minute a good thing?" I asked. He was still holding me in his strong arms.

"That you marry me officially when we come back," he said.

"What do you mean 'officially'?" I removed my hands from his.

"Like in a real western wedding, for my family and me?"

"Yes, I will if that pleases your lordship," I said and leaned into his chest.

Harvey's dad was a naturally go-with-the-flow kind of gentleman. It didn't take him long to warm to me and, a bit more slowly, me to both him and Harvey's mother. They were fine with our traditional wedding in Conakry, Guinea, and in return would attend the official wedding of their first son in the Netherlands.

Chapter 3
African marriage

Harvey and I flew into Guinea the last week of August, right before school was to start. When we arrived at Conakry International Airport, my aunt Halle and my three younger brothers, Alpha Oumar, Goudoussy and Leonis, who was now a teenager, were waiting for us, accompanied by one of my cousins, Tandy, who would give us a ride to the hotel where Harvey was staying. Then we would drive to Tandy's house, where I would stay until the wedding night. Only then would I join Harvey as a wife, at last, in his hotel.

I didn't see my younger and only sister when we landed. "Where is Nenein Bah?" I asked. Nenein was named after our maternal grandmother, Khadija, and we never used her real name out of respect.

"She had to stay home and look after our stepmother's kids," Alpha Oumar said.

"Can I see her tonight?" I asked.

"Well, how about you get some rest first. We'll go there first thing tomorrow morning. Besides, all the women are waiting to start your wedding preparations, and tonight we'll take care of Harvey," Goudoussy said.

"That sounds good, but we're hot and exhausted," Harvey answered, blowing on his T-shirt, which was already damp from the heat and humidity. The airport was crowded with people who had just landed from Europe and the USA.

We walked out to my cousin's six-seater SUV. Harvey and I took the middle with Goudoussy in the front and Alpha Oumar and Leonis in the back, filling the vehicle.

The drivers at the roundabout were impatient, and it seemed like we heard every car horn in Africa. My cousin, a big talker who had just earned her driver's licence, was eager to demonstrate her skill. The bumpy street had a lot of pot holes. You could see that it had once had a firm surface and was well made, but it had become run down due to the weather and lack of maintenance. Multiple roads branched out around it and the drivers using them would simply look at one another, wait, and then whip out the moment they saw an opportunity. The set-up appeared to invite disaster; it was disorganized and, with no proper road signs, singularly uninviting.

Tandy entered the roundabout without looking to her right or left. Harvey and I could see cars coming at us on either side, from all directions. We squeezed each other's hands and prayed we came out of the roundabout alive. Harvey swore he wouldn't sit behind my cousin ever again for as long as he was visiting.

The hotel helped him find his own driver, so he rented a car to shuttle us around. My cousin's house was big, with three living rooms, seven bedrooms and three bathrooms. Her husband worked at one of the main banks and had lived in Switzerland for many years. He returned to Africa to give back and had married Tandy.

Theirs was an arranged marriage that worked well for both families. My cousin gave birth to twin boys in the first year; they were a great anchor for the union, and her husband and in-laws treated her like a queen. Anything she wanted was given to her; all she had to do was ask, and sometimes she was given things even without asking.

Tandy had three maids and two nannies from her husband's village who cooked, cleaned and ironed; they took care of everything in the household. The nannies took turns on day and evening shifts. I wondered whether Tandy she missed her babies, because I hardly ever saw her with them. As a result, I seldom saw them myself while I was there.

She also had water and electricity even when nothing was coming from the pipes or from the city's power system. Her husband had found a way to pump water into the house for showers, toilets, drinking and anything else for which it was needed. As for electricity, he had a diesel motor on standby.

Their imposing Sony TV dominated the principal living room, where MTV was always playing. You found TV5 in the second living room and a medium-sized TV with CNN in their bedroom. The noise in this place resembled the racket at a soccer match, with sounds and overlapping voices and languages swirling from every direction.

I wondered why they would leave everything turned on and yet keep trying to hear each over the din, but I didn't say anything; I wouldn't be there for long anyway, so why bother?

I adapted quickly to their customs. Their lifestyle, wealthy and prosperous, made them the envy of many. And except for the TVs and all the noise, they lived in exactly the same manner as I had growing up in my father's house in Port Kamsar, Boke.

With all the preparation going at my cousin's, I didn't see Harvey that night. I could hardly find time to think of anything but accepting whatever they had on their agenda for my wedding. The women spent the night putting henna on my arms and feet as well as singing, dancing and telling stories of virginity and how it had been for them on their first night.

"I was 100-percent virgin, because they had to heat the blade to open me up before my husband could make it inside," one cousin from my father's village, Bouliwell, offered.

"There's no better proof of virginity than that, my dear," said one of the aunts on my father's side.

"Our Galle is also a virgin. If she wasn't, she wouldn't have brought the westerner here to get married. She respected her culture and tradition," my aunt Halle said and took me a little from the crowd.

The night was long because nobody went to bed; they just kept dancing. My ears – all my being – were yearning for a silent moment. I wondered if Harvey was thinking and feeling the same, wherever he was right then. I was in and out of sleep as they braided my hair and applied henna anywhere they felt fit. I was not to say no to anything they were doing. Since I wasn't allowed any input, I made up my mind to go with the flow. My head felt weird and itchy at times with the tight cornrows; in each furrow they planted silver and gold coins held in place with red, gold and black ribbons.

The next morning one of the old women took me into the shower to wash off the henna and give me a ritual pre-wedding bath, with all kinds of oils, scents, and candles burning. It smelled like destiny, and it was energizing. After the bath, she made me walk, naked, in a circle on top of the scent. My first meal of the day was rooibos tea with milk and a warm baguette because I had refused to eat the special cooked rice in the early morning. I couldn't swallow it; it felt too strange to have hot food for breakfast, although out of respect I tried a little.

The next day, Harvey came to get me. He was dressed in a long African sky-blue caftan the boys had insisted he wear in preparation for his big day. My brothers, our male cousins and their friends had prepared an African bachelor party for him the same evening as the women had for me. In his outfit, he looked radiant and happy, if foreign. He seemed to have caught some colour from the little exposure to the sun he had already had.

I looked at him with curiosity, as he did at me; his gaze lingered a while longer on my new hairdo. He winked, and we both smiled discreetly. We then seated ourselves, along with most members of my family, in the brand-new Range Rover whose driver the hotel had assigned us after the incident with my cousin. Harvey had kept his promise, even though I thought he had been bluffing at first or would get over Tandy's dangerous driving.

Not for an instant had Harvey and I been alone since we arrived.

At last, we reached my father's house. The compound looked as it had when I'd left. Even the tropical flowers at the entrance remained; the exterior was still canary yellow. I could see it had just had a fresh coat – because I was coming and because of my wedding preparations. A crowd sat under the mango tree, with women on the left and men on a mat on the right. In the middle appeared my father and his young brother, Hussein, while my stepmother and my uncle Hussein's wife, also toward the middle, bordered them on the women's side.

Without warning, my stomach knotted. Was it the mixed feelings from seeing my uncle Hussein after all these years and at the same time knowing all these people's eyes were on me?

"Was this only for my wedding?" I thought. "They certainly know how to throw a party and make things grandiose, and all this for me." I slowly started trusting and smiling, happy they had gone to such trouble for Harvey and me.

They sat me next to my stepmother and gave Harvey a seat next to my brothers. We were all facing each other now, ready to be served the exotic food I'd smelled since entering my father's compound. I felt my mouth watering but slowed it immediately, looking to see if my sister was in the crowd with the other women. *Where could she be all this time?*

The women wore bright white with very little colour other than their veils. The mango trees under which they lounged bore fully ripened fruit, ready to fall. In the left corner of the gathering, along the side of the compound entrance, was a small garden where my father had planted his favourite vegetables. It seemed strange to see everyone in white, because that's worn mostly at funerals, not at weddings; in my culture, pure, bright white is a sign of virginity and death at the same time. *Do they really think I'm still a virgin? Would my uncle think so as well?*

At the moment I was going to ask about my sister, my aunt Halle started crying. She reached out to me with her right hand, but it was taken and held by the ladies she was sitting with. I was apprehensive. *What was going on?*

"Your sister, Nenein Bah, is no longer with us," my father said firmly, looking right into my eyes.

"Did she get married?" I asked, thinking they had married her young, like they always did anyway, so why the fuss?

"No. She's dead!" my aunt Halle howled. All the women started crying and throwing themselves on the floor in front of me. I felt confused and deceived. Yesterday they had held a splendid party for me, and this morning these same women were moaning about my sister's death, which they had not told me about. *Why would they do this? Am I a toy to this family?*

I was dumbfounded. It was like I was in a slow-motion movie where all the characters were aliens from another planet, or lived in a ghost town, like in the song by Adam Lambert. The sad thing was that I was one of those ghosts who would never, ever, wake up; I'd keep living in their realm of misery, from which I'd run when I left for the West.

And the worst part about Adam's song: I would have danced to the rhythm, but in this spectral place my legs were numb and lifeless. Though blood coursed through my veins, I had become a living ghost. Whether I liked it or not, life was going on before my breath, my feet, my being. *How can one get past a moment like this?* I kept wondering, my hair corn-rowed with coins that had no meaning or value to me.

I scrutinized my family; they had not changed. Their pale, loveless and heartless roots and rigid consumers' way of life would always go against the way I saw the world and my place in it. I felt like an invited outsider.

I couldn't rouse myself despite the tumult around me. Harvey cast me a quizzical glance and everybody froze, waiting for my reaction. Were they expecting me to throw myself on the floor like they had done? Why didn't I? Wasn't I part of them and their culture? What in me had changed? What made me so different that I couldn't manage to behave exactly as they did? A day that had started out sunny and bright was now tarnished and lifeless. I didn't know how to react, and they waited. I wondered whether Nenein was in the hospital morgue, longing for me to see her before burial.

"Is she in the hospital?" I finally asked with a dry mouth.

"No, Galle. She died last week Friday, right after you talked to her on the phone from Amsterdam," my father replied.

"Yes. We spoke on Wednesday," Harvey said, looking at my father and my younger brothers as well as my uncle, who just sat there.

"OK. Then you talked on Wednesday and she died on Friday evening," my father said.

"Why didn't anybody tell me she was dead before I flew here?" I looked at Harvey.

"He didn't know. Nobody could tell you because it was to be kept secret until you arrived," my brother Alpha Oumar said.

"Why?" I asked.

"You had already left. Even if we wanted to let you know, it would have been impossible," Goudoussy explained.

"What happened? Can someone take me to her?" I asked again.

"She was buried the same day," Goudoussy said.

"Buried? Why didn't you wait for me?"

"Where?" Harvey changed the subject.

"She's at the same cemetery where our mother is." Goudoussy wiped away his tears as quickly as they rolled down his cheek.

"You know we don't wait to bury the dead. It has to be done the same day. Have you forgotten tradition?" my uncle interjected.

"I'm sorry, Djadja. We're beyond shocked this had to happen over your wedding trip," Goudoussy said.

"There won't be a wedding," I replied.

"You're not going home without at least getting married," my father said.

"If you don't want a big wedding after what happened, so be it. However, you can't go back without getting married to this man in a religious ceremony, since he came all this way to be with us," my uncle said.

"Can I go see my sister first?"

"Now?" my father asked.

"Yes, now," I said.

We didn't take the car, since the cemetery was only half an hour's walk. We left the crowded house.

Everybody was trying to cheer each other up, and the neighbours and other family members were bringing all kinds of food and drink to the house. Some even brought goat and sheep, some brought chicken, and some carried bags of basmati or Thai rice, as well as palm oils, shea butter oils, cornflower oils and eggs. Anything you could possibility think of animal- or vegetable-wise had appeared at our house, but not only for my wedding. My sister's death had created a frenzy of sympathy; even people who didn't know us but had heard the story through word of mouth came to pay their respects to my family.

Some wanted most of all to see and touch a white man, which Harvey welcomed graciously. Some of the people who were holding his hand even rubbed his skin to see if anything would stay with them. Harvey went so far as to bite his finger to show that his blood was red. Everybody was shocked and loved him right away.

They said he was a great white man with brown eyes instead of blue, as they often thought any white man's would be. They also thought he was extremely wealthy, since he was white, and that I was lucky to have married white. Some people said my family had sold me to him for a lot of money and that in consequence they would never be poor because of him. It's true that Harvey is and will be the light and torch for my relatives for as long as I live married to him.

We arrived at the cemetery with the usual protocols waived because the guard had been informed of my arrival. As soon as he saw Harvey was the only white man in the crowd he knew I was Nenein Bah's sister. He walked through the headstones and names. I passed my mother's grave, marked by the acacia tree we had planted – my aunt Halle and I had done this since we weren't supposed to put her name on the plot.

Nearby was a fresh grave the size of a child's. It was my sister's. At seven, she had died too soon. Hoping for some kind of solace, I knelt and touched the soft, smooth red earth as if about to pray. Taking the soil in my hands, I felt my eyes moisten and tears tingling on my cheeks. My nose was running, the salty mucus dripping onto my lips. I licked it innocently, as if hungry for something unknown – maybe for guiltless lives taken prematurely from me: my mother first, and now my very own and the only sister I had ever had, at my own wedding. *What did I do to you, God, to deserve such attention?*

I touched the burial plot head to toes; my brother had told me how her body lay. Everyone present gave me room, and nobody approached me until I deliberately started poking at her grave, like a black crow that wanted to see the deteriorating flesh of my sister's body, or maybe imagining, driven by some force, that my digging would resuscitate her. She would wake up and say simply, "Hello, Djadja. Welcome back."

"Please stop digging, Galle. You'll release what you don't want," my father said. He had tears in his eyes but they did not brim.

"I'm sorry, sweetheart," Harvey said, kneeling quietly next to me and rubbing my shoulders. "What a waste of youth," he added sombrely.

Nenein had asked for gold earrings and a necklace, which Harvey and I had taken with us. I kept digging and didn't listen. Reaching into my bag, I started putting the jewellery into her grave.

"Djadja, I think a living being would be better having that, and Nenein Bah wouldn't mind at all," Alphadjo said. He removed the gifts from the hole I'd made.

When I had first dug into the earth, ants and worms had come up. Then an unfamiliar, inexplicably awful smell came rushing out.

"Is this really what you wanted? You'll remember this for the rest of your life," my father said.

"Father, it's fine. Please, let her do whatever she feels is right," Alphadjo the pacifist said.

"I'm done now," I announced. I walked away, past my mother's grave, which I saw had been pushed aside to put someone else on top.

I'll come see you another time, Mother. As tears streamed down my face, I took Harvey's hand, a gesture my father saw; I let it go right away.

"It's fine to hold his hand, daughter. You're getting married," my father said kindly.

"OK, then. Thank you." I leaned into Harvey's shoulders.

I wanted nothing grandiose for my Conakry wedding to Harvey. He was hot and overwhelmed by all the clothes a groom had to wear. I had requested that everything be subdued in the name of my sister.

"Death doesn't mean the end of the world, daughter. It's the beginning of life, and life must go on. You came all the way here for a great wedding, and we'll give it to you," my father said.

The guests danced and ate most of the evening and into the following day. I refused to leave my hotel room once settled there the night of the ceremony. The morning after, the old ladies and my aunt Halle came to pick up my wedding dress, which Harvey had put aside as they had requested he do. They asked Harvey right away if I'd been a virgin.

"There was blood everywhere," he said innocently. I wondered if he realized the value or consequence of what he'd just announced. Halle and her friends, who had managed to plant blood stains on my gown, danced and serenaded my virginity without me being in the circle I was supposed to be sitting in. I didn't want to be surrounded by screeching women celebrating a virginity that had been stolen from me in jail.

"Why are you doing this, Aunt Halle? You're aware I was not a virgin ... you know –"

"Nobody else does, sweetheart, and you're a virgin because you didn't sleep willingly with a man. You were ... you know what I mean. ... Let's not talk about it anymore. Let's rejoice in your beautiful wedding and the man you landed. He's handsome, all right. Is he good in bed as well?" she said.

"Anyway, who says a woman without a clitoris has no feeling down there? There's so much to our body, it's beyond belief. Do you remember what I told you at the river?" She hummed while breathing deeply, as though she were orgasming.

"You haven't changed a bit," I said. "If sleeping for the first time with the man you truly love means you were a virgin, then that's what I was," I agreed.

She smiled.

The moment she and the other women left, Harvey was by my side. But as night fell, I couldn't sleep. Was my only sister really gone? How had she died? As I was later to learn, she had been cut and soiled in the name of tradition.

I wept bitterly in Harvey's arms. He could now be called Mustapha because he had been shaven and converted to the Muslim faith before we got married. He had not minded, undertaking everything he had been asked to do except for getting circumcised. In fact, everybody in the family had assumed he already was, because they thought circumcision was practiced everywhere. Harvey and I were relieved that the issue had not arisen before our African wedding.

Chapter 4
Unrootedness

Back in Amsterdam: no sense of home – December 1999

On my way back to what I now call my refuge – Eglise de la Sainte Croix, a church in Brussel's Flagey Square – I daydreamed, feeling at first like a snowflake that can't land on anything, unwillingly plummeting to earth, and then like a tree branch whose leaves were being snatched by winter, a season which Africans who emigrate North accept either willingly or, because they have been forced to flee for cultural, religious or ethical reasons, under duress. They often feel their motherland has given up on them. They will hang on to anything to survive until they accept we're all from Africa, with all its glory and all its badness, yellow fever, malaria and meningitis a part of it all.

Before Harvey moved from Amsterdam to join me in Vancouver, we had always celebrated Christmas with his parents in Oostburg, Zeeland. We also went to see his mother and father almost every weekend. His mother, Rina, who usually felt entitled to do with Harvey whatever she pleased, made it feel mandatory that we visit as often as she wished.

"My good son won't stop coming to see us, not even for you," she said proudly on one of our calls. At times, I wondered whether my mother would have behaved this way with her son-in-law and me.

On numerous occasions, Harvey had warned me about his mother and had even blamed her for his failure to settle down all these years – with his first girlfriend, Adreian, particularly, and many other girlfriends who had followed.

He had told me about her intrusiveness when we first met. With a half-genuine and half-embarrassed laugh he said, "No woman will be good enough for her."

She sounds like a Fula mother-in-law, and that won't be hard to understand, because that's a tradition I know: brutal, unmerciful and beautiful at the same time, with an immensely unfounded and misplaced love.

I couldn't help but notice – or wanted to see and believe – the similarity between us as humans, beyond the colour of our skin and eyes, when I first met Harvey's younger brother, Neil, and his wife, Madeleine. I noticed each time she wanted to feed her newborn, Nathalie, she hid her breasts under a long quilt that had strategically placed holes around the nipples. I wondered why she nursed behind a cloth. An African woman would simply sit there and mind her baby's needs without covering up. The quilt looked fancy and convenient, but using it seemed weird to me.

Every now and then in my time alone I wondered how many things I was doing that they would find awkward or strange. They always had bread for breakfast and lunch, with assortments of Dutch cheese, which I liked a lot, and one hot meal for dinner at seven, at the latest, and many snacks in between. Being on time, well-dressed and well-mannered at dinner was important to this family, and everybody had to be arrive at the table punctually. That time was mandatory to them, like it was with us to be reading the Koran at six in the morning when I was growing up in Africa. They also drank a lot during the day – coffees, teas.

For one thing, I always liked chewing on the bones of the fried fish I had for dinner, which they prepared especially for me. For another, I couldn't stop hugging them; in contrast, they liked giving three kisses on the side of each cheek, leaving a big, unhugged space between our bodies.

Since I didn't know much about celebrating Christmas other than the little I'd learned from Clay and his family, and I didn't know much about Harvey's household, I wondered what to offer them. What did one give to the wealthy for Christmas? I went ahead and presented each with a travel kit that I'd bought in Frankfurt the last time I was there with my uncle.

"Nobody ever gave me a toothbrush as a gift before. You don't know me, and you're offering me a toothbrush?" Neil said, laughing and pointing the toothbrush at his face like a little boy who had found an unusual toy.

Nobody added to his comments, nor did I. I could see and feel that they all accepted and loved their gifts, like they had accepted me and welcomed me into their beautiful family, but I remained unsure about Harvey's mother. Would she be an asset in my life or a hindrance to my marriage with her beloved son? I stayed awake thinking some nights.

Brussels, October 2015

I couldn't help but remember that around this time eighteen years earlier I used to go for a walk in Vandal Park in Amsterdam and think the same thing: *I'm getting older, but my memories are not; I can only hope and pray that it's a blessing, not a curse.*

Brussels, unlike any other Western city I'd lived in, was full of Africans. On a day like today I could hear all kinds of African dialects even though I'd forgotten mine; they sounded familiar.

"Wait a minute. Maybe I'm in search of mine; mine for me or mine from my roots?" I mumbled to myself. I realized how loudly I'd spoken when the man walking beside me wondered if I were talking to him. I smiled and kept on going. Since we'd moved to Belgium, things I thought were buried deep inside kept welling up and grabbing me – why?

As I continued striding down rue de Lesbroussard, I felt the gravity of the earth under my feet disobeying me, because I no longer knew where I wanted to be. Everything came rushing into my brain. I relived how we'd flown from Moscow to Amsterdam, and the night I challenged Harvey to show me the mountain through his lens. It turned out it wasn't a mountain but a cloud.

"We don't have mountains in Holland. It's a flat land, darling, the lowest in the world. We drained away water to acquire land," he said with some pride.

We had just returned from Africa, fully blessed by a traditional wedding. My father called Harvey "my son-in-law," and I hadn't told him, nor did he ask anything, about my jail time. But I knew something in me had died, something I couldn't put my finger on. Was it my sister's brutal death? Was it that I hadn't stood up to my father and his brother, or was it simply that I felt I'd betrayed myself again for having gotten married exactly as my father wanted instead of the way I saw fit? *God, what was it, really?*

Unable to answer my own million questions, I just kept walking, thinking of life with Harvey in Amsterdam after our wedding. I was tiring when I noticed that I was still on Lesbroussard and walking uphill.

"I really miss the mountains, Harvey. Why can't I go see the mountains?" I asked, holding him in the middle of the kitchen after dinner, which he had cooked for us.

"How about I take you to the mountain, then, tomorrow?"

I kept quiet – a little too quiet.

"How about I take you right now, somewhere special?" he proposed spontaneously. It was 8:54 p.m. and I was staring out his tall kitchen windows.

"I'll drive you to find a mountain in the middle of the night – how about that?"

"How far is it?"

"Who cares? All that matters right now is that you want to see a mountain and I'm going to show you one. All you have to do is say 'Yes, Lord Harvey, yes!'" he said.

"Yes, Lord Harvey, yes!"

He was fun in those days because he laughed and joked a lot and would do anything for me, and we had sex with as much gusto as when we ate.

Two weekends passed by in which Harvey and I hadn't gone to his parents' house. Why we hadn't gone didn't come up, but our bedtime routine started to change. We repeated the same conversations over dinner, and right after eating he'd take the phone to talk to his mother until he finally decided to go to bed or I went without him.

"How was your day?" I'd try to start a dialogue.

"Good, and the same," he'd respond without lifting his eyes from the plate. We sat at either end of the table as though in a royal sixteenth-century dining room.

"Is this about visits to your mother?" I asked.

"Not really," he said and took a sip of his Diet Coke.

"You're talking to her every evening and she has all your attention. Is it because we're not spending so much time with her?"

"Yes. And?" he said.

"How long is this going to go on?" I asked.

"She's my mother, and she'll always want us to see her, and since you don't want to go on weekends she calls every evening. I warned you about her possessiveness even before our wedding in Guinea. I didn't lie to you, so you better get used to it and to her if you want us to be happy together." He returned to his steak.

"I've had it with your mother, Harvey. I'm married to you and not to her. Or maybe I hoped to find a mother figure in her, but instead she's jealous and possessive," I said, holding my fork and knife in the air.

"Linda, you're taking this the wrong way. It's like this with every woman I've been with, and there's nothing we can do about it. I love you, and that should be all you need – nothing else, and not even her. You're wasting your time if you think she'll treat you like her own daughter," he said.

"But I *am* her daughter ... or should be her daughter. That's how it is and has always been in Africa."

"You're not in Africa, and you're not married to an African man in an African family, so get over it," he replied.

"You know, you're right, but I'm right, too, because when we met in Moscow I never hid that I planned to immigrate to Canada; that was clear between us all along." I stood up behind my chair and held the edge of it.

"What do you really expect? That I pack every time you wave your finger? My mother doesn't want me to move to Canada, and she's right. I've got a job here, a house on the best street in the best neighbourhood in Amsterdam. This is my homeland and the land of the free. No country or continent can be freer than Holland. And you want me to give all this up for –"

"For me," I interrupted.

"Please don't finish my sentence; what I wanted to say was –"

"I don't care what you wanted to say, because I can't live here in Amsterdam with you." I stomped up the stairs toward the bedrooms. He kept eating. I ran back down and roared like a tigress on the loose.

"I'm packing my suitcase. I will get the fuck out of here and then your mother will have her way, and again you'll blame her for your inability to nurture a relationship," I shouted and ran up the stairs.

"Why are you getting yourself all worked up, Linda? For nothing. All I'm saying is that I don't want to move to Canada," he said, running after me up the stairs. At the top I threw myself down on the landing but then lost my balance. For a moment I sensed his right hand reach for my leg, but his grasp failed and I tumbled to the bottom of the stairs like a ball rolling downhill.

"Are you going to kill yourself for Canada, Linda? I thought you loved me more than Canada. Once you've lived for a while with me in Holland you'll forget about moving to Canada. What's going on? We've gone too far. Is Canada really home to you?" he asked, standing over me.

"My Canada; yes, my Canada, where your mother doesn't want you to go, is my home," I said as he helped me up. We walked to the couch in the living room.

"You were willing to like it here; you're learning Dutch, taking classes. What changed all of a sudden?" He went to the kitchen and returned with his Diet Coke and water for me.

"Your mother doesn't like me and doesn't want us to live together. You know it but never want to talk about it." I took a sip.

"I know, but that goes for all the women I've been with. I warned you; I thought it best to let her do whatever she wanted. That's why seeing her on weekends would keep her quiet. But you and I love each other, and that's all I care about," he said, moving closer to me on the blue leather couch.

"Didn't it occur to you that it would take more than just going to see her on weekends?"

"Yes, it did, but, like I said, it's my mother's problem, not mine or yours. I love you and I'll always love you, for as long as I breathe –

you're everyone and everything to me, Linda. Coming from a Dutchman, that's true. I love you." He slid even closer but I moved away.

"What if *she* tried harder? I think you underestimate what she can do. Just think, Harvey. You could've married a Russian or Ukrainian. Why didn't you? They're the most beautiful women in the world, but you went for a black African with no Victorian fancy house like this one." I stood up and waved my hands in the air, running my hands against the luxurious walls he had just renovated for us – he had done the whole house – as though I wanted to scratch off the paint.

He approached me. "I'll go with you to Canada – at least for a visit, and then we'll see. Would that make you happy?"

"Yes. Then I'll learn perfect English and be a published author, finally," I said.

"Let me show you what else we can do in the meantime for your book." And with that he swept me up the stairs, like Cinderella, to our bedroom and tossed me playfully onto the waterbed. This was one of those perfect, happy moments when being a size zero suited me fine.

Harvey's first time in Vancouver

Harvey flew with me from Amsterdam to Vancouver in the spring of 1999.

We enjoyed two weeks together before I moved in with a Canadian host family arranged through the University of British Columbia, where I was to study English as a Second Language.

On the last weekend before he returned to Amsterdam, we went golfing. We were on our way home in his rented red Corvette convertible when he said, "After all those awful tropical shots I endured so I could go to Africa to marry you according to your tradition, you can't say 'I love you, too'? I even fainted on that table because of the injection, shaved my hair off and let myself be called Mustapha, and yet you haven't told me even once that you love me. Each time I tell you I love you, you bring up all the excuses that have nothing to do with me so you can keep hiding behind whatever is fragmenting you; you still don't want to share it with me."

"We're having a great day with great weather. Why are you bringing this subject up again? You know I love you. Why is it important that I say the words?" I asked, looking out the window.

"Please look at me when we're talking. Why are you avoiding intimacy?" he asked.

"You talk a lot for a Dutchman. Are you nervous because you're leaving?"

"Come with me to Amsterdam?" He looked me straight in the eyes.

"Are you asking me because you're afraid I'm going to fall for somebody else? Are you jealous?"

"I don't like long-distance relationships. You're young and beautiful and …" He paused.

"Can I ask you something, and you promise to answer it honestly?" I said.

"Yes."

"After we had sex on our wedding night, why did you tell my family that there was blood everywhere when there was none?" I asked.

"I wanted to tell them what they were expecting to hear. I hoped to honour and show respect for you, like they do when a married woman is found a virgin in your culture, and in my culture in the old days, too, of course. Your people have simply not evolved, or refuse to evolve, in that sense. Where are you going with this?" he said as he slowed his speed.

"Would you believe me if I told you that you're the only, the first, real man I've known?" I said and laughed out of nervousness.

"Well, I'm not entirely sure. But I did have to teach you quite a lot." He waited for my comment, but I remained silent.

"I don't know," he went on. "You're quite tight, but it really doesn't matter. What *does* is what's between us right now and what we're working on and looking forward to together. Is it important to you that you were a virgin when we met? It's you that I love and not that you bled or didn't bleed the first time."

We rode the rest of the way in silence. I didn't say that I loved him, but I rubbed his shoulders and smiled.

We spent the night walking on English Bay and made love on the sand once we were certain there was no patrol. We left the beach at dawn, returned to his hotel and slept for the rest of the morning. Harvey was flying back in the afternoon with KLM.

In the taxi, I could still hear his mother's voice as it had been when we lived in Amsterdam. "You know I can give you enough money to buy yourself an apartment in Vancouver and leave my son alone, because I don't want him moving to another continent or living too far away from me. Even though he often does, I don't like it."

"Do you still think I'm with your son for his money, or yours? I doubt you'll have your wish if he finds out you're trying to buy me off. I'm not for sale, so please don't even ask or suggest that to me again. I will go and leave you with your son, and if he really loves me he'll come and join me, because I'm not going to live in Holland anymore. Besides, I'm sick and tired of the time you steal from us every weekend," I'd said, holding back tears.

I looked at Harvey as if it were the last time I'd see him. Maybe I should have taken his mother's bribe; then I could leave him and move on with my life. We both knew our African wedding had no legal status whatsoever and could easily be overridden by a Western marriage if Harvey met another girl; his mom hoped for this with all her heart.

Exiting the taxi, we walked silently into the Vancouver airport. I felt an urge to tell him why I didn't want to live in Holland but kept it to myself; at the same time I struggled not to cry. *This man loves me, so why am I doing nothing to reciprocate?* We hugged and kissed; he passed through the gate but came back as quickly as he'd gone. The passengers nearby turned around and followed us with their eyes. Harvey guided me away from the crowd into a small corner beside the washroom entrance.

"I love you, and I'll be back for good next time we meet," he said.

I didn't respond but wondered whether my decision to live in Canada was in fact the right one. *Am I really this stupid to be staying in Vancouver alone? This man loves me and is willing to do anything for me, yet I'm just going to let him go? What if he's right? What if he finds somebody on the plane, a Dutch woman his mother will like better than me? What if he finds one at work? Am I doing the right thing by saying goodbye?*

I felt a slight panic rise within me and wondered what my mother would advise right at this moment. *Mom, can you listen to my heart? Do you feel my pain? Are you really here? Are there any trees where you are right now? Which tree would you be? Please tell me what to do. You have been gone so long that I'm starting to forget your face. Are you in my dreams?*

In the taxi home I kept hearing his voice as big, salty, untameable tears ran down my cheeks. "I love you a lot." And "I'll be back." The words echoed in my head, but he was gone.

Chapter 5
Children and motherhood

Finding out Linda was pregnant – Vancouver, summer 2004

I couldn't imagine that I'd conceived, because I'd sworn I'd never be pregnant or have kids, no matter what. I doubted my vagina was capable of such a thing after all it had been through, and I'd seen my mother die from giving birth.

We had been living together for ten years now, and only once had we mentioned babies – on our honeymoon in Saint Louise, Senegal. We were strolling on the beach after a delicious cassava dinner with freshly grilled fish and fried banana plantain, which we had both enjoyed.

"Do you want to have kids?" I asked, his hand in one of mine and my sandals in the other.

"If it's meant to be, yes," he said.

"Indeed: yes, if it's meant to be. I like the sound of that," I said, leaning into him. "So you're not going to ask me to have babies all the time?"

"I won't," he said and leaned into me as well. "It will come when the time is right," he added quickly, and we ambled into the Atlantic waves.

Vancouver, July 2004

After Harvey's first visit to Vancouver, I'd continued studying English as a Second Language at UBC. Right after graduation, it occurred to me that, finally, I could go to acting school, a long-time dream of mine, and not worry about being a diplomat, like my father wanted me to be.

Meanwhile, Harvey and I also realized we couldn't do long-distance for too long, so he applied for his landed-immigrant papers so he could move to Canada. Even though he was born Dutch, the immigration process was taking a long time, and I needed to do something that would make the wait go by faster. We both agreed that since I'd always wanted to be an actress, it made sense for me to attend an acting school.

I worried that my father would be upset, but Harvey reassured me that I was his wife now and he had the right to advise. With his encouragement, I enrolled in the Vancouver Film School. Consumed with the demands of classes and my love of acting, I found that time passed quickly; before we knew it, we were together again.

We settled into a two-bedroom, two-bath apartment with an open kitchen and den in Yaletown, where everything was within walking distance, including trendy restaurants and supermarkets such as Urban Fare, which stocked most of our European foods. Still in love, Harvey and I couldn't take our hands off each other. We both knew I was not on the pill; I was allergic to most of them and bled too much with others, so I stopped taking them altogether. We used a condom whenever in doubt, but most of the time, in the heat of the moment, the prophylactic would land on the floor.

In the summer of 2004, to celebrate my graduation, we vacationed in Paris – our first visit. The city exceeded all expectations and never deceived when it came to love, according to many lovers, and we, too, had the time of our lives. Sex! Romance! God, I loved it then!

A month had gone by since our return. Harvey bought a pregnancy-test kit at the supermarket, but I was unable to pee on the test stick despite trying several times.

"Keep it until you're ready, but if you can't figure it out by yourself it's time to see a doctor," he advised as he stepped out the door.

I went back to the bathroom, sat on the toilet and managed to pee on the stick, but when I was almost finished I saw blood coming out. I stood up and watched it drip through my tights to my knees, ankles, and finally the floor. I looked up and found myself in the big mirror. It felt like I was back in my old prison cell.

Wordless, incapable of moving, I waited until my feet could take one step, then a few more. Once in the shower, I watched my blood washing away, a red sea flood going down the drain slowly.

I stepped out and then back in, soaping myself again quickly without looking down. I put in a tampon, deciding to keep what had happened to myself. I had mixed feelings about the blood and the probability that I was pregnant.

That day I didn't do much but take a short walk around the sea wall to English Bay. Arriving home, I waited for Harvey and hugged him the minute he came through the door.

"What a warm welcome!" he said, smiling broadly. "Are you OK?"

"Yes, I am."

"Shall we go out for dinner?" he asked.

"Sushi," I said. Vancouver has the freshest and most delicious sushi.

"Sushi's not a good idea at the start of a pregnancy." He walked to the bathroom to wash his hands.

"What happened to the carpet here?" he asked. I came to check. "These red dots, they look like blood. They weren't here when I left this morning." He looked to me for an answer.

"I hadn't noticed them. Maybe I cut myself," I said.

"You cut yourself? Where and when? Did you try cooking again?" He entered the kitchen to see if anything was amiss.

The last time I had attempted to prepare a meal, the fire department was called. I'd dropped prawns right from the freezer into hot oil and tried to extinguish the fire with water; the more water I added, the higher the flames grew. We both agreed I should stay out of the kitchen from then on.

"No," I said, staring at the spots. The carpet was white but now it had blood on it. I wondered how I'd missed seeing this before he came home. I got the stain remover from the pantry, but Harvey took it away from me.

"I'm not asking you to clean it. I'm just wondering where it came from," he said, spraying the detergent himself. I was no longer listening. I was back in Africa with my aunt Halle having a similar conversation.

The day my first period began, my aunt had said, "Kenda, what's that stain on the back of your dress?"

"Dirt?" I asked and turned around to see what she meant. When she pulled the seat of the oversized garment around to the front to show me, I began to weep.

"Why are you crying?" she asked.

"Because I'm dying."

"Who said a bloodstain on your dress is fatal?"

"I'm going to die like my mother in the hospital," I cried, wiping tears with the back of my hand.

"No, Kenda. This isn't that kind of blood. Do you know what it could be?"

"No," I said, still drying my tears with her help.

"This means you're a woman now and can have babies and even get married. Let's go to the river and get you washed. I'll tell you all about it," she said, smiling.

"Are you having your period?" Harvey asked as we scrubbed the rug together.

"Maybe," I said, avoiding his eyes.

"Maybe what, Linda? Why can't you trust me with your secrets?" he asked.

"What secrets? I don't have any secrets, and I'm not pregnant," I insisted.

"Then you're having your period. What I can't understand is how come there's blood everywhere between the bathroom and the shower. The entire corridor has stains."

I said nothing and kept on cleaning. I silently scolded myself again for not having seen to this before his return.

"Maybe we'd better call our carpet cleaner," he suggested.

"I agree, and I'm starving for sushi," I said. I washed my hands in the bathroom and started getting ready. I love sushi, so if anybody says "Sushi," I'm on to it at the speed of light.

"No sushi for you," Harvey repeated.

"Says who?"

"Says me. Until you see Dr. Brian and he confirms you're not pregnant, no raw fish," he said, putting the cleaners and stain remover back into the pantry. The carpet looked OK, but it retained some strange patches. We may have made it worse by spreading the redness. The blood stains had become ochre blotches.

"Why do you know so much about women's things?" I asked when we were both finally ready to leave.

"My first –" He stopped. I waited.

"My first girlfriend was a gynecologist." I finished his sentence and didn't comment further.

At our favourite Japanese restaurant on Granville Street, we dined in silence, and it felt like an eternity. I sensed Harvey had millions of questions he knew I wouldn't answer.

Weeks went by quickly, but I still was unable to eat as much as I wanted without throwing up. I'd made it clear to Harvey that he should stop asking me to go see someone. Since my health was not improving, however, he insisted I see Dr. Brian.

"I hate doctors!" I shouted, almost crying.

"You don't hate doctors. You hate going to the hospital," he said.

"OK, then, I hate going to the hospital."

"Going to see our family physician doesn't mean you'll wind up in hospital. It's just to make sure you're okay. I'm worried about you, Linda," he said, holding me.

Linda confirms she's pregnant – Vancouver, Dr. Brian's office

As the weeks passed, the silence between Harvey and me grew. I continued throwing up and couldn't even keep water down. Being vegetarian didn't help. I looked gaunt, always felt tired, and was extremely moody. At last, consulting Dr. Brian seemed like a good idea. Harvey came with me, which I did not want at first.

"Please allow me, Linda. Let me be there for you," he pleaded.

"OK. If you stop asking questions, you can come along."

"I won't ask you anything anymore, but I will ask the doctor. Is that a deal?" he said.

"As long as I don't have to answer anything, I'm fine."

Since we had an appointment we didn't wait long. After I filled out the medical form and provided a urine sample, we were shown into one of Dr. Brian's examination rooms.

"How are you guys doing?" Dr. Brian asked with his usual kindly smile. He had my file in his hands.

"Fine," we both answered. He checked me without talking but was very gentle.

"Congratulations, you're pregnant!" he said, beaming at me. Harvey stood up next to him and took my hands as tears rolled down my cheeks. I was not sure what the tears were about, but at that moment I had a sneaking feeling of joy, particularly on seeing Harvey's delighted smile.

"Congratulations, Harvey!" Dr. Brian said, offering a firm hand shake.

"You'll need some blood tests. They have nothing to do with your health or anything," he went on, turning back to me. "Just routine procedure. From here on, you'll keep seeing me, but at some point we'll transfer you to an OBG, who will watch your pregnancy and help you deliver the baby," Dr. Brian said.

"She did have some bleeding last month," Harvey observed.

"Sometimes that happens, but it's nothing to worry about. She just has to take it easy and avoid heavy lifting. Again, congratulations!" Dr. Brian helped me get down off the examination table.

Harvey looked distant and thoughtful. I felt like saying something but I held my peace. Didn't he want to be a father? Was he really ready for this? Was I? Was anyone ever truly ready to have kids or get married?

Once I was into my third month, I was still throwing up, so bed rest was ordered. Harvey was worried about my inability to keep anything down and about something else he had been unable to share with me.

He often found a way to vary our nature walks, either into the forest or simply on the beach. This time, we drove to Burnaby Park in another municipality south of Vancouver. Since it was a late Sunday afternoon, the park was bustling with parents and their kids, dogs and their owners, and even some equestrians. The pond in the middle was filled with screeching geese and goslings, which the wind seemed to blow off course; with each blast, a mother goose came running to keep her babies safe.

"Mother Nature, eh?" Harvey said.

"Yes. And for somebody who didn't want to come here, you just said 'eh' like a real Canadian," I teased. He held me and kissed my forehead.

Expecting the first child – Vancouver, summer 2004

I couldn't wait for my belly to start showing and was so happy when it did, even though the first months had been tough. Each week became a celebration of sorts along with every visit to the doctor. My ultrasounds went well, and both Harvey and I were reassured by the good health of our unborn baby, whose sex we chose not to know.

"Should I tell you if it's a boy or girl?" the technician had asked, smearing cold jelly on me.

"No," I said.

"Are you sure you don't want to know?" Harvey asked.

"Yes. I kind of know anyway, you know," I said.

"What do you mean, you kind of know?" the woman asked.

"I prayed for it," I said.

"What do you think we're going to have, then?" Harvey challenged me with a smile.

"A boy," I said matter-of-factly, as if I'd peeked at the baby's sex on the ultrasound.

"Harvey, don't look at me," the technician said, smiling. She kept her eyes and hands on her task. "I haven't said anything yet. And every time you've been here, too, pocketing the pictures right away."

"Sorry. Now I remember when she prayed all night to have a boy," he said thoughtfully.

The infant's heartbeat made us feel as though we'd entered a realm beyond our control. It gave us hope that soon enough we would have a healthy mini-Harvey.

As the weeks added up to months, my restlessness found an outlet in redecorating the entire house. I didn't choose a colour, even though I felt in my heart that I was going to have a boy. God was too good to give me a girl.

Right before birth with Dr. Carter – Vancouver, April 1, 2005

In the last weeks of my pregnancy, all I wanted, all I looked forward to, was giving birth, even though deep down it was what I feared the most. I was scared of dying in childbirth like my mother. I was due this month. We had our second bedroom transformed for the infant's arrival, and the excitement affected everyone around us, including Harvey's kin and my extended family in West Africa.

Many strangers, going by how my belly looked and the shape of my body from behind, predicted I was going to have a boy. Nobody could see that I was pregnant until they bumped into me; they'd apologize once they saw me from the front.

I'd been meeting Dr. Carter, my prenatal psychologist, every two weeks since I was four months pregnant.

"Is there anything you want to talk about, Lawra Linda, other than your mother, today?" Dr. Carter would attempt to have a normal conversation.

"Yes," I said.

"What?" she asked

"I like the mountains in Vancouver," I replied.

"Why?"

"Because I feel grounded by their presence."

"Do you ski?" she asked.

"No. I've tried snowboarding," I said and shifted on the couch to my left side. We both noticed the baby's continued kicks through my stretchy shirt.

"Does your baby kick a lot?" she asked.

"Yes," I said as I rubbed my belly.

"Do you like that?"

"I'm not sure, but I think it's a good thing, because it shows that it's alive, the GP said."

"That's correct. It looks like a big, healthy baby in there," she noted with a smile.

"Yes."

"Do you know how you want to have the child delivered?"

"What do you mean?"

"Natural birth or C-section?" she asked. I sat up straight.

"Why do people always ask a pregnant woman to choose her method of delivery? Has it been an hour already?" I asked.

"No," she said.

"Can I go now?"

"Do you want to go now?"

"Yes."

"Do you want to meet every week now instead of every two weeks?" she asked.

"Why?"

"Because as the end of your pregnancy approaches, we need to prepare you psychologically for the big day. Usually, the closer we get to the due date, the more frequent the meetings."

"Is this a need or a want?" I stood up.

"It's both, if you'd like me to be honest with you," she said, standing as well.

"Oh, I see."

"Your husband is worried about you, you know, and so am I. Please trust me with your pain," she said, helping me with my coat. "How about next week, same time?"

"OK then, next Wednesday afternoon at two," I said, leaving the room with the appointment reminder on the yellow sticky note she had handed to me.

I found Harvey waiting in the hallway next to the coffee machine, sipping his Americano. I handed him the piece of paper without commenting on it. He smiled, walked me to the parking lot, and opened my door. On the way home, we shared our usual silence, but it didn't last long.

"How did it go today?" he said without taking his eyes off the road.

"I'll see her every Wednesday at two until the day I deliver," I said.

"That's nice of her," he said, retrieving the paper from his pocket and scanning it.

"Did you ask her to do this?"

"Yes. I talked to her last week, because I still see and feel that you're not there yet."

"There yet?" I said.

"Yes. You talk a lot in your sleep, or, let's say, during the short time you're able to sleep," he said, looking at me.

"I do?"

"Yes. At times you wave your hands in the air as if pushing somebody away. I'm really worried about you."

"I'm very healthy, the baby is strong and growing just fine, so what's the worry?"

"You're both doing great physically, but you're not fine psychologically."

"I wouldn't worry too much about that, you know. Psychology is white people's problem. I'm going to pop this baby out in no time," I said, rubbing my belly.

He glanced at my tummy. "It definitely kicks a lot!"

I felt a strong, unexpected pain in my upper leg and then in my vagina that I was unable to hide.

"Ouch!!"

"Are you OK?" he asked.

Since we were not far from the St. Paul hospital, he took me to the emergency department and they quickly placed me in a room. It was my first Braxton Hicks and a sciatic-nerve alarm. They didn't send me home right away, because I was bleeding slightly as well. They prescribed bed rest, so any physical activity would be prohibited. I'd already stopped my yoga class.

Since I was in the same hospital where Dr. Carter practiced, Harvey walked me over to see her. Her assistant, Magritte, a UBC student doing her practicum, had come searching for us. She took us to the doctor's office and made me comfortable, asking if I wanted anything to drink.

"Water will do. Thank you," I said.

"Harvey, are you staying or waiting for her in the coffee room?"

"You can stay, if you want, Harvey," I said.

After offering Harvey some coffee, Magritte left us alone.

Dr. Carter entered with a smile. "You look radiant, Lawra Linda. Are you staying with us today?" She looked at Harvey and me.

"Yes. She wants me to," he said.

"Then so be it," she replied. "Will you be in the same room when Lawra Linda is having her baby, Harvey?"

"Yes –" he said.

"They killed her, and they killed her by cutting her clitoris, her vulva, and sewing her vagina to keep her virginity. She bled to death because she was too old for what they did to her. They killed her in the name of tradition, and I was not there to protect her. I've failed my mother and my brothers and her for not being there when she most needed me. I wish I'd taken her away from Africa in time to prevent it, but how would I have managed on my own? How could this happen? I'm scared to have a daughter. My family will kill me if I don't do the same thing to her that they did to my sister and me."

"What are you talking about, Lawra Linda? Are you OK?" Harvey said, quickly sitting down next to me on the couch.

"I just now realized, that's what happened to Nenein! They're monsters. I'll never go back to Africa again. How am I going to have this baby? How? What am I going to do if it's a girl? Please take me home. I want to go home now," I said through my tears, holding onto Harvey.

"Female genital mutilation should be forbidden and banned like all harmful traditional practices," Dr. Carter said. She understood that I spoke reasonably despite my high emotion. "Mutilation, child marriage and unwanted pregnancies cause terrible suffering and result in thousands of young women dying in labour every day around the world. I hope you find the strength someday to encourage women like you to speak up, to become activists protecting the next generation of girls in Africa or any developing country, so we don't lose more lives because of it."

Pausing, thoughtfully, she asked, "Would you want to be an advocate for this? It could be something to look forward to down the road. You never know whose life you could change with your story."

I kept quiet and hid my face on Harvey's chest. If I couldn't understand my own pain, how could I help anyone else? Why would she even think of suggesting such a thing right now? *I should have kept quiet.* I burst into fresh tears.

"None of what happened to your sister or to you will be happening to our child, whatever sex that baby is. We'll be different parents. Please keep that in mind and know that I love you and will continue to love you for the rest of our lives. I'm so proud of you, Linda; it's beyond words. Believe me, I love you," Harvey said firmly, as if he were taking an oath aimed at erasing everything mournful from my past.

"I'll give you a call, for sure, Dr. Carter. Thank you for all your help," Harvey added, shaking her hand.

Linda is hospitalized before childbirth

My baby was due on April 10, but for some reason, he kept waiting to arrive; it was beyond our control. My sciatica was killing me, and my bladder always seemed ready to burst, pushing against my cervix. I felt I needed to tuck a bathroom in my handbag, although I'd stopped carrying one; I was too tired, and slow and grumpy most of the time.

Crossing the street was a nightmare. I hated that the light would turn while I'd still be in the middle of the road. Impatient drivers would honk, not seeing or knowing they had to contend not with a pedestrian but with a duck. I even refused to cross the street in front of my house if Harvey had the car; I loathed the intersection at Pacific Boulevard in particular. To avoid it, I'd walk around the building trying to get to Urban Fare on Davie, but that was no practical solution either.

Harvey and I agreed that from then on, he'd ensure the fridge was full of my favourite veggies, fruits and seafood I had started eating to get more protein. By the time the baby came, I was no longer a vegetarian.

One day, without telling Harvey, I went to the mall by metro. Having left home at 10 and arriving around noon, I was famished. Without thinking, I went to the food court; I wanted something Indian. Anything Indian with naan appealed to me, so I could hardly wait to reach the front of the line where a woman was serving.

"Are you having triplets?" she asked.

"I don't know," I said curtly.

"Sorry you don't seem to like my question. How can I help you?"

"I want the spinach with lentil and one naan. Do you have naan fresh from the oven that isn't burned?" I asked.

"Yes; I'll make it all happen for you, and don't worry about coming to get it. I'll bring it to you," she said.

I paid and made my way to the front of the seating area next to her food section. Fifteen minutes later, I had what I'd ordered, along with a fresh naan cooked to my liking and a bottle of water. I took a sip from it first and then bit into the naan.

Suddenly, I felt something moving deep down between my legs, like the baby's head was pushing against my bottom. Only a pinch at first, it became an excruciating pain that I tried to control with deep breathing. But in vain. Then, I went blank.

I woke in the back of a restaurant that smelled like curry with a woman who just minutes ago, or maybe it had been hours, had served me food, a dish I couldn't wait to eat.

"You fainted. Are you OK now?" she said.

"I think so; I was too hungry … and … I think I'm also having too much pain," I said.

"Is there anyone who can pick you up?" she asked.

I was unable to respond as fast as I wanted. The pain between my legs was muting my desire to speak. I pressed the redial button on my cell phone, ringing Harvey, who was working in one of his stores, Morgan de Toi, in Metrotown Metropolis, one of the largest and trendiest malls in BC. He sounded surprised that I'd gone to the mall without passing by his office first.

The woman made me comfortable on a chair while we waited for Harvey. Meanwhile, she was nervous.

"Do you want me to call the ambulance instead?" she asked.

"No. I don't want to go to the hospital," I said.

When I heard Harvey's voice at the front, the woman left to fetch him. "Are you OK?" he asked.

"A little, but I really don't know. Do you think I'm in labour?"

"It could be labour, because … what's the date?" he asked, looking around.

"It's April 20," the woman said, checking a calendar at the back of the restaurant.

"Well, you were due on April 10," he remarked drily.

"I really don't care. Get me out of this place before I have my baby in the mall!"

"She's going to have triplets; I think she's in labour now," the woman said.

Harvey thanked her and walked me to his store, where we entered from the back. He made sure I was comfortable and went to get his car from the parking lot. The pain was coming in waves, but it was inconsistent, so I could still stand up and walk around. We got in, and Harvey drove as quickly as he could without breaking the law. I moaned a bit and held my breath.

"Please don't hold your breath; instead, inhale deeply and exhale slowly," he said. I tried to keep at it but forgot, most of the time, when the pain hit me hard in the cervix. The more intense the pain grew, the more agitated and restless I became.

"Please keep breathing, and take deep, deep, deep breaths each time," he said, almost forgetting the road. A car honked and another driver shouted at him through his lowered windows. He didn't react to either and just kept racing up the bridge.

Had we been heading home, he would have exited onto Pacific Boulevard, but instead he continued on Smith toward Granville Street.

"Where are you going, Harvey?" I asked.

"To the hospital," he said.

"No. No. I don't want to go to the hospital."

"We have to go for your delivery," he insisted.

"I'll die if you take me there."

"No, you won't. You think you're going to die? Of course not – not today. Where did you get this from? We're going to emergency and then the obstetric unit," he said, turning.

"I'm going to die, and the baby is going to die as well. Please take me home!" I said.

"Nobody is going to die, Linda," he said, looking back at me.

"Take me home now!" I shouted with all my being.

He gave in. "I'll take you home, then. Please keep your energy for the big thing and don't get angry. What am I going to do with you at home?" he asked.

"You'll call our doula," I said.

"Our doula. Yes, I'll call our doula … you're right." He looked calm when we arrived, and so did I.

"Can you please check that everything is where it's supposed to be?"

I rested on the couch facing the picture window that was so clean it felt like the outside had come in. I could easily bump into it, not realizing it was there. The sun was bright, and the trees were blossoming into their predictable spring colours. I was distracted by the sea water at high tide in the distance, under the bridge. I relaxed a little because of the view, all the beauty my eyes were taking in.

"I can't find your bag," Harvey said, coming from the bedroom.

"Which bag are you talking about?"

"The one we prepared for the hospital," he said and scratched his head.

"Did you call the doula?"

"Yes. She said to keep calling her as the contractions got closer," he replied.

"It sounded like you were calling the hospital."

I went to look for the bag and Harvey followed me into the room.

"I really want her here. What if I urgently need her?" Opening the sliding closet door, I noticed something black in the right corner.

"That looks…?" I asked Harvey and stepped away.

"Yes, that's the bag." He pulled it out and put it in the middle of the bed.

"It's a black bag?!" I shouted. Harvey looked startled.

"I asked for a purple bag and you put all the things in this black bag!" I said.

"Well, I remember buying purple, but the cleaning lady must have used this one instead." He continued looking in the closets, under the bed and inside the cubby of the washroom before entering the baby's room and searching the storage space there.

"I found the purple bag," he said, returning to me. He repacked all the baby clothes from the black bag into the purple one.

Meanwhile, I was groaning in pain. He quickly put away the bulging bag. I started gagging as if I were going to throw up, but my stomach was empty.

"When was the last time you ate?" Harvey asked.

"I don't remember. Maybe this morning. I wanted to have lunch first in the mall, before I went to see you at the store, but then of course I didn't."

"You've got to eat something. You really have to do better than this, Linda. I need you to eat, and make sure you do before you get really hungry," he said.

"Not now, Harvey. I don't need a father or a mother figure."

"Yes, you're right, but I worry about you with food ... What would you like?" He headed into the kitchen.

"I'm not sure I want to eat now, Harvey. It'll take too long. Please leave me alone."

I heard my mother's voice in my head. *"What took you so long, Galle?"*

"I'm sorry that I made you wait, Mother. It was really nothing, Mother," I said, wondering why there was blood in the little red vase that had just been broken.

"What did you order in the mall when you started having pain?" Harvey called from the kitchen.

"Indian food," I shouted back. He returned with a plate of spinach salad and chickpeas, freshly cut carrots and cucumbers.

"I guess you wanted the paneer. Here's a spinach salad with stir-fried tuna. It's not the same, but it's healthy for you and the baby," he said.

"I'm not sick, you know. Why are you serving me in bed? Please help me to the kitchen," I said, lifting myself up.

Once I was well seated with a pillow at my back, I took a few bites of the salad and then a little tuna; I noticed that it was not well cooked on the inside. Everything came right back out onto my plate.

Harvey helped me clean up and take a quick shower before he rubbed some lotion on me and put me to bed. For some reason, the pain had stopped.

Our bed was full of pillows of all shapes and sizes to keep me comfortable. I put the biggest between my legs, one under my back and two under my calves. I felt Harvey leave the room and fell into a deep sleep. I woke at eight in the evening.

"That was a very long nap, Mrs. B," Harvey said, joining me in the bedroom.

"How long did I sleep?" I asked, looking at the clock next to the bed stand.

"Long enough for our doula to come see you asleep and say you're doing great."

"Why didn't you wake me?" I asked.

"She said to let you sleep as you needed and that this happens sometimes when labour stops; the mother rests to gather energy and be more relaxed when the time comes to deliver. She also mentioned that sometimes sex induces and speeds up the process."

"Don't look at me like that."

"I'm not asking for sex, even though you look very sexy right now," he said, seating himself on the bed.

"Me looking sexy … are you sure about that?" I replied. "Do you want to have sex before I deliver? Maybe it's a good idea, because it will be a while before we can have sex again, don't you think?"

"It'll depend, really, on how soon you want it, or how long it takes you to heal after giving birth. Won't it?" he said.

"How long does it take other mammals?" I asked, and he laughed.

"I wish I knew the answer. You are really Linda, my Linda, who comes up with a question like that. Only you, and for that I love you and will always love you, and, yes, you're beautiful and attractive and I want you and will always want you, my darling." He said the last part in Dutch.

He undressed and lay down behind me with a full erection, which surprised me a bit and pleased me, too; knowing he desired me right then made me feel loved and cherished. I was also a little concerned.

What if my pain starts again? What if my water breaks when he's inside me?

He was already rubbing my back and my belly down to my legs. It felt nice and relaxing, but by the time we'd finished having sex, I was bleeding all over the mattress. Had my water broken? It hadn't. He helped me into the bath and rinsed me off. I couldn't stop seeing my mother's blood under her hospital bed.

"Linda, we really have to leave for the hospital. Try to be with me always and don't think about Africa, because this isn't Africa, you know. You'll be fine. Please say yes, and let's go have our baby."

Breastfeeding right after childbirth

Following two full nights of labour, struggle and pain, during which both the baby and I fought for our lives, Josh was born. It hadn't happened the way I wanted or how I imagined it would be. I was very sleepy when I first held him. The nurse and Harvey were trying to help me feed him.

"Breastfeeding? Are you kidding?" I asked. I didn't expect an answer, because I was then in a world totally foreign to me. I had to at least try to breastfeed after failing to have Josh naturally. The C-section had made it difficult for me to sit up, and without Harvey's assistance nursing would have been impossible.

"Linda, Linda, Linda, are you awake? The baby's hungry, and the nurse and Dr. Carter are here to help you."

"Hmm, leave me alone. I'm tired. I'm really very, very tired. Leave me alone," I murmured.

Harvey begged me to wake up. "You told me to make sure that you breastfed no matter what, that the first thing our baby should have was your breast milk. Remember?"

"I don't care anymore. I don't want anything. I won't breastfeed, since I didn't give birth naturally. Everything is artificial, so I won't nurse either." I was more alert but still drowsy from the anesthesia.

"Linda. Please just give it a try. You'll be thankful you did, because it's good for both of you," Dr. Carter advised.

"Oh, yes. It's the best thing you can do for your baby right now," added the nurse.

"Do you have a name for him yet?" Dr. Carter asked kindly, leaning toward me.

"Yes, we do," Harvey said enthusiastically. "His name is Josh." He proudly lifted our son up to show Dr. Carter and the nurse.

"He's beautiful," the doctor remarked.

"With a handsome name, as well," the nurse added. "He shares it with a famous Vancouver singer. Do you know him?"

"No," Harvey said. He didn't take his eyes off the newborn son squirming in his hands.

"He's getting hungry," said Dr. Carter.

"We'll help you feed him, Lawra Linda," the nurse offered, taking Josh from Harvey.

Under Dr. Carter's watchful eyes, Harvey managed to sit me up at an angle that would make it easy to nest our infant in my arms. Once the nurse handed him to me, I gently uncovered my left breast and listened as she explained how to put my nipple into Josh's mouth. At first, I started crying and refused to do it.

I was wondering whether my mother or my grandmother had needed all this fuss to breastfeed their firstborn. Certainly not – they did it on their own, as they had given birth on their own, in their own space. Why did my motherhood have to be so different from theirs, since I was also a black woman born in Africa? This was my biggest failure. *How could this happen to me?*

As if she were reading my thoughts, Dr. Carter said, "Linda, many women have C-sections. The important thing is that you're both healthy."

"Yes," the nurse added enthusiastically while attempting to put Josh back onto my breast. I turned away and my tears kept falling.

"No. Everything went wrong, and I've failed at being a woman," I sobbed.

"Not at all," Dr. Carter insisted.

Josh started crying, so Harvey washed his hands and took him back. He had been washing them all the time – each time he was to take Josh in his arms. He gave him his thumb, and Josh sucked it vigorously.

"Look, Linda. He can suck already, so it won't hurt," Harvey said, holding the baby toward me.

"He's really hungry," the nurse reiterated with concern on her face. "I'm going to prepare a bottle, just in case, because he needs to eat."

"Not so fast," said Dr. Carter.

The nurse had been halfway out the door but came back in. "OK. Linda, let's give it another try."

Suddenly, I found myself in nurse Hellen's presence as my mother struggled to birth my brother. The memory was crushing.

"Linda. Be with us," Dr. Carter begged. "I need you to take care of your son. You love him, don't you?"

"Yes," I mumbled, focusing on Josh in Harvey's loving hands; he was still nuzzling his father's thumb.

"He needs his mommy right now. Can you help him? He's famished." She took Josh and put him in my arm. He immediately grabbed my nipple, which was big, anyway, so it was not difficult to find. I felt a pinch and bit my lips. It hurt and didn't feel nice at all.

I felt tears on my face. I didn't know if they were from sadness, pain, or feeling overwhelmed. I leaned slowly back on the bed as the nurse adjusted it and Harvey watched carefully to make sure I didn't turn over on the infant.

"Please, just remove Josh for burping when he stops by himself. If you need more help, we'll go over exercises designed to help him belch later on," said the nurse.

Linda locks herself in her room after Josh's birth

Two weeks had passed since I'd left the hospital with my baby securely seated in the back of our brand-new white Beetle. Harvey and I had had an hour's training and even watched a video on infant safety in the car seat as well as in the stroller, which I was still struggling to open. The nurse who was dedicated to helping me through and teaching me everything a new mother needed to know – things like breastfeeding, burping, changing diapers, bathing, wrapping the baby tightly and comfortably after his bath and rubbing his gums with a cloth – showed extraordinary patience and competence at her job, which she loved with all her being.

"We used to think it best to wait until the baby's teeth appeared before starting to brush, but over the years studies have shown that cleaning an infant's mouth with a cloth and massaging their gums is beneficial in the long run. It's even a great thing to do for teething because it soothes the tissue, each evening or morning when you give him his bath," nurse Emma said.

Harvey was sponging and practicing whatever she showed him.

"Can I wash him every day?" I asked.

"Babies don't really need daily washing; every other day would be just fine. If you want to bathe him more often, I highly recommend a sponge bath to avoid drying his skin," she advised.

"We'll think about it and do what's right for Josh," Harvey responded kindly, as if to avoid overstepping the nurse's boundaries.

"Yes, as you go through parenting with everybody and every book telling you what to do, you'll find your own way. Then I'll also stop my visits – when Lawra Linda feels she is settled on her journey as a mother." She smiled and kept her eyes on Josh.

"I'm fine now, Mrs. Emma. I think I can take care of Josh alright on my own," I said.

"Maybe it's best to wait until I come back from Europe; this way you won't be on your own," Harvey added.

"When are you leaving, Harvey?" Emma asked.

"Tomorrow, and I'll be back in a week. I'm going to Paris for the Morgan de Toi fall/spring collection fashion show to buy for our stores."

"Are you a fashion designer?" she asked.

"No. A franchise manager for Morgan de Toi in Canada." Being called a designer elicited a smile.

"Is this trip a must?" she inquired.

"I've asked about buying from my franchisers' websites, but so far neither emails nor calls have provided clear answers. More important, though, my father is very ill. He's in the hospital awaiting surgery. I know, considering the circumstances, I should stay here, but what if he dies? I feel I have no alternative but to fly there for at least the day of his operation and hopefully come back right away. It could be only three days that I'm gone."

Harvey was holding Josh, who had just woken up in his crib.

"It's fine to leave him alone in his crib as much as you can," Emma advised. "That way he'll learn to self-soothe and go to sleep by himself. Just make sure to remove blankets or other bedding that could interfere with his breathing."

"Well, that's good, but right now I want to hold him," Harvey replied, smiling and swaying. "So that's what I'm doing, nurse Emma. I see no harm in it. Maybe he can join us in bed tonight ... how about that, Maman?"

"Absolutely not. It's essential to leave him in his crib. I know this is the moment to bond, but you have to follow newborn guidelines," she said, taking a step toward the door. "Do you have anybody else coming to help out while you're gone, Harvey?"

"I'm fine, and we'll be fine," I said.

"Are you?" Harvey asked.

"Yes; and we have nurse Emma coming next week anyway," I added, taking Josh from Harvey to breastfeed him.

"You two look comfortable, as if you've been doing this for quite some time. The milk is flowing all right and Josh's weight is going up, even though, as a ten-pounder, he really doesn't need to put on much right now. In fact, he might lose some, but it's all part of the process. And if he doesn't, because nursing is going so well, there's nothing to worry about there, either. How about I come every day until Harvey's back?"

"Mrs. Emma, you've been a godsend to our family," Harvey said. "We thank you very much, and I'll make sure I have somebody – even if it's my assistant – to keep an eye on both of them while I'm away."

"Your employee will do it, then. What do you think, Lawra Linda?" She looked at me as I sat on the couch.

"Do you mean Misha, the store manager, or your office assistant?" I asked.

"Yes, Misha."

"Well, if you say so, but when she came to visit us in the hospital she said she doesn't like babies and would never be a mother."

"You don't need her to like babies for her to bring you water or wait while you shower when Josh is sleeping or walk with you outside with the stroller. It would be refreshing just to have somebody other than you and the baby for the first days or weeks of new motherhood. Don't you think?" the nurse countered.

"I don't want to go outside," I said.

"Have you been out since you came home from the hospital?" she asked, looking at the closed curtains of our living room. She walked past me and opened them. I saw the water through the picture window. The reflection seemed to reveal something foreign and mesmerizing in the distance, unwelcome to me.

"No," Harvey said.

"Why?" she asked.

"Can you please shut the curtains, Mrs. Emma? I really don't want to step foot outside." I kept my eyes glued on Josh, fearful he'd lose his latch and I'd need help getting him back on my breast.

"I recommend walking with them tonight," the midwife told Harvey, "before you leave tomorrow, and when I come back on Monday we'll take another stroll while Josh naps," she said.

"No." Josh squirmed in my hands, let go of my nipple and started to cry.

"He needs burping," she said.

"What's that?" I asked, looking up at both Harvey and the nurse.

"Sometimes a baby swallows air when you are breastfeeding, or he cries; then you need to burp him."

"How will we know?" Harvey asked.

"Because he'll arch his body or wiggle or cry," Emma explained.

"Can I try?" Ready to follow instructions, Harvey took Josh.

"Hold the baby against your chest, making sure his chin is resting on your shoulder. Support the rest of his body with one hand while gently pressing his back or tapping it if the rub doesn't work. At this early age, some babies won't belch, but if you keep practising, eventually he'll start."

Under the watchful eye and helpful hands of nurse Emma, Harvey kept gently rubbing Josh's back and tapping it ever so slightly, but he didn't burp.

"You can make the tap a little stronger and more precise. Babies are strong," she said.

"Oh. OK, then." Harvey did exactly as he was told until Josh gave a few big burps that made all of us laugh. Even though that was the very first time I heard the baby's burp, Harvey looked as though he had been born taking care of him.

"I have to leave now but I'll be back on Monday around nine. Please have Misha come this weekend to see them. You have a great flight!" Emma said after making sure my nipple was comfortably back in Josh's mouth.

Harvey brought me a glass of water. "She's a very nice lady," he remarked.

"Yes, she is, but I will not go outside," I said.

"Please, let's at least go through the motions, even if you just get dressed and we put Josh in the stroller and go down the elevator to the entrance of the building and come back – that will be enough for today," Harvey pleaded.

"How about you prepare dinner and we'll think about it while we eat. You're convinced it's best to take him out the first time at night?" I asked.

"It doesn't matter, really, because we'll still have daylight; he's a spring baby," Harvey said as he changed Josh's diaper.

"Shall we give him a bath only every second day?"

"I understand where Mrs. Emma is coming from with her advice, but my mother said it's best to have a proper routine from the very beginning," Harvey said.

"We'll give him a bath every day, then, and go to bed with him as well?"

"Yes, I think that will make your breastfeeding easier. Then I'll change him after you've fed him, without you getting out of bed; this will give you some extra sleep."

"But you're leaving me … us … tomorrow."

"Yes. And you're fine to do his bath, aren't you?"

"What if he slips out of my hands and falls?"

"He may be massive, but you won't drop him. Believe me, I'm very happy he's this big; I was terrified he might be tiny. Having a big boy boosts my confidence as a father," Harvey confided, lifting Josh from the changing table.

"That size almost killed me giving birth. I haven't done anything with him other than breastfeed since then, and even now I'm not entirely confident or able to relax when he's nursing," I said.

"Does your scar still hurt?"

"Only when I lift something heavy, but I still can't stand fully upright, you know, and everything feels tight down there." I tried to stretch and resume my normal posture.

"Please stop; don't force it. It's too soon." He helped me into the rocking chair next to the changing table.

"Do you want to bathe Josh while I watch, or do you want to take a bath with him?" Harvey asked.

"With Josh in the tub?!" I answered, a little surprised. "He'll be too slippery. … But can I actually do that and get my scar wet?"

"I think the shower is better than sitting in the tub, and you don't need to worry. I'm here, and we'll do it after dinner. That way you'll both have my full attention." To make sure our late afternoon nap was not disturbed, he disconnected the family phone, kissed Josh and me, took my cell into the kitchen, and began to cook.

* * *

I woke with Josh crying next to me. I rocketed into a sitting position but didn't pick him up. My first impulse was to call Harvey, who appeared even before I could. Josh stopped sobbing the moment Harvey had him in his arms.

"He doesn't like me, Harvey," I said.

"Who doesn't like you, my darling?" The last word came out in Dutch as he swayed his hips back and forth, holding Josh's finger.

"Where did you learn to do all this?" I asked.

"I learned some of it while you were sleeping after he was born. You were out for quite a while. And when you woke up, you were almost too groggy and weak to hold him. But when I put him into your arms, you looked at him and smiled; you took one of his little fingers and then fell back to sleep. Right before your eyes closed you said his hands reminded you of Leonis's, your youngest brother –"

"Did I say that? I missed everything."

"You said a lot under general anesthesia and when you were on the verge of waking up."

I started to weep.

"Please, Linda," Harvey approached my side of the bed. "Look at me. No, you didn't miss it at all! You were there, of course, and you have all the time in the world to be there now, all the way, with our big, beautiful Josh."

"Stop reminding me how big he is. I wished I hadn't eaten so much. Then I could have had a natural childbirth and seen and witnessed everything."

"Stop this nonsense. If you keep saying it, you'll believe it. I did what I had to do under the circumstances. Josh's head was stuck, you couldn't breathe because of the pain, and you were allergic to most of the painkillers they tried. Maybe, I admit, I could have stopped them from breaking your water. Perhaps we could have waited for it to break naturally."

"Where was our doula?" I said.

"She was away. After all, our due date was April 10 –"

"She was paid to take care of me and be there for me when I needed her, but she wasn't. What's wrong with people? They're never there when you need them most."

"Please look at me, darling. There's nothing and no one to blame here. What's most important now is that both you and Josh are healthy and, may I add, beautiful," Harvey said. He was still so charming.

"How did I fail at being a real woman?" I wailed.

"Didn't you hear what I just said? You haven't failed. You've done a great job! Say it after me: 'I. have. done. a. great. job!'" Harvey emphasized each word as if stamping it in my subconscious. I didn't open my mouth.

"Do you think you may need to see Dr. Carter again?" Harvey asked thoughtfully. "Although I'm not sure if you can consult her after giving birth ... and for what?"

"No. Especially since she didn't even show up when the baby was coming," I said.

"But she sent her assistant, Magritte. Don't you remember?"

"Who pretended that she was Dr. Carter? What was she thinking, that I'm some kind of crazy black woman?"

"No, she doesn't think like that. I found it a bit weird, though, that Magritte claimed to be Dr. Carter when she came to visit and when you were waking up. She kept calling herself Dr. Carter." He switched to Dutch as he looked into Josh's eyes. "Strange, eh, my darling boy?"

"It's good I had to see her only during the pregnancy. Only over my dead body would I go back to her now, because everyone in her office really thought I was crazy. Am I crazy? This is how, in the western world, they make you look unstable or think you're insane the moment you tell them about losing somebody," I said.

"Your sister and your mother were not just anybody, Linda, and nobody thinks you're crazy. You have to admit your childhood was not like that of any other person I've ever met or known. I think going to Dr. Carter certainly helped us, at least through your pregnancy. The great news now is that nothing bad can happen, because you've survived the most painful part; it's a smooth ride from here on," he said encouragingly. "And look at our big – well ..."

"Big boy. It's OK, Harvey; call him big boy – that's what he is, anyway. Sorry I asked you not to," I said.

"I think Josh is teaching me how to take care of him," Harvey replied as he danced with the child.

"Did I really say his fingers looked like Leonis's?" I asked a little distantly.

"Yes, you did. Look. Look, Linda. I'm doing what my gut tells me to do with him." Harvey kept on waltzing, gazing into Josh's eyes. He looked serene, happy, comfortable, and finally found, as if he were in love for the first time. Why was I not enjoying Josh as much? What was going on with me?

Even though I tried, I couldn't banish the thought of my little brother in my shaking hands as I climbed into the taxi and fled from my mother's hospital. I didn't cry about it, but I simply didn't understand why the images kept returning, impossible to evict from my mind. At times, when I gazed at the corner of the walls or peered out of windows, I felt as though my mother were watching me. I could even see her walking through the room, or standing next to Harvey and observing as he danced innocently with Josh.

At night, I couldn't sleep. It wasn't only because of my physical pain; the insomnia was mostly due to my mother's presence. I don't think Harvey, so intently focused on his newborn son, was seeing the same things. A couple of times I wanted to tell him what I saw, or ask if he, too, heard a voice or noticed anything unusual in the room, but I couldn't spoil the infinite joy he was experiencing with his son.

They looked like they were made for each other and this moment belonged to the two of them alone; the world had stopped, and everything in it bowed to them and danced with them. I could hear and even smell their happiness, but I was too numb and estranged from myself to register anything. I wanted to push myself to feel something a couple of times but felt I was simply an intruder. I could have walked out the door and neither would notice or miss me. Had I been simply an oven, like my mother had been for my father?

I was absent when Josh came into the world, while his father, this jubilant man, had been there all the way. Harvey hadn't once left the delivery room, according to the nurse, because he was scared he would miss something. He'd arranged for the largest possible accommodation, where he could even pee with the door open just to keep his eyes on us. But tomorrow, he was leaving me alone with this baby who didn't know who I was and, I believed, didn't like me.

"Look at this smile, Linda," Harvey said, finally sitting down next to me. "Do you want to hold him?"

"Does he want to nurse?" I asked, looking at Josh. I didn't take him.

"I don't know. Maybe. It has been a while since he woke up."

"See how he's wide-eyed and staring at me."

"He's curious about his beautiful mother."

"Beautiful mother. I'm not beautiful, and he doesn't like me."

"You're both beautiful and the loves of my life," Harvey insisted as he stood up.

"Where are you going? Are you avoiding me already? Are you getting tired of me, Harvey?" I asked.

"I'm going to check on the chicken and fish, if you don't want them Harvey's way – burned." He lay Josh next to me and left the room.

I leaned over and examined the baby closely. As soon as I held his pinky, which I found adorable, he started to cry. His fingers looked like my brother's as a newborn. I think that was the first thing I liked about him: his little fingers and toes, but he didn't like me touching them.

Harvey came back. "You both already miss me?" he said with a smile.

"He didn't like me handling his hands or feet. Do you think he's too white?" I asked.

"What do you mean, too white? All babies are born white. Maybe it's a bit cold for him outside the covers." Harvey was observant. Josh wore only his onesie, which I'd opened to reach his toes.

"Do you want to shower before or after dinner?" Harvey asked with Josh in his arms.

"I don't know."

"Are you hungry?"

"No." I really wasn't hungry, but for some reason I always felt thirsty.

"Then let's shower first. That way we can get outside on time after dinner for a walk with Josh. What do you think?" Harvey said, looking at me.

"I'm OK with the shower, but I'm not sure about a walk."

"Let's do one thing at a time." Harvey checked the shower with Josh in his arms. I slid off the bed, entered the bathroom, took off my clothes and turned toward the mirror. I didn't recognize the person I saw. She looked foreign, distant, with a dark shadow clustering around her face like an ugly wedding crasher. I was fat and ugly, with breasts bigger than my head; they were dripping all the time and I didn't know what to do with them. Josh was not taking as much as they were giving. *How am I going to manage all this milk?*

"That's a lot of milk, Linda," Harvey remarked. I kept quiet and sat on the toilet.

"Your scar is coming along," he added, leaning his head toward me.

"Do you want to hold Josh while I turn on the shower?" he asked.

"Yes." I kept my eyes on Josh like a hawk. Harvey had wrapped him in a blanket to keep him warm while preparing everything. Anticipating us stepping out of the shower, he even put two towels in the dryer to warm. He entered the stall first, then I handed him Josh, whom he held tenderly.

"I know heating your towels is great and all, but we have to consider the environment, too, so that when you're grown up you'll find the earth better, not worse. Don't you think, Josh?" He said in Dutch, almost to himself, "God, you're beautiful, and I love you."

For a moment I gazed at them under the shower. They looked so well suited to each other, as though Harvey were the mother and I a mere ghost intruding on their intimacy. Why had I been absent when Josh was born? I felt like a stranger who had woken up to a baby called mine, but whom I could only know was mine by the excruciating pain above my pubic hair and inside my inadequate vagina.

Not yet able to walk, remain on my feet or even stand straight for long, I heard Harvey and Josh talking to each other, staring in each other's eyes, in languages that felt foreign to me. Then I thought I saw my mother holding Josh in the shower and shook my head. Was

I hallucinating? Was I feeling the effects of medication? Of the tablets they had given me in the hospital?

"I don't want the pills they gave me," I said.

"What did you say?" Harvey asked without turning his head. I was relieved he wasn't looking at my body. Nothing about me or my figure could have pleased him. I felt the humidity and moisture of the shower touch my cheeks, and then the mirror fogged up; Harvey's lips were moving like an MTV video clip without sound. He was still speaking Dutch to Josh, but I'd stopped paying attention, not understanding most of it anyway.

"Can you hear me?" I asked against the sound of the water.

"We're waiting for you," he shouted and gave me a small towel to cover my scar before I joined them.

"You know the nurse at the hospital just sponge dried and disinfected it," I said.

"I'll do exactly as she showed me," he said.

Harvey poured some shower gel on Josh and me. He held Josh between us as he used his right hand to rub the soap on my shoulders before moving away. I leaned into the shower and rinsed myself before turning around to buff Josh's chubby arms. He looked straight at me, staring through my soul, and started to wail.

Does he see through me? Is he seeing my mother like I do? Maybe I'm crazy after all.

"Here, hold him," Harvey said, even though Josh was crying.

"Maybe run your hands a little under the hot water before taking him again," Harvey added quickly.

I stepped out of the shower, turned on the hot water, rinsed my hands and ducked back under the stream. This time, when I took Josh in my arms, he didn't protest. I felt happy and relieved for the first time since we had come home – he didn't howl when I held him. Harvey poured more gel on us and stepped out of the shower. I felt anxious being alone with Josh, but I pretended I was in control.

"Where are you going now?" I asked.

"To turn on the dryer. I'll be back right way," Harvey said through the open shower door.

I watched Harvey disappear before turning to Josh, who was quietly waiting for me. It felt good that he wasn't sobbing. I carefully soaped his belly and was starting to enjoy our short time together. Without waiting for Harvey, I turned the baby to clean his back, but he moaned a bit, clearly annoyed by the move. It was then that a strong pain erupted from my scar because I had unwittingly straightened up. Standing tall made me feel more grounded, but right now it seemed inadvisable.

"He's squirming too much, Harvey. Are you coming back? I'm hurting." I shouted. Had he heard me?

"I'm coming," Harvey called.

As my husband moved around the end of the shower, I wanted to hold Josh under the stream. As I lifted him with my right hand to balance him on my left arm, he slipped from my hold. I didn't know what to do or feel in that moment, and I had forgotten my pain.

"Harvey!!! He's falling out of my arms like a fish!"

Harvey caught the baby right before he landed on the floor head first. Everything had happened so fast.

"He is a fish, you know. He IS a fish," I kept saying.

"A big beautiful fish, indeed." With Josh in a firm embrace, Harvey knelt down under the water, perhaps to console himself. He'd reddened like many westerners do when caught off guard, no matter the situation, good or bad. But the baby didn't cry, which shocked us both. I, on the other hand, was shaking, and Harvey was breathless for a moment but quickly regained his composure. He looked at me and smiled with relief.

In the split second when Harvey had caught Josh and panic had shot through me, I hadn't blushed as Harvey had but rather stood up straight again, causing the stitches to tear and the wound to bleed. Red rolled down my legs as if I were having my period. I had had the same sensation when blood spilled the night I had been raped in jail. Refusing to look at it, I felt it rush to the floor like a river. I registered no physical pain at first, but I felt cold and worthless.

"You're bleeding," Harvey said, looking up between my legs.

"Bleeding?" I said, touching myself. I had to acknowledge I was, yes, bleeding, and hurting. My blood mixed with white foam on the floor to resemble pink snow, then formed a thick red line sinking slowly into tiny holes in the ground, one tributary at a time, like worms fighting over a corpse, like my sister's; they were eating Nenein's lifeless body inside her grave.

The foam turned crimson; everything turned red and began to expand in my brain, like the first time I saw my mother's blood dripping under her hospital bed. I held my temples, stood still for a moment, and then shook my head as if that would rid it of the childhood detritus that had stuck inside it. I moved to get out of the shower.

"Are you OK, Linda? Josh is fine," he said, holding out his arms for me to lean on him. He managed to rinse us both before fetching the towels, trusting Josh to my arms as I waited for him in front of the foggy mirror.

I wiped a layer of mist off the mirror; it came right back. Still, I could identify a baby and me. But was it Josh or my little brother? In the hospital, my mother's newborn was nestled in my arms; I held his cute, tiny hand under her watchful eye. I heard her voice in my head. *"Galle, be careful with his little fingers ... They are beautiful, aren't they? Will you take care of him for me? Please promise me."*

Then Harvey returned with the heated towels. I abruptly handed Josh to him and left the bathroom with my leaking breasts and bleeding scars. I paid little attention to the carpet, which was getting used to soaking up my wasted blood; in return the rug cleaners visited regularly.

I wondered what the carpet would say if it had a voice. Would it tell me to stop bleeding on it? How about these white walls? So clinical. They never tired of staring at me. I hated their silent witness to my secret life, and the worst part of all was that they did nothing. They just stood there.

I glared at the white curtains as well. *Was there anything in this house that wasn't white?* What was it with these colourless walls? Why hadn't I painted them all yellow before Josh was born? I recalled mentioning it to Harvey around week thirty of my pregnancy, but nothing really came of it before we grew too busy with my big belly, trying all kinds of pillows to help me relax at night.

"I want to paint the walls and change the curtains," I'd said.

"This far into your pregnancy, that's not such a good idea. What if you don't like the smell and it disturbs your sleep? How about we just worry about your comfort for now and forget about redecorating? Besides, I doubt we can alter the wall colour without the owner's permission. As for the curtains, according to city bylaws all the windows of the building have to look the same."

"Once I finish with Josh, I'll attend to your scar," he said now. I kept mum but put on my soft pink robe hanging in the bedroom. I was exhausted, so I accepted Harvey's help. He rinsed me off and assisted with underwear and a sports bra he had bought before Josh's birth, but it was too tight for breasts full of milk.

"I think you'll feel better if Josh nurses now," Harvey said. I agreed, and he put Josh on my nipple. He choked a little so Harvey burped him and then promenaded around to calm his crying.

"He's too hungry now to feed, I think," Harvey said.

"And my breasts are too full for him to handle the flow."

"I think you're right, Linda. Shall we call nurse Emma for help?"

"What do you think?" Meanwhile Josh had begun crying again and showed no sign of stopping anytime soon.

"I'll call the pharmacy and see what they recommend," Harvey said.

"What the pharmacy would recommend about my breasts?"

"Yes. It's not like the ER is the best place when your breasts are full and hurting. Or maybe, if the pain is intense, we should go to emergency now."

"Harvey, I refuse to go out. Why are you always inventing pretexts to get me out of the apartment when I've said so many times that I won't leave!" I shouted angrily.

"No need to get worked up about this, Linda. Hear me out. Emptying your breasts will ease the pain and then maybe let Josh feed without choking."

"You know very well that the Fula take babies out into the world only after thirty days. Why are you trying to ignore that fact? Besides, he's too white. Nobody will believe he's my baby," I said.

"Sorry. I forgot. Yes, we discussed your customs a long time ago. Parenting is challenging because no baby comes with a manual. We have to figure it out, and we will. But keep in mind, Linda, we're not in Africa and nobody is going to think that Josh isn't your baby because he's too white. Again, all babies are born white. Do you get it now?"

"Oh, all right. I see," I said with hesitation. "Let's go with whatever the pharmacy can do, because anything's better than a clinic. I'm not sick; I'm just in pain," I said as Harvey dialled his cell phone with one hand and held Josh, who continued to cry, with the other. I envied Harvey's composure through it all.

He hung up. "They said that I can buy a pump."

"Buy a pump ... for what?" I asked. "To pump my breast milk?"

"Yes, and that's a good thing, isn't it?"

"My mother and my grandmother never did that. What do you think they would do?"

"I really don't know, and I don't think your mother or your grandmother are relevant right now, because your mother isn't alive and your grandmother is far away in some lost, closed-off community in Africa." He swayed left and right to keep Josh calm, but the baby kept howling as if he were being spanked.

"Closed off?" I shouted.

"Please, Linda; stop picking on my words. I don't know what to do, either; I have a crying newborn on my hands and a mother ... a mother ..."

"A mother who is crazy and doesn't know what to do with her own baby, and you're feeling sorry for yourself and disrespecting my mother and my grandmother," I shouted again. "Call *your* mother, then, since she's one phone call away and she's not living in her grave or in an impeded world. How lucky are you?"

"That sounds like a great idea, Linda, but it's very late in Holland right now," he said.

"You're right. Nine hours ahead of us. Not so backwards, eh?" I said, laughing, which Harvey chose to ignore.

"What time is it? Ah. It's 6:45 p.m.," Harvey said, checking the alarm clock by the nightstand, which we were both staring at.

Josh persisted in his wailing and the pain in my breasts increased. I lost the desire and energy to fight; all I could do was collaborate with Harvey. Who cares about my mother and grandmother anyway? One left me before I had even reached womanhood and the other, as Harvey said, lived in a lost world somewhere. What would she advise me to do at this moment, though?

At the same time, ironically, my friend Vivian came to mind. I felt happy she had chosen to move close to her family in China for the support she and her son might need. Why hadn't Harvey and I thought of this? Would being near his mother have made him feel more comfortable?

"No need to call anybody about it right now. I'm going to buy the breast pump," Harvey announced. He put on his pants and got ready to leave. "Watch Josh while I dash out. I'll be right back."

"You're not going to leave me alone with him, are you?" I stepped away from the bed, where Harvey had deposited Josh, still crying, next to me.

"We'll all go, then," he said with a smile.

"No," I said.

"Then I guess you'll have to stay here with him," Harvey said, walking toward the living room.

I sat there like a dog and looked at Josh. I noticed the uvula in his mouth, hanging down like an uncut clitoris.

"I'm not fit for this, Harvey. I don't know what to do or how to do it, even though I knew what to do with my brother. With my own son, I'm at a loss. I even said at one time I'd never have kids, but I didn't keep my promise. Since I met you, I've violated everything I believed in. I didn't even want to marry or belong to anybody, and now I belong to you and to him. How classic.

"I failed to give him a natural birth, and now I'm going to fail at being his mother. Why do you know so much about mothering when you're a man, and a white man at that, and I don't? Why is this happening to me?

"I'm not here; I'm not feeling anything at all except pain – from my scars, in my heart, in my head. Pain everywhere. Yes, pain, pain, pain, even in my soul. Everywhere, I feel and see pain and blood. I can't sleep or shut down my mind; it can't close the door to its past and its ache, not even with these stupid pills.

"Maybe they're what's making my breasts ache; maybe they're what's making me crazy. God, I'm hurting! Harvey, help me. I'm lost, and I don't know what to do for myself. What's happening to me?" Like a wounded animal, I shouted, bawled and groaned; it was as if I were competing with Josh's shrieks.

He had cried so much he was starting to sound hoarse. *How can a baby wail so long and so loud, maybe even lose his voice?* Harvey turned around to put Josh in his crib, removing the blanket and toys, and held me in his arms.

"Please calm down. Let's –"

"Don't tell me to calm down."

"OK, don't calm down," he said, still holding me.

"Stop saying that word, and don't touch me anymore. Leave me alone. Go catch your flight and get the fuck out of my life and our lives. I smell, and I'm fat – a cow that you're going to milk with a stupid white-people's pump, a machine, another stupid machine. How about getting a machine to replace me while you're at it, huh? Are you out of your mind? You're asking a black mother, a black African mother, to pump her breasts because she has become, all of sudden, a cow, your white cow, a Dutch cow, which at least produces the most milk, cheese and all kinds of stupid dairy products that I can't eat, either."

I moved away from him as he stood there, silent and thoughtful.

"Is that why you're getting upset?" he asked softly, approaching me and Josh.

"Josh is still crying," I said.

"I know, and he's probably hungry, but his mother needs me right now. I'm sorry, Linda, that you feel the way you do. I'm sorry about what I said about your mother and your grandmother and what I said about your beloved Africa, and you're not a cow, or a Dutch cow – that's why I'm with you instead of a Dutch woman, and I hope that you never become one." He smiled, and Josh kept crying.

"I was just trying to help. I don't know what to do either. My father is very ill and I need to see him in case the surgery doesn't go well. This doesn't mean I'm leaving you, or leaving Josh, or leaving you both. I'll never, ever leave you, no matter what happens between us.

"I need you to be strong, for yourself, for Josh and for me. Both Josh and I need you to be tough for all of us. You're my life, and he's our life! Please remember that I'm also facing this for the first time. I hope to get it right in the end," Harvey reassured me, holding my hands.

"What do you want me to do? Tell me, and I'll do it." He looked at me, then at Josh crying in his crib, and paced around the room. "I'm really at a loss, Linda. Come with me to the pharmacy. We'll bring Josh. I want to make sure your breasts stop hurting so you can feed Josh when I'm gone." His hand was in his hair like a five-year-old boy's.

"You're leaving me. How can you leave me right now?" I took my hands from his and lifted Josh from the crib.

I faced Harvey for a minute before I sat on the bed, pouting because of the pain from my stitches. Harvey kept tugging at his hair, watching me and Josh.

I tried putting Josh on my breast twice before he took it. Relieved, Harvey and I exchanged smiles, and all went well until my fast-flowing milk made Josh choke.

"Can I take him?" Harvey asked.

"No. He's my baby, too; I'm his mother, but I think he doesn't like me," I said, holding him close all the same.

"Please loosen your hold. It looks tight. Maybe if you soften it he'll cry a little less. Maybe he's swallowed a lot of air; he might need to be burped before we try to feed him again."

"Are you telling me I'm not fit to be his mother? You see and feel everything and I don't, and now –"

"You really think I know how to mother him better than you?" Harvey asked. "No. The C-section knocked you out, but that doesn't make me more maternal. I'm his father, you're his mother. You'll always be his mother, and together we're going to be his parents. We'll figure it out as we go. We're the ones responsible for him, and neither of us can do it alone. Please let me be his father as much as I can without thinking I'm taking your place or that I'm a better parent than you. We're not competing for who knows best or who's doing it right. Like I said, right now it's really hit-and-miss, and I hope we don't fuck it up."

"You're swearing in front of him," I said.

"So were you minutes ago," he said. "How about we never, ever swear in front of our precious Josh again, as of now?" Harvey suggested, smiling.

I kept quiet and handed Josh, still bawling, back to him. I couldn't stand his howling any longer and began crying as well. Harvey managed to keep his calm, and I heard him again on the living room phone.

Harvey's mother intervenes – Vancouver, May 2005

"Who are you talking to?" I asked.

"My mother," he said.

"This late?" I said.

"Yes. Do you want to talk to her?" Although I nodded yes, only with reluctance did I take the phone.

"Linda, how are you?" Rina asked.

"Sorry that we woke you up," I said.

"Don't worry about that. Old people don't sleep, you know, and of course you're more than welcome to call at any hour, particularly at this time in your life. Jaapje is in the hospital anyway, and I can't sleep, because I'm worried about his surgery.

"What if he doesn't make it, Linda? What would life be without the man I married fifty years ago? He's been the love of my life and the only man I've known. How will I go on without him?" She sobbed and then paused; we all did, except Josh, in the background, still in

Harvey's arms as he swayed to the music of his cry.

"Oh, dear; sorry that I'm venting to you. You have much bigger fish to fry. I was saying I hope you'll welcome all the assistance you can get right now. You'll need it. Accepting help is what being a parent is about, and it will make you feel much better. Harvey told me that your breasts are too full and painful?"

"Yes." I cupped them in my hands. My shirt was soaked, as if broken pumps were dripping on an already rainy day. "Yes, and they hurt, and Josh won't stop crying, and we don't know what to do." I finally wept without yelling or a feeling of angst overwhelming me.

"Linda, sweetheart; don't cry. That won't help." She paused. "Or, OK, cry a little; sometimes it cleans the soul. But too many tears can backfire when you have a newborn in the house."

"You sound like you've been crying a lot yourself," I said.

"Yes, I have, because I fear my husband may die before me. I have to be first," she sniffed. "There I go again. Sorry, Linda."

"I was saying that you're a new mother; if you cry the same time your baby does, Josh won't feel secure and you won't be in a good state of mind to calm him down. Babies pick up on the emotions of the people who care for them." She and I both held our tears.

"I can hear him crying," my mother-in-law went on. "I think first things first. Change his diaper, get him to burp and then try feeding him again, with your breast or a bottle. Do you have a bottle?" she asked.

"No."

"Why not?"

"I didn't want him bottle-fed."

"It's fine to have a bottle with your milk in it," she said.

"How?"

"Let Harvey get the pump, then pump your milk out and pour it into a baby bottle, sterilized first, of course. Then get some rest while Harvey feeds him," Rina said like an instructor.

"He should do what? We don't know how to bottle-feed him, and I can't sleep."

"Harvey can learn, and you could even take a walk while he's at it," she suggested.

"I don't want to go out. Why does everybody keep telling me to go out?"

"Then don't go out until you feel like it, but how is Harvey going to buy the pump if you won't let him leave to get it?"

"The pharmacy's closing soon," Harvey shouted from the bedroom.

"I heard him," Rina said. "I'm not sure what time it is for you over there, but either you let him go alone or you all go out."

"No." I walked into the second bedroom, where Harvey was changing Josh, and gave him the phone. Harvey returned with the phone and a now-clean Josh. He had been crying now for more than two hours according to the alarm clock on our nightstand.

"Linda, how about I stay with you on the phone, with Josh, until Harvey comes back with the pump?" Rina said.

"No, Rina. That will cost you an arm and a leg. No ... you're ... no," I said, looking around and wondering what to say.

"Are you all going to go out then?" she asked.

"No."

"Then please don't worry about the money right now. Both Jaapje and I would have been there now if he were not sick, but I promise you I'll be there for the next one."

The next one already? The next one? I gave Harvey a look that said how absurd this was.

"I wish I could be there now," she repeated. "But since that's impossible, the only way I can really help is to stay on the line. I'll sing some Dutch lullabies. Josh is Dutch – he won't mind hearing them – and I hope his grandma's voice doesn't make it worse for you both. How about that?" she said, laughing.

"How?" I said.

"I'll hang up and call you on your landline. Then you put me on speaker."

"OK," I said and did as she requested.

"So, you won't be alone. Can I leave you with Josh while my mother's on the phone?" Harvey asked

"Yes, and please don't take too long," I said as I took Josh.

He had called the pharmacy and reserved their last breast pump, and once his mother was on the landline with me, he left. She sang Dutch lullabies, of which I understood some words from the few language lessons I'd taken in Amsterdam. The lyrics – something about stars and twinkling – and the melody sounded familiar. I had sung the same tune to my little brother in French while rocking him to sleep. *Why hadn't this song come to mind before? Hadn't I performed it many times for Leonis? How ironic that she's crooning the same song some African mothers sing to their babies, yet she is white.*

By some miracle, after only a few of Rina's lullabies Josh stopped crying and even started to drift into sleep. Maybe it had been a mistake moving away from her. Wouldn't it have been easier if Harvey and I had remained in Holland?

Harvey, smiling broadly, tiptoed through the door. "He's asleep, and we have a pump," he told his mother. "Thank you, Moeder." We moved Josh into our bed as Rina continued to sing.

"Keep him in your bed if that's easier, Linda," Rina said. "And don't whisper around him. Keep talking as usual. Your voices will soothe him and keep him feeling safe, calm and secure. Now get some rest. Nighty night, and remember: I'm only a phone call away. Ring me and I'll call you right back, so Grandma can hear Josh," she said happily before hanging up.

"Stay," I said, holding Harvey's hands. He lay on the other side of Josh as we stared at him, watching his chest go up and down. I was nodding off when Harvey started fidgeting.

"You're not comfortable?" I asked, lifting my head.

"I'm feeling a bit restless. I think I'm going to figure this out – this pump – and come back once I know what to do with it." Harvey left with the box in his hands.

I couldn't sleep, either, because my breasts and scars hurt, and the painkillers weren't helping. I decided to stop taking them altogether.

Maybe the bottom line was that I feared the medication would get into my breast milk and Josh wouldn't like it. And then I'd have no choice but to give him the bottle, which I didn't think was a good idea, even though Rina had suggested it. What if he liked the bottle more than me? Harvey had given up trying to convince me otherwise about my medications.

I turned to my sleeping Josh and carefully caressed his plump, pink cheeks.

Considering a second baby – Hawaii, summer 2006

When Josh was almost eighteen months old and we were vacationing in Maui, Harvey and I talked about having another child. I felt Harvey's gentle touch on my shoulder as we sat together on a whale-watching boat, his caress as light as a whisper of fresh wind.

I shrugged my shoulder a bit, as if I felt a slight chill. I snuggled closer to my husband as I felt breast milk drip into my bra. I wondered if it was time to stop breastfeeding Josh, since he was almost two years old. I also wondered why my breast milk increased each time I felt Harvey near.

Gliding away a little, I observed this man as if meeting him for the first time. I noticed he was, in fact, an attractive living being right next to me, watching the whales in the full-moon's light. Beautiful horizons and majestic mountains surrounded us, and the sun's rays, although sinking behind tall peaks, still warmed our bodies; we had had enough vitamin D today, and, I hoped, for a long time to come.

We kept watching the whales, and he moved closer. He was wearing his favourite cologne and smelled great: salty and woodsy and sweet. I caught the aroma of the ocean from his skin.

"Do we want a second baby?" he asked gently – so gently it felt as though the whales themselves were whispering in my ears.

I was about to say "No" when I came to my senses, but he quickly went on. "You know, I wish I were only two years older than my brother Neil."

Five years separated Harvey from his sibling, and he often said the two of them lived a world apart because of it. Sometimes he wished they were closer, but his mother had not been able to conceive when she and her husband wanted to. Neil arrived when they had almost given up, so he was a gift to them all.

"I see," I replied, "and I understand." I shifted my gaze to the humpbacks.

We came back from our whale-watching both relaxed and delighted with the whole adventure. We had got much more from it than either of us had expected.

A half hour later, on the balcony sipping tea and following the full moon as it disappeared into the ocean, I felt Harvey's desire for me. His penis was erect, and I couldn't resist. I approached and sat astride him.

He rose from the chair and placed me on the floor, kissing me while moving inside slowly; my vagina was aroused, a fully ripened melon. We looked at each other knowingly, smiling in silence; having sex had stopped being a natural thing to both of us.

He started kissing my eyebrows, my forehead, my eyelids, pressing his crescent lips on me. He made me shiver. Was I feeling chilled or simply a bit embarrassed by my poufy belly, leaking breasts, long-dead clitoris, and ass like an elephant's?

He gave me a tight hug, which he quickly released as he plunged inside me. I felt my body melt; his hands on my neck were like butter on a warm croissant. He paused, then pressed a little deeper into me, staying longer and reaching farther before moving up. We gazed at each other as if we wanted to speak, but instead we simply enjoyed the touch of moonlight on our bodies, aroused from the climaxing we were experiencing that very moment. We called each other's name.

For the first time in a very long time I loved his kisses and wanted him to devour me right there and then. I wore no perfume, but he kept inhaling like he was taking in the scent of my being. That night, sex had felt effortless and full of pleasure, everything about it easy and serene, like the dancing whales we had just observed. There was something even soothing about it. Helping each other up, we kissed again and walked hand in hand to the bedroom, where we placed Josh in the middle of the bed.

I played with my son's little fingers for a bit and then turned around. A feeling of pure light and elation spread through me, and I wondered if it was unalloyed life that I'd witnessed through the whales. The emotion was truly foreign to me; in my whole life I'd never known it. For the first time, I realized, motherhood and being a wife might suit me after all. It was the perfect end to our evening.

Through the window, the moon blossomed, growing fatter and brighter. The sea's songs had replaced the silence of the night on the beach. There it was, the world asleep, and I chose to tune in to the melody of the ocean's blues: strong waves lapping against rocks infusing the quiet nights of our own breaths, like a godmother crooning to her Cinderella.

After having two children – Vancouver, 2007

Did motherhood suit me? Maybe mothering Josh and Owen felt fitting, but I'd lost faith in myself as a woman and a wife to my husband – or was it my taste in men that had changed after I gave birth?

What was it about combining the duties of mother and spouse? My father had been so rarely home, and all my mother seemed to do was get pregnant each time he returned. Was that a useful example for me? Should I really have another baby? Oh, no. Out of the question. And yet I kept dwelling on it.

"How about you go see a therapist?" Harvey suggested.

"Why is everybody telling me to go get analyzed? I don't need a counsellor. What I need is to be left alone, to have space to figure things out on my own," I said, almost in tears.

Do you know what happens to a woman's body when she has given birth twice and almost died doing so? I carried those scars to the gym, which made it worse for me. Everything hurt each time I went to class. I felt fat and bloated.

Everyone who knew us asked incessantly when we would have a third child. "Here and there and everywhere they say, 'You're going to have a girl. You're going to have a girl,'" I said, pacing around the bedroom.

They said it so often I wanted to kill them all, and, in my head I did. Thank God for unrealized thoughts.

At moments like these I truly didn't know who I was. I wondered where I'd gone since becoming a mother, and what was becoming of me. Had I been lost all along and didn't know it, only to be found through motherhood and placed in these worlds: the western world, the African world – which I could say forms my roots, even though my own family won't welcome me, who sense I am different from the rest of them – and my world: the world within me, the one in which I receive no mercy, in which I feel even worse living?

Had I chosen to ignore what life was asking me or needing me to do? Had I buried my head in the sand and smuggled life's demands deep inside me, locked them up and thrown the key into the ocean, hoping the waves would never toss it back on shore? I had the feeling that suppressed life had just caught up with me, whether I liked it or not. What was I going to do with it? How had I let things get to this point? I had a brain, and I had to get my act together before it was too late, but how? I needed help.

Thus began my journey of fear into motherhood. I unearthed my traitorous conviction that my own mother, neither loving nor caring, had given up on my brother and me. As for my father, he was another heartless man who let his woman die for the sake of his own interests. I was sure my mother would have wanted him around rather than so often away pursuing money and social status.

What was I left with? The oak and the baobab tree. I didn't have to pick one now, right this moment, did I? Well, I knew very well the baobab, being from Africa and all. I thought I'd need to learn more about the oak, beyond its external beauty, inside out, before I decided which one I'd like to be, which one's life I'd prefer to live. I felt a tiny, warm, secret giggle rise inside my tummy and realized that this morning was not like my usual morning, or any other morning.

Bleeding after children

"You're aware that this spotting doesn't mean anything. You know that, right? Maybe you were having your period. Come here," Harvey said.

He gave me a hug and left the bathroom after making sure the water was the right temperature. I waited to step into the shower; I sat on the floor with my back against the door and my knees to my chest. I no longer felt a pinching pain but saw blood again travelling down my legs.

Am I having a miscarriage? I couldn't focus; I was feeling more and more tired. I lay down, still blocking the entrance. I kept seeing my mother's agonized face. *I'm going to die young like her, leaving my children without a normal family. Yes, I am.* My body felt exactly as it had when I was twelve at my mother's deathbed.

I woke up and found I was still lying on the floor. I realized I'd heard Harvey knock a couple of times; it had sounded like the echo of running water.

"Are you OK in there? It's getting late, you know. I want to go to bed now. Can you please just open the door?" he asked, pushing on it. "Why did you lock it? Are you OK in there? Open up!" Without waiting, he forced the door open.

"Oh my god! Linda, we need help! You're hemorrhaging. This isn't your period," he said, running around in panic, unable to decide what to do. "Do I wash you first, or call the ambulance and let the doctor see this, or what?"

I heard him look in on the children to ensure that the white-noise machine was loud enough; it sounded like a river and helped them sleep.

"Let's get you showered and dressed, and then I'll dial 911. Don't die on me, Linda – you hear me? You have no right! You can't. Do you hear me? We're going to grow old together, and our children and grandchildren will visit the family mansion you buy with your acting breakthrough!" he said, turning to humour. "I'm counting on you for my retirement, so please wake up!"

He showered me with cold water, which I didn't mind. I didn't say anything, because there was nothing in my mind but my mother's death and her smile. He dried me quickly and walked me to the closet to find some loose clothes.

"Where do you keep your tampons?" he asked, looking in all the bathroom cubbies. I saw him grab the iPhone next to his bed.

"What are you doing?"

"I'm calling the ambulance," he said.

"Please don't. They'll wake up the kids and scare them. I'm fine now. Let's just go to bed, and I'll see Dr. Brian first thing in the morning," I begged.

"No! We can't wait until morning for you to be seen by a doctor."

"Yes, we can, and I will."

"You see? You're fighting me even at your weakest. You're going to the hospital. I'm dialling 911 right now," he said.

"There's no need to get excited. It's New Year's Eve, and the emergency room will be packed." I grabbed his phone. "I'll go if you call a taxi instead of the ambulance."

"Alone?" he asked with worried eyes.

I felt something dripping on my knees; I walked to the bathroom wondering if it was my blood despite the tampon. It was. "Where the hell is this blood from, and what does it want from me?" I asked angrily.

"OK. I'll call a taxi and you're going to see a doctor," Harvey said in a determined voice.

Since it was so late it didn't take long for the taxi to arrive.

"Take care of the boys. Tell them I love them if I'm not back in the morning," I said slipping into the cab.

"Of course you'll be here. I told you I won't do this alone. We're in it together." He held me tight. "I'm not going to kiss you because you'll see it as 'goodbye,' and I even take the hug back. See you soon."

"OK, boss," I smiled. The taxi was starting to pull away when he sprinted after us to give me another hug. Then we left.

"Madame, we've arrived," the driver announced.

I rushed into Emergency. Luckily no one was ahead of me. I quietly passed a few patients already in the treatment area.

"Please wait for the doctor on one of the beds next to that lady," said a triage nurse. I sat down and looked around. I was feeling sorry for myself but quickly shrugged it off, as if to convince myself I was strong. Yet my confidence drained. Maybe coming here tonight hadn't been a good idea, even though the bleeding told me this was where I needed to be. My mind went back to that fateful day my mother died.

"The doctor has requested I give you some insulin," the nurse said. "She'll be back in the morning to check on you. You've lost a lot of blood, but you're going to be fine."

Doctor's visit

Every year I see my family doctor for the usual basic check-up. "What kind of exam am I having today, Dr. Brian?" I asked, longing to know the details and purpose of these tests.

"It's a pap smear, something every woman your age should have to screen for cervical cancer or detect any form of sexual disease; the blood test is for your thyroid, blood sugar, cholesterol, iron and anything else related to your blood," he explained as he did an internal examination of my vagina.

"Can you please relax a bit more? Move a little lower down the table, then take a deep breath and release it gently," he said kindly.

I did as he asked, moving my bottom farther down, spreading my legs and taking a deep breath.

"I'm still having bad cramps and long periods despite having had children. I was told that once you give birth, these issues disappear," I said.

"Well, the C-section could explain the cramps. Also, science hasn't proven that natural births prevent cramping or long periods. Birth control pills work well for some women, but others have bad reactions to them. I can give you an injection to suppress your period for three months at a time, but, again, I don't know how you'll react to it, and there's no way to undo it once you've had it. You'd have to wait until it has run its course."

Sensitivity to violence, and bad dreams – Brussels, November 2015

For years I'd done meditations and bikram yoga daily, particularly in Vancouver. Since moving to Brussels, I was thankful to have a bikram studio around the corner, but the hours were not as good as in Vancouver and, more of concern, the studio wasn't warm enough.

I'd been able to tame most of my deepest and darkest side; in doing so I managed to avoid the majority of TV shows, despite their popularity. Harvey, on the other hand, watched many of them and especially loved *Game of Thrones*. He was excited about the upcoming season. "Do I really need to see this show to learn about brutality and how to mercilessly fight for what's mine?" I asked him as we were about to fall asleep.

"I still can't understand why you freak out when you see blood in it. It's just special effects. I can see why something like the Paris attack would get anybody riled up, and particularly you, but a TV drama – isn't that a bit much? Now, my sweet little head," he said in Dutch. "Let's get some shut-eye, shall we?"

I woke up a short while later and was unable to get back to sleep. "Were you having a bad dream, Linda?" Harvey asked, shaking me slightly to wake me up.

He did that because I'd often talk in my sleep, laughing or talking about what was happening in my dreams. After being married to me all these years, he was no longer frightened by this. He called it "your silly nocturnal craziness."

He often said he could easily learn about my days because I relived and revealed them at night; he told me this transparency gave him peace of mind. He'd wake me only when I was crying, or laughing or talking too loudly.

"Do you think my father really wanted me to marry you?" I turned to face him.

"Oh, Linda. What am I going to do with you? Of course, your father wanted us to marry; otherwise, we wouldn't be here. Please, let's go to sleep now." He turned away, but I felt anxiety and panic rise within me.

"What am I going to do with myself? Look where we are again: in Europe. It's not the same as when we left it sixteen years ago. What's happening to the world, and what am I going to do here?" I howled uncontrollably.

I wanted to let my tears pour out but I held them back – it had been like this for a while; instead, I'd bleed. He leaned gently on me. I noted his weight and ignored it at the same time.

"You're everything, Linda. You can do or be anything you want. You just have to go and get it yourself; nobody else can do it for you. And, most importantly, it will have to be something that makes you money … something that has nothing to do with whatever you're doing now," he said calmly. He sounded exactly like my father.

"I don't want to judge, but look at them –"

"Look at who?" He looked around our bedroom.

"They're killing everybody in the show without giving a rat's ass about how the murder and the violence affect the viewers, or people like me," I said.

"Let me help you fall sleep," he countered, holding me. "I think they're simply great entertainers. I'd rather have writers who kill in their stories than living beings who feed terror to our children, and all humanity, for most of their lives."

I settled into his arms and slept a bit. When I awoke, I was in a sweat and, once again, could not get back to sleep. I was trying to get out of bed quietly when I realized we had had almost the same conversation the winter of 2014. In Vancouver, the season finale of *Game of Thrones* had aired. The war between the wildlings and the white walkers had been the talk of the town, in real life and on social media, for weeks.

"Have you ever lost anybody in your life? NO. You have all your family: both your parents, your brother, and even your brother's dog. What do you know about such loss? God forgive me for the words I've been spitting out this evening. And I ask him to make sure you never learn what it's like when a loved one dies." Now I was fully awake.

"Linda, please stop traumatizing yourself. *Game of Thrones* is just a writer's fantasy; it's entertainment, that's all," he replied.

"I can't sleep while the people I love in this show are being killed. I lost my mother at twelve, my sister when she was seven, and my grandfather last year ... and if you only knew what else I've lost –"

"Me? The man you loved so much when we flew to Africa to marry? He has also gone. I have no clue how to help you with whatever you're telling me. I really have no idea what to do with you."

"Then don't sit here and tell me it's OK to see people die because it's just entertainment. The press celebrates the show's writers, either for good or bad, and they keep killing characters without feeling, without remorse, without any thought of being judged. Why? Why do we have to die? Why be born on this stupid earth just to struggle and perish? I don't want to die without knowing why I'm here. I want to live, and I want to be ..." I kept ranting.

"Yes, please be somebody; go be a writer, be – well, maybe you wouldn't want to kill people in your stories. But then go be the actress you've always dreamed of being. And, please, let's get back to sleep, sweetie," he said calmly.

I cried irrepressibly, in search of a path back to myself, and I refused his help. What was happening to me? Self-control eluded my grasp.

Chapter 6
A Premonition

News from Father – Vancouver, December 2012

Over the last few days, my left eyebrow had begun vibrating. My father would say "When your eyebrow twitches it means you'll meet someone you're missing or haven't seen in a long, long time. It could also predict a big surprise, especially if it trembles on the right."

Those words stayed with me. Often, a quivering eyebrow would send me out to buy a lottery ticket, winning the jackpot the only imaginable surprise. Since I'd moved to Canada, no one from my family had visited. I'd tried several times to make it happen, but immigration always found a reason not to grant a visa, not even to my young brother Alpha Oumar. We managed to rendezvous elsewhere: in Europe or the States when he came in on one of his trips to Washington, DC. I'd never invited my father, even though I believed many of my family members in Guinea were in survival mode. In general, at any given point, living in Africa is about survival.

Something inside me had always responded with restlessness whenever I thought of my mother, but now my father seemed to take her place. I kept shrugging it off, thinking it was because of the coming holidays and our not having seen each other in a long time. He might even have forgotten me, given the other fifteen kids he had, as far as my counting goes. And God knows how many more he may have fathered since I'd left Africa.

Harvey and I had now resumed a relatively normal life, or I had simply become an expert at hiding things, like my mother and my father had done. I often kept my phone turned off, even on holidays, but this time I left it on because my eyebrow was telling me something was in the cards for me.

My birthday arrived. I was adding another year to my age but was still far from realizing what I really wanted to do with my life. I didn't even understand why I'd moved to Canada. What was keeping me from going forward? Was I my own worst enemy, with nobody to rescue me but me, a me who was drawn out from pain and the anger of knowing change could not occur until I faced my reality and my past? Could I cheat myself throughout my life and still be happy?

Why do we bury or burn the dead? Because they stink, or simply because we can't accept that we're all returning to wherever we came from, one way or another? My deeply buried secrets, flagged with the colour red, kept reminding me they were there whether I could see them or not. Some were so deep they were only misty outlines, but they kept intruding at unexpected times and places.

I'd been great at keeping secrets, hiding them, most of my life. Great at taking care of everyone but me. On my own I'd worked, worked and worked to find myself, but I was nowhere to be found. I might discover myself, on any given dawn, standing on the carpet with blood dripping down my legs yet again. What was the universe trying to teach me, and when was I going to listen? I wondered what I was doing here; had I been kidding myself that I could build a traditional family and home?

"Hello?" It was my father at the other end of the line; he was calling from Conakry. The children were already asleep, as was Harvey, who usually went to bed around eleven.

"Yes. I can hear you alright," I told him.

"I called to wish you a happy birthday, my beautiful daughter."

I was surprised by his call, and I thought his enthusiasm was forced. He hadn't spoken to or seen me in so long.

"Oh. Thank you," I said hesitantly. "You remembered my birthday. Something must be up."

"Yes; something is up. I've wanted to tell you this for a long time, but I never had the chance. I have the feeling it's something that needs to be told. It's a family secret." He paused.

"Is it a family secret or your secret?" I asked a little reluctantly.

"Please listen before you jump to conclusions," he said softly.

"Can this wait until we meet face to face, or do I really have to hear it now?" I had the urge to hang up.

"Please don't hang up. I know how you hate bad news."

"Please stop, or I really will," I said.

"OK. Again, I'm sorry, but I need to tell you this." There was pleading in his voice.

"Go ahead," I sighed. "Are you OK?"

"No," he said. "You have another brother."

I paused before saying, "AOB told me your young wife is still bearing you children. I'm not sure why you keep having kids, but that's not the secret, is it?" He didn't answer right away.

"No, that's not it. I mean I'd had another child with another woman when –"

"When my mother was alive?" I shouted.

"Yes, and I'm sorry," he said.

"Sorry?! Really, to whom are you saying 'Sorry'? To Allah, your conscience, your Fula people, my mother who can't defend herself, humanity – to whom are you apologizing?" I lashed out.

"I thought it's time you knew, because I'm not feeling well these days. Getting older and all that. He's a great boy who has asked me to inform you all –"

"To tell us about him. How could you have given me such a hard time growing up and carried on about my marrying a white man when you had such a devastating secret? Who the hell is he, anyway, to make that decision for us? Does he think we want to know him?" I shouted.

"I already gave your brothers the news, and they insisted I tell you directly," he said quietly.

"They're right," I said, trying to calm myself down. "How old is he?" I asked after a deep breath with my hand over the phone. I glanced out the window to distract myself, but nothing interesting caught my eye.

"He's twenty-five."

"He's much older than Leonis – the son of yours I had to take from the hospital by myself while you were with the mother of your bastard child. And he was old enough to be left with his mother so that you could have stayed with mine when she most needed you. But you chose to be with them instead?! Father, I wish you hadn't told me. I'm very upset." I was furious.

"I know about all that, but please remember I'm your father and you can't talk to me this way, particularly over the phone. It wasn't my fault she died. People die because their time is up," he said in tears. *Had he gotten weaker with age?*

"Says who? Your Allah? People die from lack of hope, Father, and lack of proper medication and care. You went to his mother instead of staying with mine!" I said angrily.

God, how am I going to calm myself down? Should I just hang up? Should I just stop listening to him? And then what? Would I be running away again?

"I know how you feel, and I also didn't know about this," he said through tears.

"Really? God!" I took the phone from my ear and looked up at the living room's blank white ceiling. I wished I could fly, or turn into a bird or an autumn tree that would never shed its leaves. What was I going to do with this news?

"My darling girl, please listen to your old father. The young man came to see me recently. He was on his way to Germany ..." He kept speaking as if he were talking to himself.

"Did you really just call me your darling daughter?" I sat down on the couch next to the window, remembering our phone conversation of eighteen years ago, but this time I was in a better position.

"Why was he going to Germany?" I asked irritably. It was as if I wanted to undo his words by repeating them to myself.

"He lives and studies over there. He doesn't need your money, our money," he assured me.

"Why did he reach out to you, then?" I asked a little more calmly. The leather couch was comforting, and I let myself be hugged by it, bringing my knees up to my chest. I continued listening to my father, who seemed to be talking as if he were at Sunday confession in a foreign land.

"He told me it was for him rather than me," he said.

"He said that to you?" I said in surprise.

"Yes, he's really a great boy," he replied.

"And he's your son for sure. No blood test needed." It was as if I were talking to myself now.

"We're not white at this end, you know," he chuckled.

"Well, what do you want me to do with this news?" I was in denial, but I tried to keep my composure.

"Nothing, really; I just want you, and your mother, to forgive me. I think if you pardon me, your mother will, too, from heaven," he said tearfully.

What is going on with him? This doesn't sound like my father. Is this what happens to people when they age?

I couldn't listen to him anymore. "Father, I need to go to the toilet." I released my knees from my chest, because the pose reminded me of my body's fetal form during an endlessly lonely night a few years ago. I hung up without saying goodbye, and he didn't call back.

Once in the bathroom, I sat sobbing on the floor and realized I'd just peed myself. I crawled into the shower and peeled off my clothes under the near-scalding water.

I was aching for my mother, yearning to connect with her and talk to her. What would she say: that it was fine I'd not spoken to my father or seen him all these years? Would she have forgiven him, or had she forgiven him already? I let the shower run, moving just enough so the hot water didn't burn. The stream's patter let me cry without waking anybody up until, eventually, I managed to join Harvey in our bed.

I'd had many sleepless nights, but none like the one I was having now. I wished for the superpowers of a flying black horse; I'd ride swiftly to my father and strangle him with my bare hands. Would killing somebody who hurt me make me feel better? I'd loved him and, worse, I felt a treacherous awareness that I still loved him even though he had been around so rarely. As usual, he had selfishly dumped his venom on me, like he had with my mother during each of her pregnancies.

I kept reflecting on my mother's death together with my father's details and elaborate loving message. Whom should I forgive first: my father, for cheating on my mother; for not standing up for me and confronting his brother who put me in jail when I was twelve, the same year my mother died; and for never asking me how I felt about that time and if anything had happened to me in that hellhole. Or should I forgive my mother, who stole my childhood by not fighting for us?

I was starting to understand that being 'only' a mother wouldn't be enough; my children were growing and they would one day leave, like I had left my family all those years ago. Then what? Would I still be happy with their father? How could I be happy with him if I wasn't happy myself? Why did I expect him to be the one to make me happy?

I'd heard Harvey say something like "What is happiness, anyway?" I'd always known the answer when it was about my kids, but was there anything else, aside from my children and being the best mother I could be to them? Would forgiving my father and my mother make any difference to my journey through life? And if so, how?

I had tried. I had told my mother many times that I forgave her, but did I really? Or did I say so only because that's what I wanted her to hear?

God, I'm grateful to you for giving me only boys, because I wouldn't have known what to do with a girl. "Thank you!" I said out loud, like my brother AOB would have done.

Maybe I wouldn't forgive my father or my mother until the day I joined her. I hoped I'd be much older and healthier than she had been when she passed. Right now I could neither forget not forgive her for letting go instead of fighting to stay with me and my brothers. She gave up on all of us because of a man who didn't care enough to be there for her when she needed him most.

Besides, I was already older than she had been, and I intended to grow older still. I'd do anything to see my children as happy adults. I would cheat death by taking care of myself: eating healthy, exercising, meditating ...

I felt Harvey's hands graze my inner thighs. I sighed, lifting my head slightly. Usually, New Year represented a threat to me, an added year to the ones that I wanted to live and be there for my children, family and friends. Despite Harvey's caresses, I couldn't relax. The day my mother died possessed my thoughts.

Name change – Terrorist-attack anxiety – Brussels, March 28, 2016

The clock struck three. I had another two hours before I went to pick up the kids from school. They were heading into their first spring break in Belgium. I decided to nap or at least lie down before collecting them, since I'd gotten up at six for yoga.

I looked out my new high-ceilinged window. Brussels was in full bloom; spring had been beautiful and unusually warm. Today was so sunny it felt like mid-summer. The weather had been unlike anything we had expected when we moved here; it was unpredictable, still, inexplicably, snowing at times. Perhaps we could blame global warming, since we were great at blaming anything but our actions.

The sounds of passing cars, buses, trams and construction vehicles through the wide-open French doors made the promise of a busy and eventful summer more palpable. The sun shining directly inside, heating our home, made me feel like I was on vacation; my quiet time ended when I heard Harvey walk in the front door.

"Linda, are you home?" he called.

Why is Harvey here at this time of day? I rolled off the bed to meet him in the living room.

Since I had begun to change my name officially – I wanted nothing to do with the previous one, Lawra Linda – I didn't like him calling me 'Linda.' But his refusal to use the new one had forced a wedge between us.

"Stop calling me 'Linda.' And what's brought you back home?"

"When we met in Moscow in 1988, you introduced yourself as Linda, not Lawr … a name I can't even pronounce." He spoke quickly as if he wanted to avoid the topic. "We've been given an extra day off because of the attack."

"That's nice. But please stop calling me 'Linda.' I'm not her anymore and will never be her. I'm Lawrelynd."

"Why are you dwelling on a name when our world is falling apart?" he asked.

"Because that's the only thing I can control right now; otherwise, show me what's more important than the death of my old name. Besides, death is trendy right now."

"Don't change the subject. I've known you as 'Linda' for the last eighteen years; do you expect me to create a new habit overnight?"

"God will pray for us, for my brother to get better and for all the mothers around the world who lose children to terrorists or to whatever else is beyond their control. How many are still dying in childbirth in Africa, and how many girls have been mutilated and deprived of their childhoods? How many of those girls lived or died?" I lashed out like an old wound bursting.

"Terrorists, or perhaps your own demons … which is it, Linda? You're totally off again … Have you gone to yoga today? When was the last time you meditated? For all the years I've known you, you've wanted to save the world while you can't even save yourself!" I stood and listened to him rave.

"And you mention God?!" he went on. "'God' seems to live on the tip of your tongue, but is he really here? Has he ever been here, Linda? Most of the chaos that has visited humanity, as far I remember, occurred in the name of God. But where was he when terrorists plotted to kill innocent people and fill us and our children with fear, Linda?"

"Stop calling me 'Linda'! Yes, God has always been here for me."

"Please don't try the patience of your god, Linda! Whatever is done to humanity in the name of God is unforeseen, and unforgettable and unforgiveable to you. You of all people should know that because you lose everything."

"I lose everything? Are you insinuating I have some kind of curse on me because of the people in my life who have died? Are you accusing me of killing them, one by one – that it was my fault? Please take it back, Harvey. Please. I've worked on myself all these years to escape the guilt of being the one who survived; now, again, it's all my fault because I'm cursed. What you're really saying is that I'll never have peace of mind no matter where I go. Please take it back. I'm no longer the same, and I'll never be the Linda or the Lawra that my whole family in Africa remembers. You can't –"

Harvey moved forward as if to embrace me, but I stepped back.

I thought of everything he was willing to do for his sons, and how he'd dashed off to school to fetch them after the terrorist attack. "At times I envy the boys for what you are to them and for what you do for them. I wasn't fathered like that," I said.

"Any father would have picked his children up on that day. However, I want to make one thing clear, Linda: I'm not *your* father, and what went on with him is your father's problem, not mine. We have been over this – your mother, your father, your uncle, and now your brother AOB is sick. I've heard it over and over, for the last eighteen years, and I'm tired of it." He sank to the couch as if he had finished running a marathon.

Is it this hard to live with me?

"Do you really mean it, Harvey? My own ghostly and tormented destiny; whatever you call it … my mother, my father, my uncle, my brother – who else do you want to bring up?" I didn't expect an answer. I'd not only combined my first name and middle one but also changed my last name, never taking his.

Is something really wrong with me, or do others want me to believe something is wrong with me?

"When I first met you, you introduced yourself as Linda, and that's the Linda I know and still love. You can't ask me to call you by any other name."

"Can't you at least use the whole thing, Lawra Linda? I'm tired of being one half or the other. Everybody calls me as they please; maybe that's why I seem missing to myself, unable to know who I am."

"You're Linda and will always be Linda to me," he insisted.

"Are you sure about that? Who would confirm that for you? My mother, my father, my cousins, my brothers, my family in Africa? Whom did you meet at our African wedding who called me by any name you know? Who? Tell me. No, wait; you don't know, and you can't answer."

"They all call you a different name, but that's not my problem, really –"

"It is mine, and I'm going to change my name to whatever I please because it's my turn to decide who I am, what I am and what I want to do with my life. You'll call me by my new name whether you like it or not. Now, If you don't mind, I have to make an appointment with my name-change counsellor." I picked up the phone.

"All I'm hoping for by changing my name is to be at one," I continued, "and being called by a single name will make it easier to be whatever and whomever I choose, to actually love the new me simply because I chose to be that person and not who you or my father or my mother or my grandmother or any other person or culture wanted me to be. You know, a friend of AOB's, when we were kids, couldn't stand even a nickname because he believed so strongly in his own name. He was absolutely right in his stand."

"Knowing you well enough by now, I'd simply call this one of the projects you take up to distract yourself from facing exactly what's underneath it all –"

"What do you mean, underneath it all?" I was still holding the phone.

"You make it sound like having many names is a disease. Well, queens, famous people and many others have had a variety of names without making them official, as you're about to do."

"If everybody had stuck to one name, out of all of mine, maybe I wouldn't feel so lost. … Aren't you supposed to be somewhere this morning?" I said.

"Maybe if you believed that you're Linda and forgot all your past traumas, you'd be fine."

"I don't want to be fine, Harvey. I want to be happy with my name and myself and with you. The only thing I'm definitely happy about and proud of is being mother to Josh and Owen, but that's not enough for me."

"How absurd, Linda. The only thing you're best at being isn't good enough? The grass is always greener …"

During breaks in the argument with Harvey I was managing to carry on a conversation with a gentleman at the Kabalarian society. He told me, "It's good that you want to change your name, but it takes time. Make sure the new one is exactly what you want and that nobody else in their right mind is asking you to change your old one. Why do you want it altered? Did you use the online sample of name balances, as I asked you to do before we meet?" he asked.

"Yes." *This feels like going to a shrink, which I really hate.* No shrink had ever made me feel good. *God, what am I getting myself into again?*

"I can see it here," he confirmed. "Did you read it all?"

"Yes, I did. And, yes, I did think about it, to anticipate your next question."

"Well, we aren't actually changing your name. We're balancing it, given that you wish to continue after this meeting," he explained.

"If I understood you correctly, a balanced name will bring me wealth, health and happiness, right?" I said. "I would like to have this done before I leave."

"If you insist, at least we'll start the process and hope that you get some of it off the ground before your departure."

Lawra Linda fears dying the same age as her mother – Vancouver, December 25, 2013

My chest constricted; a strong pain squeezed my heart. Starting to wheeze, I saw two people in front of me instead of one. Maybe I was getting a migraine. *Just take a deep breath. It's only the start of a migraine.*

I struggled to breathe, but each inhalation was shallow and I still felt breathless. *No, I've never had migraines.* I stood in the middle of the kitchen where Harvey was making himself an afternoon espresso. I walked toward the children's bedroom, needing to be close to them. I wasn't feeling good.

What if this was the end of me because God was punishing me? Was I really on the same path as my mother? I had been a great mother, and I wanted to share my life with my boys, to be there for them for many years to come.

Was this my last chance to tell them I loved them and hug them? I tried to calm myself down, because, despite my premonition, I knew this wasn't the day I would die, but the pain in my chest kept growing.

I'll fight this. Where is the ache coming from? I'm struggling just to reach their door.

"Are you OK?" Harvey asked as he trailed behind me. I ignored him and kept going. "Do you want to go to the kids' room? You're sure you're all right? You look bad. Can you breathe? Can you hear me? Do you want me to call the doctor?" He followed me down the hall.

"Hmmm, no…" I forced myself to speak so as not to leave him hanging, but the corridor felt unusually long. Determination alone kept me purposefully moving toward my sons' bedroom. I knocked at the door.

"Come in," I heard them say enthusiastically. They had mounted a sign, "Knock before entering." When I walked in they looked up and raced toward me.

I wanted to smile, but too late. I fell to the floor. The back of my neck hurt, and it didn't feel like I could get up by myself anytime soon.

I heard some talk, and crying from my kids, and Harvey on the phone to 911. It seemed like I was fighting for my life. I thought about how old I was. God, I'm not yet ready to go. I'm too young – but my mother had died at 33.

You have to give me back; my sons need me. Maybe their dad doesn't, but my sons need me. You can't take me now. You have to let me be their loving mother for many years to come. I won't be like my mom; please bring me back to my kids and my husband. I promise I'll behave myself and not do anything to compromise my presence in their lives. Please, God: one more chance with my boys. Please, please, be merciful, please …

I felt someone's hand on my chest, pushing it up and down. People were talking. The ambulance had arrived fast, or maybe it wasn't fast, but I knew paramedics were there and trying to get me back to my family.

Then an attendant was asking my husband to arrange for someone to look after Josh and Owen so they wouldn't have to witness the worst. In the meantime, I was busy with God:

You heard that? Please close Harvey's ears. My sons are supposed to be with me, and with me all night, not afraid I won't be able to get back. I need them – they are my oxygen! You have to return me. I want to stay, and I want it now. I'm not ready; I'm not going anywhere. Please bring me back. I beg you, God, please.

I saw myself on my knees pleading with God to let me return to my family. *I promise I'll be a great wife, mother, friend, daughter – a worthy person for humanity – and I'll behave thoughtfully and honestly. I promise! I promise!*

I couldn't understand why nobody heard me. I believed my kids were tuned in, though, because they ran to me, each holding one of my hands. The attendant started to pry them away when Josh pleaded, "Please don't separate us. She needs us both with her right now!"

"Please let us stay with her," added Owen, a little more quietly.

"OK," she said as though something more powerful had induced her to accept the request. I felt them lifting me into the ambulance; the siren had stopped. I was awake now.

Looking around, I showered kisses on Josh and Owen like never before. I wanted to return them to my belly and never look back. I'd be fine with that if we all went together to the next world. Harvey was wordlessly trembling, massaging my legs as if to warm them.

I've always had cold hands and feet. Whenever anyone asked why, I'd blame my warm heart for having given away too much love with only a little left for me, but I'm fine with that.

This time, though, I wondered if it were a sympathetic reaction to my mother's last hours, her body rapidly chilling. Something came to mind that I'd kept from everyone. It had become Harvey's habit to reach for my hands or feet whenever he felt powerless with me or when we fought. If we were sitting, he'd massage my fingers or toes. I wasn't sure whether the present gesture was meant to remind me of us, to reassure himself that we were still together, or to confirm I was still alive. A corpse is icy cold, from what I recall of my mother.

Brussels-attack stress leads to bleeding – Brussels, March 23, 2016

I'm really, really frightened because I'm losing too much blood again. A phenomenon I'd thought I'd put behind me is right here again between my legs. I haven't had sex with my husband for months, so why do I have to swim in my own blood? Does every woman's period give her such a hard time? Don't you realize, God, that I'm tired of wiping myself, and of my husband seeing me bloody all the time? What am I holding on to with this bleeding? Have I still not healed from my past? I thought I had ...

"You're bleeding ... are you having your period? Are you scared? I am, too, but you don't see me drenched in red every time something happens beyond my control. What's going on? Didn't you tell me this had stopped? Have I been too tough on you, Linda? I'm ... should I call a doctor, an ambulance? Should I do that?"

I was half conscious, watching, drenched in my blood, feeling it flow down my calves and onto the floor, as though a nomad had just cut off a goat's head so his family would be sustained while he was away. Harvey helped me to the bathroom, where I took off my pants and underwear to step into the shower. I heard him open the bathroom cubbies. "What are you looking for?" I asked as I turned on the shower.

"Tampons or pads," he said. I didn't respond.

I can't believe I'm bleeding again and that Harvey is looking for tampons. What's happening? I thought this was behind me. Why am I again losing so much blood when I don't have my period? God, I'm tired of it; whatever this is, it has to stop. Haven't I exorcised all my demons and ghosts, or are they still lurking? Why in Brussels? Why? Is Harvey right about me after all? Have I lost all sense of myself? Will I ever catch up and be simply me?

"You're talking to yourself again, or you're thinking too loud," he said.

"I don't know; since you seem so sure –"

"Sorry, Linda. We shouldn't be arguing with all that's going on around us. I'm sorry; I'm heading to the store to get you some tampons."

"Maybe try checking the reserve suitcase first."

"Please just wash ... and listen to me this time around. I'll be right back," he said.

While the shower ran, I pulled down the bathtub handle to plug the drain, sat down and watched the water turn crimson as it rose. At first I felt like I had with my aunt in Africa, the day I almost drowned, and then as though I were floating in a shallow scarlet ocean.

I watched the tub fill up quickly, the water growing redder and redder until it reached my knees; then it covered my stomach, my breasts and my neck, and I didn't flinch. I saw myself walking into a pool with tiny ripples like a sleepy lake; it was turning icy cold, like my mother's toes in her hospital bed, so cold that goosebumps formed on my skin, and the water was rising to the crown of my head.

Before totally submerging myself in the sea, with waves now strong and slapping each other like galloping dragons' wings, I whispered, "Paris attack ... Brussels attack, and now my brother ... *Game of Thrones* ... move over. Death will never be as beautiful as it is right now ..."

I felt the whitecaps lift my feet, which I started to wiggle, since fighting for life seems to be a human instinct, yet all the while I kept calm. *Death can never be as trendy as it is now, AOB. You're right, baby brother. Leave some room for me*, Game of Thrones *heroes; here I come with an endlessly bleeding vagina.*

As the currents captured my torso and my hands let go, flat into the tub, I heard Harvey's voice.

"What are you doing, Linda – sorry, Lawrelynd? I know how hard it is being here for all of us, not to mention for yourself, sweetheart, but remember, the kids and I need you, always, and your brothers' kids are going to be fine. Lawrelynd is strong, and Lawrelynd isn't a victim; she's a happy person, no matter what." He pulled me out of the tub and started spreading towels on the floor.

Linda in the hospital – Vancouver, spring 2015

The ambulance had been called again for the ongoing, unpredictable chest pains I was having, and I had been hemorrhaging almost to death, though I was keeping that fact to myself. I hadn't told my doctor or Harvey about it for fear my jail time would be revealed and what had happened to me then. Although I was in denial about my past, sometimes I was driven, one way or the other, to face it, but I kept it hidden as it dug ever deeper into me, to the point where my hurting, damaged soul seemed to merge with my physical self. I felt caged in shame; perhaps it was eating away at me. Did I subconsciously wish to join my mother? One thing was certain: I'd rather be dead than tell another soul about my rape.

I wasn't sure why Harvey was rubbing my feet, but it didn't matter now. I just wanted him to be there for me, as well as for our sons. I scrutinized him carefully. He looked a bit older and sadder all of a sudden. He leaned in and murmured in my ear.

"I can't do it alone. We need you. You know we need you." He stopped. "You're the love of my life. Don't ever think of leaving me again. Please don't take the easy way out. We'll work it out; I love you. Do you hear?"

I kept silent and listened. He wasn't an emotional man and didn't usually talk like this. The only time he had was when I was labouring with Josh, when Josh was stuck between our world and the passage to it from my uterus. We were both calling for life, but my strong desire for a natural birth blinded me until things grew much, much worse.

"You, and me, and the kids, together always and always forever; do you hear that? Do you understand how much I need you – we all need you in our lives?" There was a tear on his cheek.

"Yes, I do," I said in shock.

"I'll come in after you with my family, if that's OK," Harvey said to the paramedic who was attending to me.

"You guys can stay where you are. Your mother is fine, and she'll stay fine," she told Josh and Owen.

"Can we please just go to the hospital too? We're her oxygen," Josh said confidently.

"She'll be stronger if we come," Owen added without any shyness in his voice.

"Can't we all come?" Harvey asked gently, his eyes full of tears.

"OK, then." The paramedic caved.

"We'll all meet over there," Harvey said.

"Can one of us be with her in the ambulance?" Josh asked.

"Yes," said the attendant while looking at my three guys. "Josh, do you really want to go with Mom?"

"Yes. Owen, do you want to go with Papa?" Josh asked, looking at Owen, who was holding his dad's hand.

"Yes." Owen nodded.

"Thank you!" Josh said to his brother with a quick hug.

I looked up and said, "Thank you" to God. *This is why I'm not ready yet. It's beautiful to see them negotiate so kindly with each other. I want to be here to enjoy more of this and to guide them through their lives.*

The pinch at the left side of my chest was stubborn but manageable with the deep breaths the paramedic had asked me to take as she prepared me for transport to the hospital. She watched me carefully even as the kids pleaded with her to let both come along in the ambulance. There just wasn't enough space. The urgency in her voice won out; she wanted to get me to emergency as fast as she possibly could.

Harvey followed the ambulance with Owen in the back seat. Josh never let go of me; he had convinced the paramedic to let him hold my hand. He was staring at me like a hungry bear hunting for salmon in spring.

On arrival at St. Paul's Hospital, I was seen by a doctor right away. It reminded me of the clinic in Paris I had gone to when I was stung by a bee. This was on the trip to France where Josh was conceived. Now I was whisked into care – a good sign? I hoped for my children and worried about myself, but Harvey would surely manage without me; he'd remarry right away. Why wouldn't he if I died in surgery? What made me so special that he'd wait even a month – but, then, what would become of my kids? What?

I must live! It's my duty to raise my children. I won't be like my mother who gave up on me and my brothers and her newborn child.

A nurse entered and told Harvey, "We think Lawra Linda had what we call an anxiety attack. She ought to take it easy or get more help with the kids and relax if anything is bothering her. She could see Dr. Carter again; without a proper consultation and X-rays, we can't say for certain what happened. It seems that at one point she was gone. It's strange. We want to make sure she's okay, so we're keeping her here to monitor over the next twenty-four hours. Once our cardiologist has seen her, you can pick her up. For now, go home and get some rest. And take the kids to the park. It's a beautiful day outside."

"Do you guys want to go play some soccer?" the doctor on duty asked Josh and Owen. They hesitated.

"She's young and very healthy," the nurse added.

Harvey looked dumbfounded. He followed the physician out into the corridor, asking him several questions as he made his way to the next room. With no other words to express his shock, Harvey wanted to know what was next. Would a specialist see me before we left the hospital? "Who is the doctor we're waiting for?" he asked.

"I'm almost done for the day, but Dr. Greg from cardiology will be here soon. She usually starts in the early evening on the night shift."

"Can a woman my wife's age have a heart attack?" Harvey asked, his eyes focused on the nurse, who was a little surprised by his delayed reaction. In situations like this, Harvey had always been a little slow to respond.

"I'm not confirming it was cardiac arrest without a complete examination, but it does happen to women." The nurse and doctor were both answering calmly, even as they began interviewing the next patient in line.

"Heart attacks occur in young woman who are healthy, too. Maybe too much stress?" the doctor asked. "Do you know what took place prior?"

I started thinking about what had really happened, other than our arguing. I wondered why the clinician wasn't asking me directly. I was still here; I had not died yet. I chose not to interpret this, however, since he might have his own reasons. I turned my back to them but kept my ear on the conversation.

"She went to her early-morning yoga," Harvey started to explain.

"How early?" the doctor asked.

"She leaves at 5:30 for a 6 a.m. class."

"That's really early. Why? Does she eat before leaving?" the doctor asked.

Harvey shook his head. "I think it buys her time. I'm home then, but I really don't know why she doesn't go during the day," Harvey said.

"How often does she go?"

"Over the last few months, daily."

"Why?" the nurse asked.

"She told me she loves it and feels great afterward."

"You're right; she seems very healthy and in good shape, too. I don't think it could be the yoga. What kind of yoga does she do?" the doctor asked.

"Something called bikram," Harvey said.

"Hot yoga is sometimes too intensive if the person isn't hydrated or can't sweat enough to keep themselves cool in the room and then replenish their body with good food and minerals. Now I'm even less sure why this would happen," the doctor admitted reluctantly. "Did you argue?"

"We had an incident a few weeks ago, or maybe it was last week. ... Recently, not that I know of," Harvey said with a gentle smile. "You know women; sometimes they can be upset with you for days and you'll only find out about it later, down the road. But with her I don't seem to be able to crack what's really going on. I'm a little lost myself," he added, and they gave a small laugh.

Josh and Owen were more relaxed now that even the doctor seemed merry. He had ordered an insulin IV for me; the fluid was dripping slowly into my vein.

I turned around but couldn't see Harvey. "Do you know where your daddy is?" I asked the boys, who were leaning on my bed.

"He went call to Grandpa and Grandma, I guess," Josh replied.

"Or maybe he went to call his brother," Owen added. "Or he's trying to get hold of one of your brothers – AOB, Goudoussy or Leonis – or other family?" Owen listed with his fingers as if he were counting all my brothers. It made me think about my twin brothers who had died in a miscarriage, for whom my mother grieved for the longest time, and the death of my only sister, whom nobody talked about, even on the phone, because of the way she had died, even though Fulani families went on cutting hundreds of girls each year. I wondered why my dead kept invading my thoughts. Was I destined to join them soon – was that the meaning of their presence in my life?

Yes – my brothers. It has been a while since I've spoken to or seen them. They're all grown now with families of their own, except for the youngest, Leonis. Has he found out our mother died giving birth to him? I wondered if that had been added to the many family secrets we had accumulated over the years.

"What time is it in Africa right now?" Owen asked.

"For them it's night time, my love," I said gently, smiling at both sons.

"Look!" Owen pointed his finger. "There's Daddy in the corridor, talking to the nurse who was in the ambulance with you."

"Yeah, Maman; there's Daddy. Do you want me to call him for you?" Josh asked.

"No. It's fine. He'll be with us once he's done with the doctor," I said before drifting off into deep sleep.

What had truly happened that morning? We had argued about something and nothing, but one thing was certain: I had been seeing my mother and her dead children constantly during my days and in my dreams.

She'd be holding them at her side: my sister, Nenein, and the twins she had lost through miscarriage, something only Alpha Oumar and I knew about. Sometimes it looked like she was waving. Sometimes one of the children resembled AOB, and all of them were beckoning me with gentle, soulful smiles, surrounded by light so bright I thought I was going to burn. I approached but wasn't scorched; I had a sense of tranquility and a desire to join them, but my mother seemed more interested in what AOB had to say. My frustration would grow and I'd leave them.

I'd wake up in a sweat, upset that she hadn't hugged me like she did her other children in the dream.

Had I kept my promise? Was all I had done not enough for her? I'd been wondering more than anything what she really wanted from me or what message she was trying to send that I was unable to catch without guilt, fear and blame.

Chapter 7
A Butterfly

Sick brother – Sense of responsibility – Vancouver, August 1, 2015

The month of August was loaded with endless to-do lists, and each day seemed to be short on time. Harvey had gone to San Francisco for training; we were returning to Belgium to further his career. At times I worried that Harvey and the kids would be late for our flight to Brussels. To make it even worse, my brother Alpha Oumar had pneumonia.

"How did you get pneumonia, Alphadjo?" I'd asked him over the phone in July when he was hospitalized.

"I caught it in Guinea when I was visiting some of the villages. I should have worn a mask like Goudoussy advised, but rest assured, I'll beat this in no time. We'll meet in Europe as soon as I recover."

Since Goudoussy was a doctor, and AOB himself was working for the International Monetary Fund, I tried to get him a medical visa to Europe, but the French embassy refused to give him one.

When Harvey came back from work in San Francisco, I ran into his arms and hugged him tight.

"Are you OK, or is this all because I'm home?" he said, squeezing me back.

"The French embassy refused AOB his medical visa, Harvey."

"Oh. That's not good news at all."

"He's going to rot there; he'll die, and nobody will give a shit. Why didn't I chain him here in the Western world? Why does he think *he* can save Africa?"

"Of course, we've got to do something, anything we can, to help him, but you're not obliged to take care of your brothers anymore. He's in the wonderful position of being able to move half of Guinea with him if he wanted to, but he hasn't. They all made the choice to live in Africa, and you made the choice to be here. That's something you have to respect. Let them be responsible for their own lives; it's not yours to decide. Our life is at times a living hell because you feel guilty and are in constant fear of what will become of them."

"No. I'm not afraid. One day while you were gone, I was in the park with the kids and I understood that I have nothing to fear anymore. But if AOB is sick, then I have to do something, you know. I need to go back, Harvey."

"Maybe it's something to consider if it would put your mind at ease, but right now let's focus on the move. We'll deal with the rest as soon as we at least find a school for the boys," he said.

The importance of children and life's meaning / Treeing people – Vancouver, fall 2013

It was autumn, and my birthday was fast approaching. I was questioning my life choices and my health issues; I had no clue how to solve my bleeding problem, but my life continued to unfold. I walked around our bedroom wondering if it needed painting or a new set of linens. I noticed, to my left, the walk-in closet by the entry. Without thinking I stood up to approach it. I felt the softness of the champagne-coloured carpet under my feet. It reminded me of the walls. They were painted a light brown I'd loved when we moved to this house six years ago, but now I couldn't stand it because it made everything seem dark, distant and indifferent to my feelings.

The only great thing about this place these days was how much bigger it was than our previous condo. My sons' giggles, scampering and playfulness were present in each room. Memories of them crawling in the long corridor, room to room, and now their running from one to the next and their loud, crazy imaginary stories gave me an even more expansive and brighter breathing space.

There was so much more to it, though, than the latte-coloured walls. Here we had experienced our many firsts, and I had always looked forward to bringing my children home when I picked them up from school. Their presence in my journey, in my house, filled me with oxygen, love and light. But when they were away I couldn't feel it.

I often wondered, or admitted to my little inner voice, I truly didn't know what to do with myself when they weren't around. What would my life be without them – their beauty, their genuine love of life, their grounded and well-rounded minds and spirits directed toward themselves, me, their father, their relatives and their friends, and their curiosity about the world, about which they had endless clever questions.

Sometimes all I could tell them was that I really didn't know. For my children's sake I'd strive for life as long as I could wake up in the morning, lift my head from my pillow and leave the bedroom.

I walked back to my bed as if I were going to get back in it; maybe I was a bit disoriented because it was getting darker faster now than it did in summer. Outside my window, leaves were turning yellow, brown, red and orange. Seasons change so fast in the West, in each country and city I have lived in. The trees were robbed of their beautiful green layers, disrobing before my eyes each day, falling into a beautiful multi-coloured autumn.

I could feel the air pressure change and wasn't sure if this explained why I was feeling unsettled this morning. Was I a treeing kind of person, shedding my leaves unknowingly like the trees, getting naked, letting myself be seen – me, who was always fearful of change? Or did I actually like fall? It made me think about all the sombre grey jackets, all the gloomy faces and, in some areas of the world, all the endless white snow. In Vancouver, it was the abundant rain that felt never-ending.

I'd see people striding quickly side by side, indifferent to each other. What could be weighing on their minds so much they couldn't give themselves a second to lift their face and acknowledge someone else, thereby creating a more loving world?

I looked back to what had become of the trees around me. I have always been fascinated by their transformation in fall. Do they like the change? Do they like losing their leaves? Do they call for anyone to witness the loss of their most precious part? Does it happen without their permission or does something invisible ask for their go-ahead first? How could I tune into that kind of talk if it existed? Maybe the trees have a way to negotiate it all, so it looks to me, and everybody else passing them by, that things happen effortlessly.

When it's time for my children to leave the nest, will I be able to let go of them as easily as these trees humbly accept being stripped of their leaves?

Oh, no; I'll do anything to prevent it, maybe buy a big house where we'll all live forever and ever. Harvey says we won't change; is he right? Am I distancing myself from him, living only for the children? I fear the dreadful idea that one day they'll move out. Wait a minute – for now I have them, and I have time for them. Yes, I do have time no matter what. Don't I?

They were growing so fast; at nine, Josh was almost my height, and Owen was not too far behind. Soon, for the sake of their father's career and their heritage, we would cross the Atlantic. Should I have said no to going to Belgium and taking them from their homeland and the friends they cherished so much? Was I doing the right thing? What would have been the alternative? Letting their father go alone to Belgium while we three remained in Vancouver? They had made the answer clear to me.

"Maman, we're a family, so we stay together," Owen said the night we discussed the move; Harvey was away in San Francisco.

"I agree with Owen, Maman. Besides, we'll be close to our father's family and learn proper Dutch," Josh said.

"We'll see grandmother Rina, grandfather Jaap, uncle Neil –"

"And aunt Madeleine and our cousins." Josh cut Owen off in his excitement. Jaap was Harvey's father's nickname; his real name was Jacob Cornelius.

I contemplated how great it would be to have the life of a tree. What kind would I be? What type of tree was I, really? A baobab, an apple tree – I do love apples – or perhaps an oak, because it's strong and powerful. Maybe a mango, one that feeds African people and their animals. Perhaps a palm tree in the sun, because it's tall, vivid, lively and flexible, able to angle itself in any way – the wind decides and yet it stands – and because people relax underneath it, when they take the time to look up at it. How about an evergreen, the Christmas tree? It dries a little, lets off steam with its cones and yet is used as decoration and celebrated in the coldest season. It is a tree everybody loves and cheerfully welcomes into their homes each year. Could I live my life like one of these trees? How long would I live, then? I would not want to die early and leave my children, like my mother had done. The image of her death will never disappear. I sometimes feel like I'm still at a door, listening to my parents' conversation or awaiting my mother's demise.

I was agitated and wanted to calm myself down. I slipped into the boys' room, gave them each a long kiss on their foreheads and sat on the rocking chair that was still there between their beds. I wondered what my mother would think of the little girl whose childhood she had stolen. Her man had abandoned her. Mine had always been there for me no matter what, but now I had to agree to support him in Europe. Would she have lived if my father had given her what she wanted that night I overheard their conversation? Would a C-section have saved her? Would she have taught me how to be a mother, or did motherhood teach itself? I missed her beyond belief. My body ached for her with every breath and at every event focused on her grandsons. My children would get to know their paternal grandparents, and for that the move to Brussels was worth it. My mother would have loved them and cherished them, nurtured and spoiled them. She'd have been a perfect grandmother to them. I felt tears pouring down my cheeks, but I checked them; this was not the time to cry. I needed to be strong.

Motherhood – Family life – Wandering soul in Brussels – April 11, 2016

I'm not an avid reader of anything related to violence where blood and human heartlessness is at the core of the story. I've never intentionally watched the news. I have spent so many years working on myself that I've learned to shove the things I don't want to reveal down into a deep sea. But it seems that within the sea is an untameable turmoil of waves that erupt like a volcano. I have learned to see the waves as a passing storm.

***

My kids were growing at a shocking rate, more swiftly than I'd anticipated, especially since we had moved to Brussels, much as they had done in the first years of their lives. Each morning I'd see something that had changed overnight: their noses, their mouths, their hair, their eyes or their height.

Also growing was their sense of the world around them and the complexity of Belgium's population and number of languages to be heard. I was hearing them as I walked down Rue de Lesbroussard. I reached down discreetly under my coat to reassure myself that my tampon was still in place. I checked the time on my phone. It was six in the evening, and we had been asked by Owen's best friend's mom, Laurence, to come for dinner – an invitation we had accepted two months ago and couldn't change because we had had all the time in the world to plan for it.

"Maman, did you have a great walk?" Josh asked, giving me a hug at the door.

"Maman, you know we can cancel this dinner because of AOB's death. Laurence will understand. We want you to be happy, Maman." Owen ran into my arms as well.

"Thank you, Owen, for your understanding, but you know we promised them two months ago. Happiness isn't perfect, either, so we're going." As we stood there, the main entrance door opened and we moved a little so Harvey could come in.

"We're going out? Where?" he asked, opening his arms to the boys.

"To Laurence's house for dinner; do you remember?" Josh took a seat while Owen, as usual, lingered in Harvey's embrace.

"Josh and Owen, can you please get yourselves ready? I'll wash up and then we're out of here," I said, walking to the bedroom and into the shower.

"Lawrelynd –"

"Did you just call me 'Lawrelynd'?" I drew the shower curtain aside so I could see him.

"I'm trying, Law…"

"Law-re-lynd." I helped him pronounce my name correctly.

"Thank you, Lawrelynd. You really don't have to keep this promise, since you couldn't have foreseen your brother's death. AOB died on April eighth, and today is only the eleventh. It's too soon for anything," he said.

But as I stepped out of the shower, he added, "Whoa – you are still bleeding?!"

"How about you go with the kids to get a small gift, and I'll be ready by the time you're back," I said as I applied some lotion.

Owen came into the bathroom. "Let's get a comic book for my friend and something for his older sister," he suggested.

"Let's not forget they're Belgian kids who might already have all the collections. We'll need luck, or a receipt in case they want to return or exchange it," Josh said as he joined us.

"Maman, do you feel better now that you've had your shower and put your cream on?" Owen asked as he sprinted out of the bathroom door to catch up with his father and brother who were halfway out of the house and calling for him.

We could have walked to Laurence's, but we took the bus three stops. The hosts welcomed us the Belgian way, with one kiss on the left check, as Owen and Josh climbed the stairs of the three-and-a-half-storey home, passing us oldies like they were running on flat ground. *You're guaranteed European stairs like I'm guaranteed oxygen.* The house was filled with the great smell of fresh baking, roasted chicken and French baguettes still in the oven.

"I hope you're all hungry, because we've prepared a real Belgian spread," Laurence said in French.

At her insistence, we first toured the house. Tycia's room looked anything but girly; it had a big telescope right beside her window, like Harvey had had in his Amsterdam house. She also collected all kinds of butterflies. As she told us about them, her green eyes grew expressive; their light could have illuminated even a dark room. I couldn't help but drift out of our conversation into a day I'd picked up Owen and Josh at their soccer practice in Vancouver.

The unexpected visit of a yellow butterfly – Vancouver, August 8, 2015

I was hustling across the soccer field to collect my sons when Josh and Owen jumped at me with unexpected hugs. I fell on the grass to deflect their weight; they were tickling me wherever they could to make me laugh, and I couldn't help but beg for mercy, attracting the attention of almost everyone nearby.

"Maman, you're a crazy nice person," Josh said reassuringly, looking into my eyes as I squinted in the bright August sun.

"You're the craziest and nicest person on the planet, Maman," Owen added, now on top of Josh, who was on top of me. I asked them to move so I could give them the pony ride my father gave me when I was little. We had always played horse or choo-choo train. I lost myself momentarily as I remembered giggling with him under the loving, watchful eyes of my mother. I could feel and hear my kids' happy laughter above me as I savoured those memories of my mom right beside us, ready to catch me if I fell. I felt exalted and expanded as I recalled my parents playing with me.

I suddenly came back to the here and now. It was a big day for my brothers and me, and I wanted to touch base with them – August 8 was the date our mother had passed away. "This very same date my mother died" was on repeat in my head.

The thought of her slowed me down a bit, so I let go of Owen and Josh. Where had this abrupt sadness come from? It had happened so long ago, and I didn't know why I had this feeling of profound loneliness. I looked around as if hoping to show her how busy I was and explain, in my thoughts, that if I didn't call my brothers today, I would when the time was right – but would that be fair to my brothers or enough for her? She would have wanted me to drop everything. Does she see me with her grandsons here and now in this soccer field?

The sky was clear and blue. The trees were still, as though politely and patiently waiting for fall's arrival and its invisible command. Their leaves were slightly dry, which made me wonder when it had last rained. It had been a while now, because the smallest and lowest branches were almost bare of foliage, but some were growing new shoots, tiny and shiny. The space between the soccer field and the woods was claimed by a fenced-in "dogs-only" area. Although most canines were kept on a leash, some animals still managed to escape their owners and run to us. Both Owen and Josh, under my watchful eye, would gently pat the approaching dog and give it some cuddles, inspiring many people, including the owners, to say, "Your sons are exceptionally beautiful and kind."

"It's time to go, boys. Please, let's call it a day." I knew their willingness to leave would be slow in coming, but it was time to at least start preparing them for our departure.

I held up my left hand to wave them over, then looked around to see why my kids had suddenly fallen silent. They were quietly watching dog tricks behind the fence. A brown dog emerged, a true beauty: tall, slim, with short hair like bronzed silk, and tiny, round, hazel eyes that seemed almost green. He was gorgeous and looked expensive. I watched him, too, but a little distractedly as I tried to find its owner. I was in two worlds: mine and my children's.

We were fascinated by the creature. All of a sudden Owen exclaimed in French, "This dog is truly beautiful. Are we ever going to have a dog, Mother?" Josh and I exchanged glances and laughed, knowing that Owen would seize any excuse to ask for a dog.

"Yes, it's a golden retriever," said Josh.

"Can we have that kind, Maman? I'm not saying 'some day,' because there's no such day on a calendar," Owen said. *Some day.* I smiled at him.

"I'd like a Labrador retriever – in chocolate," I said, and they both laughed as if I were tickling them.

"Now that we're moving to Belgium, everything will be about chocolate. We're going to have Belgian Labrador retriever chocolate!" Josh declared.

I had changed the subject to let them know I agreed it was a pretty dog, but we couldn't do more than think about a Belgian chocolate version. I planted tiny kisses on their cheeks. For some reason, time had stopped for us to enjoy it. It seemed I was waiting for something. Instinct told me not to rush myself, and I listened.

"Oh, Maman. Look at the butterfly – he's stunning!!!" Josh, excited, screamed in French; the winged beauty had just flown by us.

"Josh, that's Grandmaman!" said Owen assertively.

"Oh?" Josh asked, curious.

"Josh, you know. Maman always says that when a butterfly's around, it's our grandmaman visiting her." Owen with his big, bright eyes explained it to Josh, who listened attentively.

The moment was priceless to me; the pride that my children had acknowledged my mother through this butterfly let me move on. And I realized she was really, truly here, encouraging me, no matter how busy I was, to call my brothers that night.

If not for the chaos of the move, I would have been preparing some gesture or sacrifice with my siblings to mark the anniversary of our mother's death. For many years I had been opposed to this, but I'd given in to their entreaties without figuring out why I had been against the idea in the first place. Maybe because I had been upset with her and still wondered if I'd ever heal from her dying and leaving me alone with her young children to care for. It was a promise I'd kept against my will. "Why didn't she fight for us?" I asked myself again. But I quickly willed away that persistent and agonizing thought. The butterfly was here; so was she.

Is she seeing my kids? On my cheeks I felt a soft breeze, fresh and cold, and took a deep breath, realizing she might be next to me right now. We watched the butterfly swirl and twirl with its beautiful yellow wings again and again.

"Maman, I'm not so sure the butterfly is your mother, but if you believe it, then I will, too," Josh said, his reassuring eyes twinkling. "And it *could* be her. You told us your maman loves yellow, and that butterfly has yellow wings." I turned my head back to the field just in time to see her disappear as if she were never here, yet I knew she had been there and has always been with me.

I drifted back to Tycia who was wondering whether I had been listening to her stories about butterflies.

"Lawrelynd, which is your favourite?" she asked. As I was about to answer, Josh and Owen bounded over to us.

"Maman, it's snowing!" Owen shouted breathlessly.

"Yes, it's really coming down," Josh said, taking his younger brother's hand before they thudded down the stairs together. Without a word, I looked out the window. I took the telescope and saw the snowflakes fall as if somebody were on the roof shaking snow from a bucket. They looked crisp and shiny, like freshly ground sugar, and sweet, like life itself. We all rushed outside and started a snow fight, like kindergarteners free from rules, under the watchful eyes of an angel.

THE END

Afterword

By Tobe Levin von Gleichen

I was named for a great-grandmother who died in childbirth. My Grandma Frances had been only 13 when her mother Taube passed. That was in 1911.

Often growing up, I would notice grandma's inward turn and overhear her murmur about how, "to this day," – sometime in the 1950s – she still missed her mother. Taube had left eight living children; the last one didn't make it, and no one still alive knows how many pregnancies might have miscarried. But in that New York City era, immigrant wives not infrequently became maternal mortality statistics.

Those casualties occurred, however, more than 100 years ago, and in North America. The feisty if wounded protagonist of *Swimming in a Red Sea* lost her mother on another continent in the late twentieth century in a way that would count as malpractice, if not criminal negligence, had it occurred elsewhere than in the 'global South'. A respected midwife in Guinea already a multiple mother, Lawra Linda's mom Djenab is denied a C-section despite her knowledge that the operation could save her life. Following a lengthy struggle to expel the infant, hemorrhage rages rivers on the bedding, invades the mattress and pools on the floor in the presence of the sufferer's daughter. As Lawra Linda watches, warmth drains. Legs and hands grow glacial until, in place of her mother, a corpse remains – and a baby. The compelling episode rewinds itself over and over in the coming years; that the harrowing scene might trigger PTSD is all too apparent.[1]

And alas, cementing the event's life-altering power is a promise the dying mother extracts, an oath resented because the twelve-year-old had replaced her father as companion at the birth. The previous night, despite his wife's pleas, he had insisted on leaving town, and it is revealed later that he had not gone on business as announced but spent time with another wife and child.

Mother Djenab, meanwhile, aware of the coming farewell, beseeches her girl to nurture the surviving boys, including the new little brother. Only with reluctance does Lawra Linda swear to do so, and the pledge will haunt her throughout her life.

Among immigrant women's memoirs, the death-bed tableau gestures toward themes that make this work unique. The first is female genital mutilation, the bane of nearly all Fulani.[2] At present Guinea's prevalence rate is 96.9%.[3] Thus, Lawra Linda's mom, who had surely endured it in her youth, now suffers obstetric consequences, for FGM is known to delay the second stage of labour, thereby elevating the risk of maternal and infant mortality.[4] Although Djenab, an outlier, strives to maintain her daughter intact, the cutting takes place to 'restore' virginity following rape with strong hints of punishment in the motives of both male physician and vindictive contracting uncle.[5]

Virginity is a second major theme linked to FGM. A virgin, defined as a person whose vagina has never known a penis, can verify her 'purity' if skin at the introitus bleeds when pierced. Even today, Fulani expect untouched brides and can require proof at defloration. Anticipating this, the considerate Dutch husband at the traditional wedding informs his new wife's family (ironically given the aftermath) that the first night spilled a significant amount of plasma.[6] In fact, gynecologists affirm,[7] bleeding is rare and for that reason often staged. For instance, no more than 30% of girls enter the bridal chamber with vulvar tissue apt to stain the sheets and, according to pioneer anti-FGM advocate Dr. Nawal et Saadawi,[8] hymens can be missing at birth, atrophy or rupture from daily activities. The widespread desire of grooms for reassurance – that they are the first, the fathers of their offspring, and uncontested sexual partners of too often unwilling wives –, rests on fiction, not fact.

But this deceit is perilous, a fabrication that can wound. In some cultures, newlyweds are killed if not repudiated for failing to 'prove' their 'innocence'. What then does virginity connote? Underlying the obligatory ignorance of heterosexuality is censorship, i.e. mandated unfamiliarity with both women's and men's bodies.[9] Only legal possession by a man warrants women's deployment of sex aimed not at her pleasure but at pregnancy and motherhood, with offspring possessed by the father.

Lawra Linda confronts this hostility to women's erotic inheritance. In youth, respect for her dad motivates compliance, but discomfort with his directive to guard her virginity remains. And in maturity, feeling claustrophobic as 'merely' a wife and mother, she finds awareness blocked by trauma derived from having witnessed negligent homicide – a developed nation would have saved her mother's life – and having had her desires suppressed. As a female she is muted by patriarchal fiat; her body, however, speaks for her. Defiant, it bleeds.

The Virgin Complex

Because in *Swimming in a Red Sea* the virginity complex[10] exercises such decisive influence, unfolding it in multiple cultures over time is helpful. For all characters, including the protagonist, chastity is a pre-condition for marriage. Disagreement arises only regarding the means to preserve it – by restricting a girl's freedom or by trusting her? Lawra Linda's mother and uncle Hussein argue about these alternatives. Reasoning with the irate man, Djenab points out how misplaced are his suspicions based on Lawra Linda's innocent flirtation with her school friend Clay. After all, not only is the girl a prize student and conscientious older sister who willingly helps at home, but also she "hasn't yet developed breasts," signs of a sexual awakening, and hence "she won't bring us shame."

Djenab's brother-in-law disagrees, convinced that no young women can be trusted. To suggest that his niece has indeed had intercourse, he invokes a syllogism: Only married women – i.e. females with sexual experience – swim in the river. Lawra Linda's aunt takes her swimming. Thus, the youth must resemble wives and be sexually tainted. The brush with drowning even confirms his malicious avuncular misgivings: he views the near catastrophe as punishment for the girl's having changed status of her own accord. "She almost drowned the other day when only married women go to the river," he offers to substantiate her guilt. Well before he has her arrested, he places her in the dock.

Seeking to relieve his own distress – and given entrapment by the 'social norm', the threat of 'dishonour' is real[11] – he challenges Djenab to confirm the virginity assurance, that is, the genital mutilation of his niece.

> "Can you swear to me that she's still a virgin? Sometimes I even doubt you've cut her like any clean, decent girl should be. Have you? Is she clean? When was she excised?"

According to a DHS survey from 1998-99 covering the situation during the protagonist's youth,[12] female genital mutilation "is nearly universal in Guinea. ... [and] among ... [the] Fulani ... all girls were expected to be circumcised."[13] The study found one ethnic exception in the nation, however: "The only significant opposition ... [appeared] among Guerze Christians in Forest Guinea." Let's remember, although the boyfriend Clay was Mandingo (who cut) and not Guerze, his family was Christian, placing Djenab's opposition within the realm of possibility – and 3-4% spared is a significant real number of girls.

Returning to the uncle's challenge, Djenab deflects the conversation from the blade to her daughter's character, refusing even to acknowledge the phallocratic stance on 'purity'. For Djenab, hygiene is literal.

> "Yes. Of course, she's clean; why would she be dirty in the first place? Simply because she has a clitoris, a vulva ... a full vagina doesn't make her filthy. And she almost drowned because nobody taught her how to swim – end of discussion. How could you think otherwise?"

How could he think otherwise? In her 1966 magnum opus *Purity and Danger*, Mary Douglas explores how metaphors of stainless innocence embrace not soil but spirit. They differentiate among binaries that become indexes of power in a fixed hierarchy whose aim is to maintain order. Douglas catalogues, among other duos, clean/dirty and male/female,[14] contrasts that stabilize governance by dominant males for whom women are ontologically unruly.

Behind the desire for order is the threat of chaos, and pandemonium in turn is associated with the female. In *La jeune née*[15] (1975; *The Newly Born Woman*, 1995), Hélène Cixous and Catherine Clément expand Douglas's list of opposites to explore the influence on reality of words that inventory women negatively, and although calling their analysis "Western," what they say is valid globally. They point to "the violence of hierarchical binary[ies], ... dualistic pairs such as activity/passivity, culture/nature, head/heart, superior/inferior [that gesture toward ways in] which philosophical systems are organized around … 'the' couple, man/woman'."[16] Coded as erratic, the latter terms are feminized, devalued and, often, feared as dubious and unpredictable.

Unpredictability manifests in the psychosomatic affliction the heroine confronts: an irregular spontaneous menstrual flow induced by stress and distress.[17]

Not coincidentally, Claude Lévi-Strauss, when describing elementary structures of kinship that depend on the exchange of women, suggests that male domination answers the challenge of "'women's periods, their uncontrolled flow, too close to nature and therefore threatening'."[18] The anthropologist interprets measures to obviate this danger as "stabilizing" for society. If taming the rebelliousness of nature and, hence, the female requires strictures deleterious to women, the alternative is worse: social mayhem.

Thus, returning to the uncle's interview with Lawra Linda's mother, when he rages, "Is she a virgin or cut clean or both? Which one is it, Djenab?" he uses language carelessly, 'virgin' and 'clean cut' having been established not as alternatives but synonyms. In his implacable schema good character has no agency. Women are caught in a cultural catch-22.

A prime example is the mother/whore dichotomy[19] that underlies the value of sexual abstinence and the threat to all females of devaluation as BOTH mothers and whores. An ideal – The Virgin Mother – that can never be met, the image is nonetheless deeply anchored not only in the cult of modesty upheld by Lawra Linda's uncle but also in the iconic Mary and her Greco-Roman predecessors: Athena and Minerva, the Etruscan counterpart to the Greek goddess.

Athena, as many are aware, is considered a virgin born fully formed from the head of Zeus. What is less familiar is her motherhood, and "as it appears in connection with Athena, motherhood must be understood in terms of father-right."[20] With intercourse forbidden, the story goes that Hephaestus ejaculated on the thigh of the goddess; she in turn passed the fluid onto the earth who gestated Athena's son Erechtheus.[21] And the improbability of virginal maternity notwithstanding,[22] etymology preserves it. According to "G. Neumann … the name Athena is a compound of the Lydian word 'ati' (mother) and the Hurrian deity 'Ana'… a fertility and mother goddess … [Thus] unit[ing] virgin and mother in one and the same divine person,"[23] a convention sustained by Mary but presenting a distressing role model for all mortal females.[24]

Gendered Distress

Although Lawra Linda's conflict between desire for Harvey and allegiance to pre-marital chastity is resolved by marriage, gendered distress is visited upon the heroine, especially in parturition. An inflexible ideal of maternity molds her unfortunate birthing experience. A first-time mother unable to dilate and therefore delayed in the second stage of labor – I emphasize, a known side effect of FGM due to scar tissues' inelasticity – the primigravida cannot come to terms with having to forego a 'natural birth'. After all, the head nurse had assured her mother, "No C-sections for African women! Not necessary for a Fula mother. We're born strong with hips to bear children and give birth naturally!" Now, Lawra Linda has every reason to nuance this cliché, certain that Djenab might have lived had an intervention in Port Kamsar's underequipped hospital been possible. Moreover, the story's multiple migrations answer the drive to escape her origins. Yet the 'failure' to produce offspring without technical assistance torments her. Discouragement deepens when breast-feeding also proves a challenge and the first born won't stop wailing. To a Western reader, she may also seem stubborn, refusing to go out with her husband in quest of a breast pump at the local drug store. Only after several pages do we learn why: not only has she negative feelings toward a milk extracting device, but also her upbringing taught her to observe 40 days of sequestration. Africa won't let up on its demands even if repressed.

Producing so much mental turmoil is a divided mind, holding court within itself yet inaccessible to consciousness. In Lawra Linda's case, the body expresses what thinking can't: it bleeds. In one telling episode, the heroine craves Vancouver's Sushi, "the freshest" in the world. But "Sushi's not a good idea at the start of a pregnancy," her husband warns before spying flecks on the carpet. "What happened?" he asks. She has bled again, and although not unusual early in gestation, a suspicious pattern is beginning to emerge.

Ineffective stain remover transforms the carmine into smudgy ochre while a defensive Lawra Linda maintains her innocence.

> "I'm not asking you to clean it. I'm just wondering where it came from," [her husband remarks], spraying the detergent himself. No longer listening, I was rather back in Africa with my aunt Halle having a similar conversation.
>
> The day my first period appeared, my aunt had asked, "Kenda, what's that blot on the back of your dress?"

Like many uninitiated girls, Lawra Linda bursts into tears, for blood loss augurs death, conflating pregnancy and childbirth with mortality. "I'm going to die like my mother in the hospital!"

Psychologist Ernest Becker has examined the "rumble of terror"[25] that seethes in everyone but with greater vehemence in people intimate with dying, – as Lawra Linda learns at age 12 –, amplifying "how death looms over life – every life."[26] Coping strategies are needed. As Dexter Dias explains:

> ... For Becker one of the 'great rediscoveries of modern thought' is how the terror of death – invariably without our realising – lies at the heart of so much human activity. The question is how serious a challenge to functioning it is.[27]

Terror Management Theory (TMT) investigates "how we build defences against the incapacitating intrusion of death anxiety in our lives." For Lawra Linda, anguish sits uneasily with its anti-dote, as TMT acolytes define it: creating meaning. "Terror is then managed by embracing cultural values, or symbolic systems" that provide an enduring sense of worth and identity from which self-esteem follows.[28]

In other words, Lawra Linda counters the destruction of what human beings are, the grim reaper's prey, by creation, what she does, or at least tries to do: first, escape (her origins); next renounce (selected values of her upbringing); then recreate herself (as a Western wife, mother, and professional), all the while being pulled back to what she's left by somatic subterfuge – the message of, and in, her blood.

Not the flow itself but rather the surprise, inconvenience, and lack of control matter more. The protagonist is repeatedly ambushed by values anchored in her past, especially by the promise offered in a time and place where one's word was binding. As sociologists would argue, Guinea provides a 'high context culture' whose codes of mutual responsibility weigh on both sexes but disadvantage women more in their gender-specificity. Women are subordinate to men; they must be 'cleansed' in order to marry as virgins. Their self-worth is measured by conformity to a standard incompatible with personal unfolding as is now increasingly possible in the West.

For Terror Management Theory, salvation lies in moulding life's meaning. Difficult after deleting earlier cultural inscriptions, reinventing the self from a tabula rasa poses a challenge – but Lawra Linda tries.[29]

Good sex

Not only as a mother but also as a wife, despite occasional domestic spats, Lawra Linda succeeds in this quest. The emblem of happiness is – surprisingly given prior genital trauma – good sex. The couple enjoy satisfying sexual relations charmingly conveyed, a startling element for readers aware of the dyspareunia frequent in women who have suffered FGM. Many accounts of sequelae take for granted clitoral amputees' loss of sexual appetite, the patriarchal aim of the pruning. But testimony culled, for instance, by Hanny Lightfoot-Klein[30] among more than 400 infibulated women in Sudan during extended journeys in the 1980s defies this generalization. "A body is a body," one informant tells Hanny, whooping with laughter at the very suggestion of deleted capacity for arousal. In fact, Sudanese wives, more than 90% infibulated and forbidden to ask openly for sex,[31] can express desire with perfume dispensed by the *dukhan*, or smoke bath. Under a tent-like cover, straddled above scented charcoal, open pores are enabled to absorb the aroma that spells lust. In what may be Lightfood-Klein's most amusing anecdote, her ignorance of the meaning of the odour leads to a disconcerting error whose multiple dimensions expand in the age of #MeToo.

A guest for several months in the provincial Sudanese home of a factory-owning husband and wife, Hanny begs the woman's permission to experience *dukhan* and ultimately, despite strenuous repeated refusals, Hanny wins, only to learn too late why her hostess had said No. The husband, on returning home, quickly sheds his impeccable good manners to engage in relentless pursuit of the hapless, star-crossed researcher! What was going on? she wonders, abashed and annoyed. In fact, he is merely being courteous, responding with gallantry to her unequivocally expressed desire.

This sketch comments on Lawra Linda's story in so far as its protagonist faces a similar task: to decipher non-verbal cultural cues. Reinventing ourselves in cultures whose youth isn't anchored in us is a challenge because so much of importance remains sub rosa.

How have other FGM survivors managed the cultural switch?

Migrant women's memoirs

With varying degrees of success.

A revealing comparison to Lawra Linda's tale can be found in a manuscript originating not in Guinea but Somalia. "Countries with the highest prevalence among girls and women aged 15 to 49 are Somalia with 98 per cent, Guinea 97 per cent and Djibouti 93 per cent."[32] Thus, Nura Abdi's *Tränen im Sand* (2003), translated as *Desert Tears*,[33] features similar fraught encounters between the cultures of home and host.

In Abdi's chapter called "Am I even a woman?" the Somali has asked for asylum in Germany and spends the first few weeks sharing housing with other refugees where "nothing" in the experience "rocked [her] as much as learning that not all women in the world are circumcised" (260). The discovery, to be sure, is distressing. As a rumor spreads that Nura "was the only one who wouldn't sleep around," an Ethiopian friend challenges her:

> "What's the matter with you? Why don't you have a boyfriend?" Hanna wanted to know. ... Then she looked at me as though a light switch had been flicked and said, "Oh, right, you're Somali." I was taken aback. "What do you mean by that?" "You're circumcised," she said. An awful premonition shook me. "And you're not?" I asked, doubt in my voice. ... So out it came.

And I learned that there are two kinds of women. (260)

> Soon the pre-fabricated 'containers' in an asylum colony for Afghanis, Africans, Balkan refugees and Iraqis, was, despite the language barrier, abuzz with the news of Nura's genital wounding.

And from all sides I was met by shocked, disbelieving, pitying glances. Above all the Yugoslavians couldn't contain themselves. "How can anyone do a thing like that to such a pretty girl?" they wailed, shook their heads and felt obliged to offer comfort. As for me, I'd fallen into a nightmare. It appeared that not even the Afghan women had been circumcised! O.K., Ethiopians are Christian, I thought, so that might be why. But Afghanis are Moslems like me, and they don't do it? I felt myself hurled into hell.

But the worst of it was, they appeared to consider me a cripple, half a woman incapable of any feeling. They behaved as though I had been the victim of a crime, as though it were shameful to be circumcised -- whereas I had always believed, circumcision made me clean!

I wasn't going to stand for that. It came to verbal blows between Hanna and me. "You're running around with all your filth," I hammered into her, "and proud of it?! Maybe you think it's better to stink like the uncircumcised? At least ... I don't smell!" I was angry. "Aren't you ashamed to be like a whore down there?" But Hanna countered scornfully: "You're as smooth as a wall between your legs. They killed your sensitivity. They've destroyed you." I was shaking with rage. "Look at me!" I screamed. "I'm every bit as much a Mensch as you are! I have feelings just like you! And I'll bet I can love even better than you can!" ... Didn't I *have* to defend myself?

But to tell the truth, I didn't know what I was talking about. As a matter of fact, I knew nothing at all. Nothing about my body and nothing about sex. I'd wound up in an unimaginable situation. In Somalia you talked about *gudniin*[34] in lovely language, as you would about good fortune. Yet here I was, surrounded by people who reacted to it with horror. But putting two and two together, I drew the same conclusion as everybody else: There was something wrong with me. I became foreign to myself. (260-263)

Demanded of the excised immigrant woman is a hairpin mental turn. What she thought right is wrong, what she thought good is evil and what she thought beautiful, ugly. And yet, despite the strain and monumental risk of backlash, numbers of FGM survivors are writing memoirs showing how the erstwhile beneficial truly harms the girls subjected to it. Among these courageous voices are Hibo Wardere, *Cut. One Woman's Fight against FGM in Britain Today* (2016); Soraya Mire, *Girl with Three Legs* (2011); Khady with Marie-Thérèse Cuny. *Mutilée* (2005) [*Blood Stains. A Child of Africa Reclaims her Human Rights*. Trans. Tobe Levin (2010)]; Fadumo Korn, *Geboren im Grossen Regen* (2004) [*Born in the Big Rains. A Memoir of Somalia and Survival*. Trans. and Afterword Tobe Levin. (2006); and Waris Dirie. *Desert Flower* (1995), first volume in a series. Now Lawrelynd Bowin's *Swimming in a Red Sea* (2018) enhances this list – to which many more texts can be added.

Literature also illuminates burdens that FGM places on cultural nomads. The best among those with excision at their heart include Jeanie Kortum, *Stones* (2017); Halimata Fofana, *Mariama, l'ecorchée vive* (2015); Fatou Keïta, *Rebelle* (1998); Alice Walker, *Possessing the Secret of Joy* (1992); Evelyne Accad, *L'excisée* (1982), and Ngugi wa Thiong'o, *The River Between* (1965), to name but a few spanning a half century and several continents. By revealing excision as deeply-anchored and complex, these tales fruitfully escape nonfiction's rules; they "witness by the imagination."[35] Certainly, field research and statistics are essential, but they are also insufficient. "Fiction can lead to clarity," author Alma Katsu asserts. "I don't think we understand life well head-on." It's better, she suggests, "when you tell a story."[36] Decades of effort – severely underfunded, but vehement and tenacious – have failed to stop FGM.[37] Social science, politics, law enforcement, human rights, the hippocratic oath – these approaches have helped staunch the march of blades but, so far, have fallen short.

Abolition could accelerate once we expand favoured sources of insight beyond social science and prevalence statistics to include memoir and fiction. In 1988, as soon-to-be Nobel Laureate Toni Morrison told the BBC, "There are some things only writers can deal with." Then, thoughtful, she repeated, "*only* writers can deal with. And it's their *job*."[38] Lawrelynd Bowin has done hers well.

Endnotes

[1] In Chapter 4 of *The Ten Types of Human. A New Understanding of Who We Are and Who We Can Be* [London: William Heinemann, 2017] Dexter Dias describes Terror Management Theory to show how confronting death affects the rest of the witness's life. Regarding FGM and mental health in a broader sense, Alice Behrendt and Steffen Moritz, applying the Mini International Neuropsychic Interview, uncovered an elevation in PTSD among 'circumcised' women. Of 47 Senegalese, "the circumcised … showed a significantly higher prevalence of PTSD (30.4%) and other psychiatric syndromes (47.9%) than the uncircumcised women. PTSD was accompanied by memory problems. [Thus] within the circumcised group, a mental health problem exists that may furnish the first evidence of the severe psychological consequences of female genital mutilation." "Posttraumatic Stress Disorder and Memory Problems after Female Genital Mutilation." *The American Journal of Psychiatry*. Vol. 162 Issue 5. Pp. 1000-1002. Online 1 May 2005.
https://ajp.psychiatryonline.org/doi/abs/10.1176/appi.ajp.162.5.1000
Accessed 26 May 2018.

[2] The Fulani, also called Peuhl, found in 18 African nations, comprises a majority nowhere but a plurality in Guinea. UnCUT/VOICES' first book by a Senegalese, Khady, *Blood Stains. A Child of Africa Reclaims Her Human Rights* (2010), was originally titled *Mutilée* (2005), and is also authored by a Peuhl. *Mutilée* has been translated into 17 languages.

[3] According to the country report *Guinea* by 28 Too Many.
https://www.28toomany.org/country/guinea/
Accessed 25 May 2018.

[4] "Female genital mutilation and obstetric outcome: WHO collaborative prospective study in six African countries" *The Lancet*, Volume 367, Issue 9525, 1835 - 1841.
https://www.thelancet.com/action/showCitFormats?pii=S0140-6736%2806%2968805-3&doi=10.1016%2FS0140-6736%2806%2968805-3 · Accessed 25 May 2018.

[5] See Omar Ibrahim Hussein. *The Virginity Blade*. Baltimore: PublishAmerica, 2007. This male Somali's novel is fierce in combatting FGM, the narrator convinced that the virginity obsession is a major cause of genital torture.

[6] Invoking the multiple cultural meanings and taboos surrounding 'blood' could assist in interpreting defloration rites and the protagonist's affliction, spontaneous bleeding, but would require a plethora of examples exploding this essay's page limit. Here I'll simply mention one influential source – the Old Testament equation of blood with the spirit of the Lord, distinguishing the sacred from the profane. Applied to the story, vaginal blood throws the heroine back to her mother's exsanguination as also the desertion of her spirit. The migration theme is invoked as well, because exile is the punishment for violating commandments regulating interactions with blood. "Whosoever of the house of Israel, or of the sojourner sojourning among them, eateth any manner of blood, I will set My faces against that soul that eateth blood and will cut him off from among his people; for the soul of the flesh is in the blood; and I have given it to you upon the altar, to make atonement for your souls; for it is the blood that maketh atonement for the soul. The soul of all flesh, it is the blood thereof; whosoever eateth it shall be cut off" (Lev. 17:10, 11, 14).
https://www.biblegateway.com/passage/?search=Leviticus+17%3A10-14&version=NIV
Accessed 27 May 2018.

[7] As noted by Professor Dr. med. Sven Becker, Director of Goethe University Hospital Department of Gynecology and Obstetrics. Personal communication. 12 May 2018.

[8] Nawal El Saadawi. *The Hidden Face of Eve. Women in the Arab World.* Trans Sherif Hetata. London: Zed, 1980. A venerable opponent of FGM, Nawal el Saadawi reconfirmed her opposition to FGM on BBC's HardTalk with Zeinab Badawi on 23 May 2018. https://www.bbc.co.uk/programmes/b0b3q58n Accessed 24 May 2018. See also Leila Ahmed, Rev. of *The Hidden Face of Eve: Women in the Arab World.* Nawal El Saadawi, Sherif Hetata. In *Signs: Journal of Women in Culture and Society* 6, no. 4 (Summer, 1981): 749-751. https://doi.org/10.1086/493844 · Accessed 25 May 2018.

[9] What really lies behind the trappings, I suggest, is awe of women's sexual potency – and men's fear of women's eroticism, though offering examples here would generate another chapter. See H.R. Hays. *The Dangerous Sex. The Myth of Feminine Evil.* NY: Pocketbooks, 1965.

[10] I encountered the "Virgin complex" in Beijing when a guest professor at China Women's University in 2011. The faculty requested a public lecture on 'FGM and the Virgin Complex'. Briefly, after decades of sexual liberalization, Chinese men are now making virginity a precondition for marriage. See "Why Is China Still Obsessed with Virginity? Shifting sexual mores mean young women are shamed both for having too much sexual experience and too little."
http://www.sixthtone.com/news/1000261/why-is-china-still-obsessed-with-virginity%3F
Accessed 25 May 2018.

[11] The dishonor alluded to here is that which manifests in acid attacks, so-called 'honor' killings and the like.

[12] Yoder, P., Stanley and Mary Mahy. 2001. *Female Genital Cutting in Guinea: Qualitative and Quantitative Research Strategies.* DHS Analytical Studies No. 5. Calverton, Maryland: ORC Macro.
https://www.dhsprogram.com/pubs/pdf/AS5/AS5.pdf
Accessed 20 May 2018.

[13] "… the practice … forms part of the expectations of most individuals. In the open-ended discussions of the formative research, women talked about circumcision as important for being pure, clean, and properly educated about behavior appropriate to a wife. Many women as well as some men mentioned the importance of circumcision in terms of parental responsibility: parents must educate a daughter, have her circumcised, and find her a husband. In the DHS survey, women and men were asked if they thought the practice should be continued. Two-thirds of the women and one-half of the men said that it should be continued." Ibid. P. viii-ix.

[14] "Mary Douglas." https://de.wikipedia.org/wiki/Mary_Douglas
Accessed 20 May 2018.

[15] Cixous, Hélène and Catherine Clément. *La jeune née.* Paris: Union Générale d'éditions, 1975.

[16] Katarzyna Marciniak. "Introduction to Hélène Cixous." *Sorties. Out and Out. Attacks/Ways Out/Forays.*
http://homepage.westmont.edu/hoeckley/readings/symposium/PDF/201_300/219.pdf
Accessed 20 May 2018.

[17] Among innumerable medical references, "Extreme emotional stress and excessive exercise can cause abnormal bleeding." Women Living Naturally.com
http://www.womenlivingnaturally.com/articlepage.php?id=189
Accessed 24 May 2018; see also Mark Shapley, Kelvin Jordan, Peter R. Croft. "Increased vaginal bleeding and psychological distress: a longitudinal study of their relationship in the community." *BJOG: International Journal of Obstetrics & Gynaecology.* June 2003. Vol. 110. Pp 548-554.

[18] Sandra M. Gilbert. "Introduction. A Tarantella of Theory." *The Newly-Born Woman.* Hélène Cixous and Catherine Clément. Trans. Betsy Wing. London: I.B. Taurus, 1996.
https://books.google.de/books?id=hzJHtq6jGHEC&pg=PR3&source=gbs_selected_pages&cad=2#v=onepage&q&f=false
Accessed 24 May 2018.

[19] This reminds me of the ire I felt when reading, just this morning – 21 May 2018 – the following links sent by the UN Women's Report Network: WUNRN "High Fashion and Hijabs – Mixed Response." Modesty per se condemns 'whores', i.e. women defined by the use to which they put their sexuality. Viewed through a feminist lens, gender equality is incompatible with 'modesty'. See
http://www.wunrn.com
http://www.independent.co.uk/life-style/fashion/new-york-fashion-week-hijabs-islam-immigrant-fashion-show-anniesa-hasibuan-a7583321.html
https://www.jihadwatch.org/2017/05/now-some-muslim-women-are-outraged-over-high-fashion-hijabs

[20] "The Shrine of the Goddess Athena."
http://www.goddess-Athena.org/Athenaeum/Psychology/Athena/Mother_Mistress_and_Protectress.htm
Accessed 26 May 2018.

[21] "A myth links her with the son of Hephaestus, Erichthonius a.k.a. Erechtheus. Hephaestus, the lame smith of Olympus, attempted to rape her. She fended him off, but he ejaculated on her thigh. ... Athena took up the child formed from Hephaestus' semen and kept him in her sanctuary."
https://www.quora.com/Did-the-Greek-goddess-Athena-have-children.
Accessed 21 May 2018. Gratitude to Dr. Vincenz Brinkman for bringing this legend to my attention while touring the ancient Greek shrines in Athens with Rotary Städel, 19 May 2018.

[22] Though rare, impregnation in the absence of ejaculation into the vagina can take place. "You can get pregnant without intercourse – you know that," warns the clinician who mutilates Lawra Linda in jail.

[23] "Ancient Greece."
http://www.ancientgreece.com/s/Athena/
Accessed 21 May 2018.

[24] The sheer number of virgins who receive greater veneration than 'ordinary' women – Iphigenia, Mary, Joan of Arc, to name a few –, when considered alongside the Sheela-na-gigs, provides evidence of patriarchy's fascination with the status of female genitalia in relation to power, underscored by the chastity preference of the Christian Church that confirms danger emanating from the temptress Eve.

[25] Qtd in Dexter Dias, p. 159.

[26] Ibid. 153.

[27] Ibid.

[28] Ibid. 160.

[29] *Wikipedia* defines "Terror Management Theory" in a manner to illuminate *Swimming in a Red Sea:* "The simplest examples of cultural values that manage the terror of death are those that purport to offer literal immortality (e.g. belief in afterlife, religion). However, TMT also argues that other cultural values – including those that are seemingly unrelated to death – offer symbolic immortality. For example, value of national identity, posterity, cultural perspectives on sex, and human superiority over animals have all been linked to death concerns in some manner. In many cases these values are thought to offer symbolic immortality either a) by providing the sense that one is part of something greater that will ultimately outlive the individual (e.g. country, lineage, species), or b) by making one's symbolic identity superior to biological nature (i.e. you are a personality, which makes you more than a glob of cells). Because cultural values determine that which is meaningful, they are also the foundation for all self-esteem. TMT describes self-esteem as being the personal, subjective measure of how well an individual is living up to their cultural values. … Self-esteem provides a buffer against death-related anxiety."

[30] Hanny Lightfoot-Klein. *Prisoners of Ritual. An Odyssey into Female Genital Circumcision in Sudan.* NY: Harrington Park P., 1989. Hanny is one of the world's foremost researchers on FGM.

[31] Admittedly, outspoken anti-FGM activists who have endured infibulation suggest that victims are more likely to experience intercourse as torture, but significant exceptions exist. See the extraordinary animations on FGM launched on 12 September 2017, hosted by Janet Fyle MBE in the House of Commons.
https://www.wovenink.co.uk/endfgm-animations/
Accessed 25 May 2018.

[32] "New statistical report on female genital mutilation shows harmful practice is a global concern – UNICEF." Press Release.
https://www.unicef.org/media/media_90033.html
Accessed 27 May 218.

[33] Nura Abdi and Leo Lindner. *Tränen im Sand.* Bergisch-Gladback: Ehrenwirth, 2003; *Desert Tears.* Trans. Tobe Levin (Excerpts) in *Feminist Europa. Review of Books.* Vol. 3, No.1, 2004.
http://www.ddv-verlag.com
Accessed 24 May 2018, and Tobe Levin and Augustine H. Asaah. *Empathy and Rage. Female Genital Mutilation in African Literature.* Banbury, Oxfordshire: Ayebia, 2009. Pp. 173-176.

[34] Somali for infibulation, literally female + circumcision, the same syllable used for men.

[35] Thanks to S. Lillian Kremer who develops this concept in *Women's Holocaust Writing. Memory & Imagination.* Lawrence, KS: U. of Nebraska P., 2001.

[36] Jarret Bencks. "A Hunger for Storytelling." Alumni Profile of Alma Katsu. *Brandeis Alumni Magazine.* Spring 2018. P. 65. See also "Female Genital Mutilation and the Arts: Rich Resource in the Fight to Stop It."
https://uncutvoices.wordpress.com/2017/12/10/female-genital-mutilation-and-the-arts-rich-resource-in-the-fight-to-stop-it/ · Accessed 27 May 2018.

[37] What's being done in Guinea against FGM? Despite domestic legislation and international pressure, authorities continue turning a blind eye. In fact, "in Guinea the number of women supporting [excision] has increased ... from 65 percent in 1999 to 76 percent in 2012." "Female Genital Mutilation in Guinea on the rise."
http://www.ohchr.org/en/NewsEvents/Pages/DisplayNews.aspx?NewsID=19869&LangID=E
Accessed 26 May 2018. In the meantime, the CPTAFE (Cellule de Coordination sur les pratiques traditionelles affectant la santé des femmes et des enfants), Guinean branch of the IAC, continues to lobby, teach, and advocate for ending FGM. "CPTAFE's main target groups are grassroots-level men and women in rural areas, heads of families, community leaders, community health workers, social workers, traditional birth attendants, traditional healers, students and youth organizations, policymakers, journalists, and government officials concerned with the health of women and children."
https://www.popline.org/node/381379 Accessed 26 May 2018.
Finally, Alpha Amado Bano Barry has studied FGM in Guinea.
https://www.euractiv.de/section/entwicklungspolitik/interview/guinea-weibliche-genitalverstuemmelung-noch-immer-an-der-tagesordnung/
Accessed 25 May 2018.
https://www.taskforcefgm.de/wp-content/uploads/2011/05/Statements_IAC-Mitglieder.pdf

[38] Toni Morrison. BBC interview. Video recording. 1988.

Acknowledgements

I thank God for giving me a clear mind, a bright spirit, and a healthy body able to author this personal story. I pray it serves each and every one who reads it, given how painful it was for me to write.

I thank my publisher Dr. Tobe Levin von Gleichen for being among the greatest activists for women's rights and well-being I've ever known. I'm humbled and enriched by your loving commitment to ending FGM, and I'm thankful for your having taken a chance on a new author. Your mentoring throughout the process of my first publication made the effort fascinating as well as enjoyable.

I would also like to acknowledge my priest Abbe Mario Rosas who gave me the freedom to be myself and encouraged me, throughout this spiritual journey, to dive into the deepest fears and darkest secrets of my being. I thank my writing-group gals Gayle Decoursey and Sarah Lawtons-Peert who insisted on accountability as well as fun at each of our Sunday meetings. My gratitude goes as well to Dr. Sonia Zghli, the psychologist who eased me into becoming whole once more. Coline Diane, Laurence Thomasset and Marie-Laure Leto deserve credit for always being at my beck and call when I needed you most. And last not least, I thank my editors Lucia Terra for keeping me focused and true to my own story-telling and Joanne Howskin who knows the essence and the cadence of my voice.

UnCUT/VOICES Press gratefully acknowledges Rebecca Sue Levin for proof-reading and penning a synopsis of the memoir; to Naomi Rosen and Kelly Benguigui for proof-reading; and to Godfrey Williams-Okorodus for early cover concepts.

Special mention goes to Kaye Beth, not only for her talent in design but also for generous financial support of the website, www.uncutvoices.com

THANK YOU!

Each UnCUT/VOICES Press book supports a specific project against FGM. Sales of *Swimming in a Red Sea* contribute to the **Clitoris Restoration and Fistula Repair Fund** that sponsors operations by Dr. Pierre Foldes and other qualified surgeons at the Institut en Santé Génésique in St. Germain-en-Laye outside Paris, France.

In the United States, your donation is tax deductible. Send a check in any amount made out to **Healthy Tomorrow** with a clear notation that you are contributing to the Clitoris Restoration Fund.
The address: Healthy Tomorrow, 14 William St., Somerville, MA 02144 USA.

You can also make a tax-deductible contribution in Germany by bank transfer to FORWARD – Germany with the clear notation **Clitoris Restoration and Fistula Repair Fund and your email or snail-mail address.**
Transfer to
FORWARD – Germany e.V.
Frankfurter Sparkasse
BLZ 500 502 01
Account # 200029398
IBAN: DE20 5005 0201 0200 0293 98
BIC SWIFT: HELADEF1822

In the UK, you can contribute to a new tax-exempt charity, the Clitoris Restoration and Fistula Repair Fund, charity number 1169186. Trustees are Hilary Burrage, Tobe Levin von Gleichen, Dr. Phoebe Abe and Nolan Victory. See
http://opencharities.org/charities/1169186.
The website will be ready in September 2018. For further information and bank details (tax exemption in the UK) contact Hilary Burrage: Hilary Burrage hilary.burrage@btconnect.com

Hearty thanks to Steffen Schenk, MaynPrint (Frankfurt, Germany) for generous support with design, lay-out, and production.

Other Books from UnCUT/Voices Press

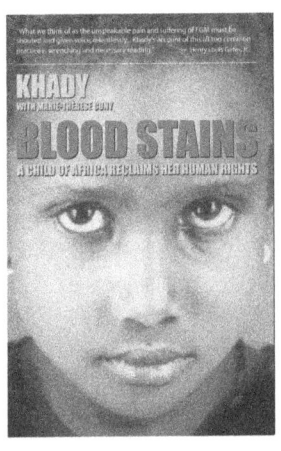

Khady with Marie-Thérèse Cuny
Blood Stains.
A Child of Africa Reclaims Her Human Rights.
Trans. Tobe Levin. 2010.
ISBN: 9783981386301

Hubert Prolongeau
Undoing FGM: Pierre Foldes,
The Surgeon Who Restores the Clitoris.
Foreword Bernard Kouchner.
Trans. and Afterword. Tobe Levin. 2011.
ISBN: 9783981386318

Nick Hadikwa Mwaluko
WAAFRIKA 1 2 3.
1992. Kenya. Two Womyn Fall in Love.
2016. ISBN: 9783981386387

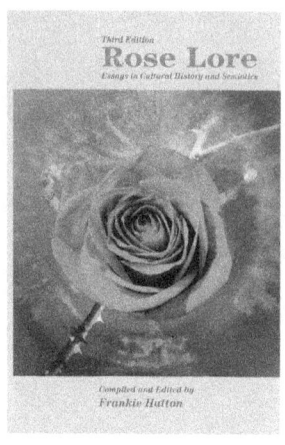

Frankie Hutton, ed.
Rose Lore.
Essays in Cultural History and Semiotics.
2015. ISBN: 9783981386349.

Barungi, Violet and Hilda Twongyeirwe, eds.
Taboo.
Voices of Women in Uganda
on Female Genital Mutilation.
Intro. Rebecca Salonen. 2015.
ISBN: 9783981386356.

Maria Kiminta and Tobe Levin.
Photographs by Britta Radike.
Kiminta.
A Maasai's Fight against
Female Genital Mutilation.
2015. ISBN: 9783981386363

Tobe Levin, ed.
Waging Empathy.
Alice Walker, Possessing the Secret of Joy,
and the Global Movement to Ban FGM.
2014. ISBN: 9783981386332

Kameel Ahmady
In the Name of Tradition:
Female Genital Mutilation in Iran.
2016. ISBN: 9783981386370.

Jeanie Kortum
STONES
A Novel
Foreword by Tobe Levin. 2017.
ISBN: 9781631521805
Co-imprint with She Writes Press

www.ingramcontent.com/pod-product-compliance
Lightning Source LLC
Chambersburg PA
CBHW031316160426
43196CB00007B/555